Praise for *Winter's Graces*

"Dr. Stewart's *Winter's Graces* gives us all a persuasive and satisfying guidebook on aging, uniquely presented through a rich synthesis of personal story, solid research, and myths and legends spanning time and culture. This writing represents a clear voice characterized by the very same powerful qualities it encourages in order to cultivate an attitude of agelessness: healthy defiance, optimism, and openness to change. Dr. Stewart invites us to question our collectively reinforced assumptions and face our fears about becoming older. We are reminded to invoke wisdom, compassion, humor . . . and a little necessary fierceness."
—**Eve Maram**, PsyD, Clinical and Forensic Psychologist
 and author of *Psychopathy Within*

"Dr. Susan Stewart's work has inspired me to watch for and to celebrate the many wonderful gifts and graces that come with the process of aging. Our society is prone to seeing the 'disadvantages' of age. What a joy it is to focus rather on the many reasons to embrace aging in light of the continuing development and deepening of the human being in later life."
—**The Rev. Jeannette Myers**, Episcopal priest

"In this wise volume, Susan Stewart offers a compelling vision of what aging can be, not only for women, but for us all. In particular, the eleven qualities she dubs as 'the Graces of Winter' articulate a profound depth-psychological model, rooted both in contemporary cutting-edge research and ancient wisdom."
—**David Van Nuys**, PhD, Emeritus Professor of Psychology
 and creator/host of the Shrink Rap Radio podcast

"At last—a glorious look at the gifts of aging! *Winter's Graces* takes readers on a magnificent journey through the later years, in all their joy and fullness."
—**Mary Ann Clark**, RN, retired

"Susan Stewart guides her readers through the thorny thicket of aging in America to a quiet clearing where misconceptions are peeled away, and our fears are not denied, but embraced. We're led with gentle hands through contemporary science and solid cross-cultural, age-old traditions that help to re-awaken our own forgotten memories and understandings of the richness and value of each season of life. With the skill of an alchemist, Susan invites us to explore eleven qualities that ripen in later life and can transform the leaden fear of aging into a grateful recognition that the 'golden years' are indeed gold. This book is to be read and then reread, one chapter at a time, whenever we need an infusion of audacity, contentment, or courage."
—**Jackie Cato**, bi-lingual teacher

"*Winter's Graces* is full of grace. For me, reading it was like opening a treasure box and discovering that a time of life I was anticipating with some dread is actually rich in beauty and many other blessings. I envision groups of women coming together to receive its reassuring wisdom and to be awakened to the inviting possibilities that age has to offer."
—**Margaret Potts**, retired teacher

"Dr. Susan Stewart's book is a gift to all of us who are making the transition to late adulthood. Written in a beautiful, moving, personal, and descriptive style, her work is inspiring, healing, and filled with timeless wisdom. Susan's writing has reaffirmed that I am not alone with the challenges that I am facing in the second half of life, and has given me the courage and perspective to forge onward with a renewed optimism about life and all that it has to teach me."
—**David F. Sowerby**, PhD, adjunct faculty member,
   Sonoma State, Sofia, and Dominican Universities

Winter's Graces

The Surprising Gifts *of* Later Life

Susan Avery Stewart, PhD

SHE WRITES PRESS

Published 2018
Printed in the United States of America
ISBN: 978-1-63152-379-3 pbk
ISBN: 978-1-63152-380-9
Library of Congress Control Number: 2018944203

For information, address:
She Writes Press
1569 Solano Ave #546
Berkeley, CA 94707

Cover and interior design by Tabitha Lahr

She Writes Press is a division of SparkPoint Studio, LLC.

In memory of my grandmother Winifred Gregory Avery and my mother, Wilma Lou Nichols, who grew even more loving as they aged.

And in gratitude for my sons, Avery and Logan, and their children, Natalie, Madison, Lona Louisa, and Lukas—my greatest teachers and blessings.

Contents

Introduction

"Grow old along with me! The best is yet to be,
the last of life for which the first was made."
—Robert Browning, "Rabbi Ben Ezra"

What if the winter of life really was the best season—a time of completion and fulfillment, rather than a misery or a failure? And what if the primary problem wasn't aging itself but the misguided tale we have learned to tell ourselves about it?

In many cultures, elders play a variety of valuable roles and are respected, even revered. The Japanese, for example, regard their elders as "national treasures" and even have a word—*shibui*—for the beauty of age. And in societies where elders are valued, "You look old today" is a compliment. In the United States, though, a number of factors, including an exaggerated fear of death and the overvaluing of autonomy, appearance, and achievement, have led to an inaccurate view of aging as a humiliating decline into misery. Demeaning ageist stereotypes reflect our collective aversion to age and cause enormous suffering for older as well as younger people. Being an old woman is seen as a particular misfortune, rather than the blessing that it can be.

In an environment where fear-based attitudes toward old age are so pervasive, it is easy to internalize them without realizing it. Some women resist these negative stereotypes by clinging to youth, hoping to avoid what is increasingly construed as the sin of aging. A multi-billion-dollar industry promises redemption, capitalizing on women's fear of "losing their looks"—and therefore their value—as they age. Most consider it high praise to assure a woman that she doesn't look her age. But the subtext is hardly a compliment: to *be* her age is bad.

At the other end of the spectrum are those who buy into the misconception that when youth fades it's all over and who simply resign themselves to an inevitable downhill slide. Sadly, the belief that the winter of life is necessarily a time of debilitating decline usually goes hand in hand with a lack of health-promoting behaviors. Thus, many of us help bring to pass the very losses we dread.

Thankfully, resistance and resignation are not the only ways to approach the last season of life, and there is mounting evidence that the dread of aging is more rooted in fear and fallacy than in fact.[1] Another more encouraging version of the story of old is gaining momentum, one that acknowledges the losses of later life but also celebrates its gifts and graces.[2]

This counterstory is apparent in the lives of many of today's elders who are living far beyond the boundaries prescribed by ageist stereotypes. It is also illustrated by little-known folktales from around the world that depict the old woman as a multifaceted and valuable character—a far cry from the stories of wicked witches and ugly hags that most of us heard as children. And a growing body of research is confirming this heartening view of later life and yielding some surprising findings:

- Most so-called problems of age are the result of inactivity and illness, not years, and can be prevented, delayed, or offset by not smoking and by regular exercise and other health-friendly practices.[3]
- Catastrophic conditions mistakenly equated with age, such as severe dementia and debilitating physical frailty, are the exception, not the rule. The vast majority of people over sixty-five do not experience them.[4]
- People age in widely different ways, becoming less alike as they grow older. We are not determined by our

years, and chronological age is a fairly poor predictor of how people feel and act.[5]

• Best of all, there are many positive trends in later life that have received far less attention than its losses, such as increased self-acceptance and tolerance toward others, enhanced creativity, a growing ability to savor life and to ride its ups and downs with equanimity and humor, and a deepening willingness to set aside our own interests for the greater good.

The Graces of Winter

Winter's Graces are eleven qualities that reach their fullest expression in the last season of life:

- Agelessness
- Audacious Authenticity
- Compassion
- Contentment
- Courage
- Creativity/Ingenuity
- Necessary Fierceness
- Remembrance
- Self-Transcending Generosity
- Simplicity
- Wisdom

These characteristics are not exclusive to later life, and their seeds are best planted in earlier seasons. Some of them (increasing self-acceptance and heightened creativity, for example) often begin flowering in midlife. And these trends can be seen in the young as well, especially those facing catastrophic illness, serious addiction, or other life-altering challenges.

Still, later life provides a particular set of conditions conducive to the growth of these graces: long years that tend to lengthen, broaden, and deepen our perspective; a rich store of experiences (including so-called mistakes and failures); diminished social demands and expectations that we look and act a certain way; a somewhat slower pace; a growing taste for reflection; and a keen awareness that time is limited and life is precious.

Winter's Graces are not inevitable, however, any more than catastrophic losses are. These gifts of later life are developmental tendencies that ripen most fully when we recognize and cultivate them. Some of them may arrive wrapped in unexpected or unappealing packages though, and we may find that opening them may require opening ourselves to things we might be reluctant to face.

The Grace of Agelessness, for example, entails owning our age so that we can move beyond it and discover its gifts. Necessary Fierceness may mean risking comfort and even safety in order to advocate for those who are suffering injustice. And the Grace of Remembrance involves making peace with the whole of our life, including the parts of our history (and ourselves) we would rather forget. This is hard work—yet good work—because Winter's Graces benefit those who nurture and embody these qualities, as well as the people around them.

An Accidental Crone

My own exploration of late life began by accident at the age of fifty-four—and with great resistance. At that time, I had no interest whatsoever in old age. And then a series of events occurred that changed everything.

On May Day weekend in 2000 I attended a workshop at a local nature preserve, where we were instructed to find a spot to which we felt drawn, sit there for a few hours, and simply pay attention to what occurred within and around us. Afterward we met to tell stories of our experiences. Mine was humorous, but not especially significant, or so I thought.

I was immediately drawn to a huge, beautiful old willow tree, bright with budding leaves. Walking toward it, I anticipated the peace and stillness sure to pervade such an idyllic setting. To my surprise, the tree was not in the secluded sanctuary I'd imagined; instead it stood in a place where three paths intersected. Finding myself at an intersection was a telling reflection of my overly busy life at that time, as a university professor, single parent, grandmother, and caretaking daughter. I longed for quiet solitude but had very little of it then.

One of the workshop leaders commented that my experience was "a wonderful crone story." I wasn't sure what he meant by *crone*, but it sounded old, which I didn't like. (I had no idea what an apt late-life image that old tree with bright new leaves was, and it wasn't until much later that I learned about Hecate, an ancient crone goddess, who is the guardian of remote places, especially those where three paths intersect.) At the time, the facilitator's comment puzzled and annoyed me, and I forgot all about the crone—until she crossed my path again two years later.

That spring as my fifty-sixth birthday was approaching, a graduate student at Sonoma State University told me that in the Celtic tradition, fifty-six is the age associated with becoming a crone. This time I wasn't insulted but was still puzzled. How could I—with an adolescent son living at home and still feeling young myself—possibly be considered old?

Naturally curious and a lover of all things Celtic, I decided to look up *crone* in the dictionary and was horrified by its definition: "a withered, witch-like old woman." I vehemently pushed the crone out of my mind, convinced she had nothing to do with me. I certainly wanted nothing to do with her.

But shortly afterward, I was reading Edain McCoy's *Celtic Women's Spirituality* and found an intriguing interpretation of an Irish myth about a young warrior and a three-headed serpent goddess: "When the warrior severed the crone, or third head, he effectively cut [humankind] off from the understanding and acceptance of the natural cycles of life, death, and rebirth."[6]

In spite of my resistance to the word *crone* (and to thinking of myself as one), I found myself fascinated by the old woman's connection to the cycles of nature. Also, this was my third encounter with the crone, and I knew that three is considered a significant number—or a wake-up call—in folklore, dreams, and often in life. So I decided to pay attention this time and see what I could learn about this insistent character.

McCoy had described the crone as the devourer aspect of the goddess, so I started by reading goddess literature and then the mythology of various cultures, hunting for grandmother goddesses. My resistance to the crone was quickly replaced by fascination. Some of these ancient goddesses were devourers, as McCoy had suggested, but they were not senselessly destructive.

The fierce Hindu goddess Kali, for example, is known as the Mother of Death, and yet the terror she instills can be a gateway to integrity and freedom. And Coatlicue, the ancient Mexican Death Mother, is also revered as the Mother of Life. I was captivated by this curious intertwining of death and life and was delighted to discover many grandmother goddesses who were not destroyers at all—Huitaca (the Columbian goddess of joy and intoxication), for example; "The Beautiful Old Woman in Red Garments" (an ancient hearth goddess who taught the Chinese the arts of medicine, herbology, and cooking); and the African goddess Mawu (the Old Woman of the West, co-creator of the world, and bringer of the cooling western winds). Most remarkable were Sheila na Gig and Tlazolteotl, Celtic and Aztec goddesses of sexuality—both old women!

Heartened and inspired, I then explored what psychiatrist Carl Jung called the "treasure trove" of the world's folktales and once again was amazed by the myriad marvelous qualities that older heroines and supporting characters exhibited. Some were witches and hags to be sure, but most were wise, audacious, compassionate, courageous, patient, ingenious, funny, and bawdy, and a few were even described as beautiful.

I was moved by these stories and found myself feeling different about aging as a result of reading them. It became clear that although I had been blessed as a child with a wonderful grandmother, I had unknowingly absorbed the negative stereotypes of older women so prevalent in our culture. My grandmother's being old hadn't been a problem for me, but I was not comfortable with the prospect of growing old myself—and I knew I was not alone.

The characters in the crone tales were revealing some exciting possibilities for aging, and it became important to share what I was finding. Once I discovered that a growing body of research was also revisioning later life in a more balanced and heartening way, writing this book became something I had to do.

Good News and Bad Words

As often happens in stories and in life, hopeful heroines who set off on journeys rather quickly find themselves in trouble of one sort of another—being chased by a monster, getting lost in an ever-darkening forest, or being forced, under pain of death, to perform a series of seemingly impossible tasks. My unforeseen trouble was this: how to share good news about growing old, without using words that would send the very people I wanted to reach running in the opposite direction.

I shared early versions of this manuscript with several women in their fifties, sixties, and seventies. They loved the stories and appreciated the information, but the younger ones especially balked at the language—not just *crone*, but words like *old*, *aging*, even *grandmother*. One asked, "Do you have to say 'old'?" Another suggested, "Can't you just share the good parts without using the word *aging*? I don't want to think about that." And a friend in her seventies said, "'Grandmother' is my grandmother, and she was very old—maybe not in years, but she was *old* old."

The message was loud and clear: We don't want to think of ourselves as old. That presented me with an enormous conundrum: how to talk with women in midlife about what lies ahead without using words related to *old*.

I haven't solved the riddle of how to speak about later life without using problematic words, but grappling with the challenge has been important. It brought home how deeply imbedded our aversion to old age is, especially our own oldness. It also spurred me to do some research on terms associated with the old woman, and that helped de-demonize words like *crone*, *witch*, and *hag*. And ultimately the struggle with offensive language led to the metaphor of winter and its graces.[7]

Crone is a particularly problematic word, though Jean Bolen has done a great deal in recent years to destigmatize it.[8] Some dictionaries trace *crone* back to the Old French *carignon*, which means "rotting flesh"! However, Jungian analyst Marion Woodman and others argue that *crone* is more likely derived from the Latin *corone*, meaning "crown."[9] Thus, a crone is she who belongs to herself and wears the crown of sovereignty in her own life. This theme of sovereignty is also reflected in the tradition among some African Americans of referring to an older woman as "Queen."

Hag and *witch* have been used for hundreds of years as derisive terms for old women. However, the etymology of both is unclear, and some suggest that the root and original meaning of each was reverential. *Hag* may have derived from the Greek *hagia*, meaning "holy," and the words *witch* and *wisdom* may share a common root.

Within these pages, three words will be used to refer to the older woman. The first is *crone* because it was the initial whisper that caught my attention and kept after me until I agreed to write this book. Another helpful word is *grandmother*, a term of respect for a mature woman—not necessarily related by blood—used by many Native American and other tribal groups. The third, *winter's woman*, emphasizes the older woman's participation in the endlessly renewing cycles of nature. In the phases of the year, each season has its beauty and strengths, its lessons and limitations, and its graces. So it is with each season of a woman's life.

An Invitation to Travelers

Winter's Graces is intended primarily for women in their fifties and sixties who are dreading what lies on the far side of midlife. Rare is the woman of any age who looks forward to growing old, but the need for good news about the winter of life is especially pressing in middle adulthood. We who are in the autumn of life are the wise women of tomorrow, and the world needs us to step into our courage, creativity, wisdom, compassion, occasional fierceness, and the rest of Winter's Graces. The growing number of people over sixty-five represents an enormous potential resource for the human family, which desperately needs the steady, ingenious, compassionate wisdom of its grandmothers and grandfathers.[10]

This book is also intended as a celebration of late life and of the old woman in particular. It has been my experience in talking and working with elders that they have discovered many gifts in their seventies, eighties, and nineties. Even so, they have expressed gratitude for having the graces of age confirmed and honored, and they have enjoyed hearing folktales of inspiring older heroes and heroines because they often feel dismissed in our culture.[11] It is my hope that this book will contribute to the growing shift toward celebrating and honoring our elders and their graces.

Finally, I hope that men and younger readers will find value here as well. If you are a young woman or one just entering midlife, may you be inspired to age in your own way, unencumbered by the constrictions of ageist stereotypes. Meanwhile, many of Winter's Graces can be cultivated at any time, for your own and others' benefit, and they do not spring up overnight.

Ageism and sexism affect older men as well, especially the measuring of a man's worth in terms of his income and productive power. My focus on the older woman is not intended to exclude anyone, but rather to honor the crone whose repeated "visits" inspired this project. Almost all of the research and theories of aging included here apply to both genders, unless otherwise specified. Male readers can find a wealth of elder tales and information on late-life development in Allan Chinen's *In the Ever After.*

Regardless of age and gender, I invite you at least to peek through the keyhole of the imposing door marked *OLD AGE* and see for yourself what might lie on the other side. Listen to the words of elders, ponder the scientific evidence, allow the stories of the old ones to permeate your soul, and give winter a chance to bless you with her graces.

Why Stories?

Folktales are a rich repository of humanity's most enduring and healing wisdom. Details shift somewhat over time and vary slightly across continents, but the essential nuggets of truth and understanding are remarkably similar in folktales around the world. If we listen to them with an open mind and heart, stories can help us navigate the inevitable challenges of human life, learn to live in harmony with our fellow creatures, and become what my son Logan (at age six) called "a full grown-up."[12]

The grandmother stories are particularly rich in wisdom because they feature the wise old woman as protagonist or essential supporting character. They are important in other ways as well. First, the crone tales contain delightful older characters that are unconstrained by our limited and limiting ageist stereotypes. In these old stories, we glimpse heartening possibilities for aging with grace, zest, humor, courage, flexibility, and a host of other qualities. In her collection of elder tales, *Gray Heroes*, Jane Yolen writes,

What the folk stories do is give us a narrative—often rife with familiar images or themes or adages—that play out enormous possibilities. An active, engaged, and powerful old age is one such possibility . . . Elderly heroes fight dragons, make love, set things aright with a bit of well-worn wisdom. They save their grandchildren, a city, a kingdom, a castle, a king. They meet the enemy with courage and compassion and cunning.[13]

Stories speak directly to the heart and can inspire us to "get moving" in new directions. The root meaning of *emotion* is "to stir up, to cause to move," and often the stirring of emotions does go hand in hand with the stirring up of lives. "The Midwife of Dakar," for example, might inspire you to venture into unknown territory, in spite of fear. Or "The Wise Woman" might encourage you to stand firmly with what you know in your bones, despite others' doubt or criticism.

Another gift of the grandmother tales is that they pull us out of our isolation and remind us—much like a good friend—that we are not alone. Many elder stories open with a statement of loss or struggle—poverty, mistreatment, loneliness, or the threat of imminent death at the hands of a powerful enemy. They bring to light our shared dilemmas and take us into the heartache of humanity, in a gentle way. They enable us to watch—from the safer distance of the third person—these age-old dramas that are the stuff of life, the heroine's life and our life. These tales help us to remember that we are not the only one who has been mistreated because of age and gender ("Tell It to the Walls") and that we are not alone in our loneliness ("The Woman in the Moon"). Recalling our membership in the human family can be profoundly healing.

And the grandmother stories also offer assurance and comfort because in them we witness not only struggle but also coming through. The ever-optimistic heroine in "The Hedley Kow" shows that even in the face of repeated loss, contentment is possible. And

"The Rope of Ash" is a heartening reminder that seemingly impossible situations often contain hidden seeds of solution. Like a warm blanket, or a cup of cocoa on a winter's night, these stories assure us that through wandering we eventually find our way, and that somehow, despite hardship, "all shall be well."

Folktales have a naturally healing effect on the human psyche when we open ourselves to them. If we take a little time to reflect on a story and notice our responses to it, its effect is enhanced. Questions to encourage such reflection follow each story. Like dreams, stories have multiple meanings for different people and even for the same person at different times. Listening to what a story touches in you is a most reliable guide for uncovering its particular message for you and releasing what Clarissa Pinkola Estés calls story's "medicine."[14]

At the same time, listening to others' responses to a story can be beneficial. In classes and workshops, I've often seen how a comment made by one person in response to a folktale can enrich the experience of others. As a supplement to your reflections, my own are included as well.

The Lay of the Land

Chapters 1 through 11 are devoted to eleven gifts of later life, beginning with the foundational graces of Authenticity and Self-Transcending Generosity and ending with the crowning grace of Wisdom. These chapters each contain one or two stories that illustrate a particular grace; snippets of research that validate it; and examples, quotations, and poetry that amplify it. Each chapter closes with user-friendly tools and practices for cultivating the grace—for those who find that particular quality challenging, or those who are in a situation calling for an extra dose of it.

The final chapter, Blessing, is a grateful acknowledgement of the rich legacy of the world's elders. It is also an invitation for readers to discover and develop the gifts of later life and to grow into wise old women and men, for their own and others' sake.

Winter's Graces may be read in many ways—from cover to cover, or grace by grace, in whatever order you wish; playing with the questions and tools, or exploring the book in your own way. However you travel through these pages, may you find encouragement and nourishment. May you come to appreciate the graces of winter in yourself and in others and dare to share your unique version of them with the world.

—Susan Stewart, PhD
Petaluma, CA
May 1, 2018

1: The Grace of Authenticity

"More and more I belong to myself . . .
It's taken me all the time I've had."
—Florida Scott-Maxwell,
The Measure of My Days

To be fully and freely ourselves is one of the most joyful and hard-won gifts of later life. In the first half of life our primary psychological tasks are establishing an identity and making a place for ourselves in the world. Outer-focused, we take cues from family, friends, and societal standards, often wearing "other people's faces"[1] in order to feel accepted, to belong. We make compromises, play games, keep up appearances, and pretend a little, or a lot.

But in the second half of life, fitting in and pleasing others become less important than being at home in our own skin. The joy of being and trusting ourselves is heightened for women because, traditionally, we have been socialized to value relationships and others' needs ahead of our own.[2] After decades of living for and through others, belonging to ourselves, at last, is an especially precious gift. As we work free of the need for others' approval, we move toward becoming our own authority and the author of our own life. Anne Lamott conveys the joy of coming home to herself as she's aged:

> Age has given me what I was looking for my entire life—it has given me *me*. It has provided time and experience and failures and triumphs and time-tested friends who have helped me step into the shape that was waiting for me. I fit

into me now. I have an organic life, finally, not necessarily the one people imagined for me, or tried to get me to have. I have the life I longed for. I have become the woman I hardly dared imagine I could be.[3]

The French have a wonderful term—*women of a certain age*—that reflects the growing ability in the second half of life to know who we are and to live accordingly. Author and activist Paula Gunn Allen describes a similar trend in the Native American world. "Middle age frees a woman for making choices congenial to her experience, circumstances, and nature. There she can choose who to be, now that her learning, practicing, and nurturing tasks are accomplished." What emerges as women grow older, says Allen, is the "ever-more-evident being of just who they are and who they always have been."[4]

Many women report liking themselves better in midlife, as the youthful hope of perfection gives way to a mature contentment with being good enough, as they are. And winter affords the opportunity to deepen our relationship with the authentic self and to become more attentive and faithful to her promptings. Decreasing demands of childrearing and career in later life allow greater freedom to discover our preferences and follow our own rhythms. Lessening social pressure to look and act a certain way brings a sense of liberation and a daring to live by our own lights, regardless of what others think. And growing awareness of our limits and mortality heightens the desire to devote the time and energy we have to what genuinely matters. The Grace of Authenticity ripens in the winter of life, bringing with it a refinement of power and greater freedom to be ourselves, even to the point of audacity.

Refined Power

Power is a natural outgrowth of living from the inside out, rather than in terms of others' expectations and standards. As a woman comes to know, trust, and honor herself, she grows more effective, more powerful. The power that becomes accessible to winter's woman flows from her deepening fidelity to what holds meaning and value for her. As she focuses on what matters, she becomes a force with which to be reckoned. Refined power is not bullying, nor self-serving, however. Tempered by compassion and wisdom, it is practical, discerning, and, above all, concerned for the greater good.

Human history is so filled with examples of abuses of power that it has become associated with egotism, willfulness, control, domination, and destruction. In addition, with the rise of patriarchy, power has been encouraged in men, but regarded as dangerous and malevolent in women. Fear of "the Old Woman who acknowledges no master," as feminist author Barbara Walker describes the crone, culminated in the torture and murder of over fifty thousand old women and other suspects during the witch hunts of Europe and North America.[5]

Due to its abuse and negative connotations, we have lost a sense of the true meaning of the word *power*. Its root is related to potential, suggesting that power is something natural and latent within that enables us to be effective. As we become more authentic, we can harness our power to do what we must and to deal effectively with obstacles that arise. And as we grow more at home with who we are, we can stand firmly *with* ourselves, rather than stridently *against* others—like the heroine in the following folktale from Norway:

The Little Old Woman Who Went to the North Wind

A little old woman wished to make a loaf of bread, so she went to the miller and bought a bowl of flour. Eager to make her bread, she hurried home. Just as she neared her house, the North Wind whisked by, blowing her flour to the four corners of the world.

The little old woman was dismayed at this bit of bad luck, but she took a coin and returned to the miller and bought another bowl of flour. As she neared her house she held her bowl very carefully, but again the North Wind blustered by, scattering her flour to the four corners of the world.

Once again, the little old woman took a coin to the miller and bought a bowl of flour. And again, despite her care, the North Wind swept the contents of her bowl to the four corners of the world.

"I will go to the North Wind and demand that he give me back my three bowls of flour!" declared the little old woman. She set out and walked a long way until she came to a mountain where she found the North Wind.

"How are you?" asked the little old woman.

"I am quite fine. What might I do for you, dear woman?" asked the North Wind.

"I would ask only that you return to me the three bowls of flour that you blew away," replied the little old woman.

"I am afraid that I cannot fulfill your request, for I have blown those bowls of flour to the four corners of the world. But I will give you something so that you will never be hungry again. Here is my magic tablecloth. Whenever you say to it, 'Cloth, spread yourself!' it will be covered with the finest of food and drink."

The little old woman thanked the North Wind for his kindness and the magic tablecloth and started for her home. Having had no rest for some time, she stopped at an inn for the night, and, feeling quite hungry, she spread out the cloth and said, "Cloth, spread yourself!"

In the twinkling of an eye, the cloth was covered with a feast of such delicacies that the old woman hardly knew where to begin. As she ate, the innkeeper smelled her food and peeked through the keyhole, and when he spied the tablecloth he decided to have it for himself.

When the little old woman went to sleep, the innkeeper sneaked into her room and took the tablecloth, hiding it in his cupboard.

The next morning the little old woman was distraught at finding that her magic tablecloth was missing. She made her way back up the mountain, telling the North Wind that she feared it had been stolen.

"I will give you my magic staff," said the North Wind. "All you must do is return to the inn and say, 'Staff, dance!' The staff will dance on the toes of the thief."

The little old woman thanked the North Wind for his assistance once again and returned to the inn. There she found the innkeeper entertaining his guests with a magnificent feast provided by her magic tablecloth. The little old woman wasted no time in saying, "Staff, dance!"

The staff danced right over to the innkeeper, dancing on his toes. No matter what the innkeeper did, the staff continued to bounce up and down on his toes.

"Please stop this staff!" cried the innkeeper.

"Then return to me what is mine!" cried the old woman.

The innkeeper gladly gave over the tablecloth, and the little old woman left. The staff danced back to the North Wind, and the little old woman returned to her home.

From that day forth, she was never hungry, for the magic tablecloth provided her with the most sumptuous meals until she died.[6]

Some Questions for Reflection

1. What part of the tale speaks most strongly to you, and how is that related to your present life or something (perhaps unfinished) from the past?

2. Is there a situation in your life right now where you need to stand up to a powerful force like the North Wind and assert yourself? How might you apply this heroine's ability to be firm yet kind, assertive yet respectful?

3. When has accepting the loss of something important (like the old woman's flour) led you to something of even greater value (like the magic tablecloth)?

4. When have you refused to surrender to changing circumstances and stayed focused on trying to recover or recreate what was lost? What happened as a result?

5. What helps you in discerning when you need to stand your ground or to surrender to life's unfolding? (Answers might include meditating, walking in nature, talking with a trusted friend, writing, or listening to your body or your dreams.)

6. When have you been like the innkeeper, resenting another's good fortune, rather than being glad for her or him?

7. If you were to incorporate the message of this story and its "medicine"[7] for you, what action or internal shift might you make in your life?

Reflections

The heroine in this tale exemplifies the refined, focused, yet flexible power that emerges in the winter of life. Even though she has been thwarted three times in her attempt to bake a loaf of bread, the old woman goes to the North Wind determined, but not belligerent. Instead of "How dare you!" her first words are "How are you?" She sets a tone for conversation and cooperation rather than opposition. And the North Wind responds in kind: "What can I do for you?" he asks.

The story demonstrates that authentic power is not insistence or force. It is collaborative, and it sometimes entails not getting exactly what we want. This woman stands up for her needs, yet she is willing to accept loss, limitations, and changing circumstances. She does not become attached to a specific plan or outcome.

This interplay of being committed to our own needs and also willing to work with what life brings reflects a fundamental paradox of later life. In winter, we grow more deeply into who we are (Authenticity) and at the same time become more willing to surrender or alter our own agenda when appropriate (Self-Transcending Generosity). The crowning Grace of Wisdom helps us to discern which is needed when and in what proportion—tenacious Authenticity and/or gracious Generosity.

The North Wind is an important and paradoxical character in this story. He appears initially as a troublemaker, but in fact he is an ally who has the old woman's best interests at heart. In many of the world's myths, the wind is a powerful and unpredictable sacred force that pushes the hero or heroine in a new direction that is necessary for the fulfillment of his or her destiny. And the term *true north* is sometimes used to describe the path we must follow, regardless of practicality, other's opinions, or our own plans and preferences.

The North Wind's blowing away the old woman's flour but giving her something far more valuable is a beautiful image for a shift in focus that often occurs in later life (see Chapter 2: Self-Transcending Generosity). Like the woman buying her flour and making her own bread, in youth we tend to focus on making things happen. With age, we recognize that we are part of a Greater Mystery that is a far more reliable source of inspiration and nourishment than our own plans and efforts—like the magic tablecloth.

The end of the story is touching to me. When the old woman has recovered her tablecloth from the unscrupulous innkeeper, she does not waste her time and energy berating him or making sure he pays for his misdeed. She simply takes back what is hers and goes on her way. I've noticed that when I'm tending to my authentic business, I am less likely to be concerned about how others' lives are unfolding. Most of the time, it is none of my business.

Audacious Authenticity

As we grow into knowing, trusting, and honoring ourselves in later life, we give ourselves more permission to be audaciously and unapologetically who we are. In a sense, we come full circle as older women, recovering an uncensored way of being, like young children who have not yet learned to hide parts of themselves and to pretend to be other than they are.

One of the deepest delights of my life is spending time with my grandchildren. The two youngest, Lona and Lukas, were three and one when I was editing this chapter, and I was struck by how clearly they expressed their authentic preferences and emotions, using very few words. And there were moments when curiosity and determination carried them into territory that was dangerous or destructive, and it was necessary to set limits, lest they hurt themselves or someone else.

In a similar way, the audacity of late life is not simply self-indulgence or the reckless acting out of personal whims without regard for others. It is the freedom to be and express ourselves in authentic and unconventional ways, balanced and tempered by the recognition that we are not the center of things, but part of the web of life. Gerontologists, anthropologists, and others have observed that this late-life "license for eccentricity" is often expressed in ribald humor, unselfconscious dancing, and forms of play such as climbing trees and jumping rope with children.[8] The old heroine in the following folktale from Algeria responds to a dire situation with a masterful blend of courage, wisdom, and audacity.

The Wise Woman

The people of a village in Algeria were under siege. Lack of food, water, and medical supplies had nearly reduced them to total destruction. Many had already died, and the remaining few were losing hope.

The mayor called a meeting and said, "My dear friends, the end is near. If we don't surrender immediately we will all die anyway. Perhaps the enemy will take pity on those of us who are still alive if we submit to them now."

The villagers listened with heavy hearts, bowing their heads with their latest burden. Then Aicha came forward. She was an ancient woman, her eyes were still bright, and she walked with dignity.

She turned to the people. "We must not give in just yet. I have an idea, and if you will help me, I believe we will be saved."

"What is your plan, Aicha?" the mayor asked.

"First, I will need a calf!" said Aicha firmly.

The mayor was dismayed. "How can you request a calf? There hasn't been a calf in our village for months."

But Aicha insisted she needed a calf, and the villagers searched far and wide for one. After some time, they found a calf in the shed of a stingy old man who had hoped to sell it later for a healthy price. The villagers triumphantly brought the calf to Aicha, leaving the old man sputtering in anger at his loss.

"You have done well," praised Aicha when she saw the calf. "Now bring me some corn."

The villagers groaned upon hearing her request. But she entreated them to search everywhere. And soon they all returned with bits and pieces of corn until there was enough to fill a bucket. Aicha added some water to it and fed it to the calf.

"How can you feed that calf when children are crying for a bit of food and people are dying of hunger each day?" asked the mayor.

But Aicha continued to feed the calf, stating, "Have faith, sir, and you will see that this will save our village."

The mayor resigned himself to giving in to her. When the calf had finished eating, Aicha led it to the city wall and told the sentry to open the gates. The mayor had followed and nodded to the sentry to do as she requested. When the gates were opened, Aicha pushed out the calf, which then began to graze on the grass outside the gates.

The enemy was watching and wasted no time in capturing the calf and taking it in triumph to their leaders. The enemy king was stunned when he saw what they had brought.

"How can this be?" exclaimed the king. "I thought the villagers were starving, and yet they have a calf they can spare. They must be better prepared than we assumed. However, let us not waste it. We shall feast tonight."

The men soon slaughtered the calf and were shocked to find that its stomach contained undigested corn. They took this news to the king, who became even more concerned.

"If these villagers can feed corn to this calf, they must have more food than we do. We cannot outlast them, or we will be the ones to starve." The kings' men agreed, and he gave the order to retreat.

The next morning the sentry ran to the mayor with the grand news. The mayor gathered the villagers and announced that as Aicha had promised, the enemy had departed. The villagers cheered the old woman, and she lived the remainder of her days in honor and comfort.[9]

Some Questions for Reflection

1. What speaks most strongly to you in this story, and how is that reflected in your life, present or past?

2. When have you felt hopeless and given up, as the mayor suggests the villagers do? What effect did your giving up have on the situation, on you, and on others?

3. When have you persevered in a difficult situation, as Aicha urges the villagers to do, and found resources you hadn't known were available?

4. What helps and what hinders you in standing firmly with yourself in the face of others' doubt and criticism?

5. Where, in your present life, might an audacious, creative ruse like Aicha's plan be just what's needed, for your own and others' benefit?

6. If you were to incorporate the "medicine" of this story for you, what action—large or small—would you dare to undertake?

Reflections

What touches me most in this story is Aicha's ability to stand with herself, trusting her sense of what is needed when others do not understand. It takes enormous courage to pursue an audacious and uncertain course, especially in the face of suffering and of accusations like the mayor's: "How can you feed that calf when children are crying for a bit of food?"

Aicha's plan shows the interplay of the graces of Authenticity, Courage, Creativity, and Wisdom in the winter of life. Authenticity is the foundation of courage, and Aicha's solidarity-with-self helps her to be an effective and courageous instrument. The situation in the village is dire, and necessity demands an unusual, indirect, and creative approach. Materially, there is very little to work with in the village, so Aicha must think practically and, at the same time, audaciously.

Like many older heroines in the world's folktales, she draws on her knowledge of herself (Authenticity) and of the human heart (Wisdom) and correctly senses how the enemy might interpret the presence of a calf with undigested corn in its stomach. There is also great wisdom in how she approaches the villagers. They are frightened, hungry, and hopeless, and her gently asking them to take on one task at a time is very skillful. She praises them for each success as well, which lends them strength and courage for the next step.

Aicha's story also foreshadows the Grace of Self-Transcending Generosity. She is concerned for the well-being of the whole village, unlike the stingy old man who is motivated by selfishness and greed. She understands that they will all survive or die together. This tale offers a powerful lesson in community: each finds something to contribute, even if it is a single kernel of corn. Together, the villagers discover that they have far more resources than they realized.

Aicha's outlandish, ingenious plan is risky, yet it saves them. Even if it had failed, working together to the end, in cooperation and dignity, might have been preferable to surrendering and begging for mercy from an enemy unlikely to be merciful.

Cultivating Authenticity

The journey toward authenticity is a theme that has long fascinated philosophers, poets, psychologists, and other pilgrims, especially in the West. Fortunately, many of these seekers have left behind words of wisdom about the vital importance of knowing and daring to be oneself. In *Hamlet*, for example, Shakespeare advises, "This above all: to thine own self be true." We are beneficiaries of a rich legacy that identifies the attitudes and practices that nurture authenticity and the obstacles that arise as we seek to honor who we really are and to let go of the inauthentic.

Allies of Authenticity

Nurturing the authentic self entails pausing and reflecting, welcoming what disturbs us, letting go of attachments, and daring to heed the promptings of the authentic self, even when they lead to upheaval.

Reflection: Stop, Look, and Listen

Back in the 1950s, parents and teachers urged elementary school children to Stop, Look, and Listen so that they might learn the secrets of passing safely through intersections. I have found this to be a good formula for cultivating authenticity as well.

Stopping is the first step. In our warp-speed and multitasking world, to stop doing and accomplishing may sound foreign, or impossible. And yet it is essential to take breaks from busyness if we are to become acquainted with ourselves. Spending just a few minutes each day doing nothing except simply being quiet can make the difference between a life that is authentic, joyful, and purposeful and one that is distracted, hurried, and unsatisfying.

Step two is turning inward, looking and listening with openness and curiosity. The purpose of this kind of inward attending is simply to notice and acknowledge what is there, without judgment. As we pay closer attention to our emotions and thoughts, to our breath and other physical sensations, to our dreams and daydreams, even to the lyrics of songs we find ourselves spontaneously singing, we glimpse more of what is alive within us. Elizabeth Cady Stanton, an early women's rights activist, observed: "To develop our real selves, we need time alone for thought [and meditation]. To be always giving out and never pumping in, the well runs dry."[10]

Keeping company with the self on a regular basis can bring awareness of unused potential and gifts within us, of defenses and rough edges that need attention and softening, as well as parts of ourselves and our lives that no longer have value for us and need to be relinquished.

Over time, we may come to know some of our frequent inner visitors by name. (Some of mine are Wise Witness, Worry Bird, Little Red Hen, and Undertoad.) By paying attention, we may come to understand the origins of some of these parts of our-selves, to sense what they might need from us and what they have to offer. And if we keep our inner eyes and ears open, we may be surprised as well—by the presence of an insistent longing we did not know we had, by lingering distress over a situation we thought we had resolved, or by an unexpected moment of joy. Our task is to acknowledge all of these; each can teach us something about who we are—if we are willing to learn.

Welcoming the Disturbers

Some inner visitors are more welcome than others. Self-observation brings awareness not only of aspects of ourselves we are pleased to discover, but also of qualities and tendencies from which we would rather run and hide. Psychiatrist Carl Jung called these disturbing, previously unacknowledged parts of ourselves the Shadow, and he observed that they begin to clamor loudly for attention in the second half of life. Shadow elements come calling in the service of authenticity and wholeness, but they also shake the foundations of who we think we are.[11]

In the first half of life, said Jung, our sense of self (ego) is lim-ited, based largely on messages from family and society about what is acceptable and required of us. For example, many women—especially those now in the fall and winter of life—were encour-aged as girls and younger women to develop their emotional skills and their capacity for selflessness, while their intellect, fierceness, and autonomy remained largely unconscious and underdeveloped.

Beginning in midlife, however, all the dimensions of the self that we have disowned begin to demand acknowledgement and inclusion. It can be both frightening and excruciating, for example, for someone identified with being a generous caretaker to admit her resentment and to begin to resurrect her own unlived dreams. For a hardheaded thinker, recognizing her vulnerable, sometimes irrational heart could be equally troubling. However, if we are willing to pay attention to these disturbing, atypical (for us) feelings and longings and acknowledge them as parts of ourselves, we grow toward a more balanced, whole, and authentic self.

The willingness to bless the disturbing, awkward, inconvenient, untamed, contradictory, and embarrassing parts of ourselves also benefits others. The kindness we learn to show toward our inner disturbers spills outward in kindness toward others and their troubling tendencies. As many an elder has discovered, age tends to make us more tolerant of others' faults, as we become increasingly aware of those same tendencies within ourselves.

Relinquishing Attachments

Another ally in the journey toward authenticity—and a counterpoint to embracing the disturbers—is letting go of our attachment to roles, activities, and abilities that have shaped our sense of self for decades but are no longer vital or viable. There are losses in the winter of life as surely as there are graces, and when these losses occur close to the heart of who we have known ourselves to be, we are shaken.

For many women, the fading of physical attractiveness causes a major shake-up, especially in midlife. I can still remember the sense of invasion, embarrassment, and annoyance I felt as a young woman when construction workers sometimes made approving sounds as I walked by. However, when the noises stopped, it was an adjustment. I had never thought of myself as beautiful, but it took time to accept that in my sixties I had become invisible. There is, however, an upside to invisibility: the delicious freedom to be audaciously myself.

Losses in the winter of life may include the inability to do certain things as well or as quickly as we used to. It has been painful for me to recognize and accept that I am not as quick on my cognitive feet as I used to be, nor as good at keeping track of multiple ideas at once. These skills served me well as a teacher. As they diminished, I realized that they had also contributed to my sense of self and worth. Thankfully, accepting those losses has opened up new territory. Along with the loss of speed I've discovered a way of thinking that is slower but richer, sometimes wiser, and often more creative.

Daring to Heed the Authentic Voice

Psychologists such as Abraham Maslow and Carl Rogers, storytellers like Michael Meade, and others describe a potent tendency within each person to become the self he or she must become. Although myriad internal and external forces, like fear, inertia, and coercion, can thwart this actualizing tendency, it keeps nudging us toward authenticity—especially after sixty-five, says Maslow.[12]

When we pay attention, this deep self lets us know when we are living in line with our authenticity. We feel whole, at peace, content, even in the face of outer opposition or internal struggle. This same intrinsic conscience also sends signals when we veer away from what is true for us; we may feel diminished, depressed, off-kilter, angry, at odds with life. In Maslow's words, these small and large acts of self-betrayal "register," and in acknowledging them we begin moving back toward what is authentic and of real value.

It's as if we have a wise and reliable guide residing in our heart and bones who knows what is true and right for us. As we listen, we grow more familiar with her voice. I highly recommend Mary Oliver's poem "The Journey"[13] for an eloquent and powerful description of the deep contentment that comes with listening to that voice and the upheaval that so often ensues when we consent to follow it.

Obstacles to Authenticity

There are many developmental shifts in late life that contribute to the Grace of Authenticity, including the inclination to turn inward and take stock of ourselves and our life, a shift toward the valuing of being over doing, a felt-sense of our mortality, and increasing selectivity about how and with whom we spend the later years of our life.[14] However, despite these developmental nudges toward authenticity in the winter of life, there are obstacles too, internal as well as external ones.

The Tyranny of Niceness

For decades feminists have passionately urged women to throw off the burden of niceness, recognize their value, and reclaim their authority. Even so, early training can be tenacious, and I suspect that the attachment to niceness and the fear of selfishness still lurk in the psyche of many of today's older women. I still feel their presence in my own at times.

We who grew up in the sugar-and-spice era were taught to be nice. That meant being considerate of others, hiding our so-called naughty qualities, and sacrificing our own needs for the sake of others. To do otherwise was considered selfish. What a choice: self-sacrifice or self-ishness! The good news is that those are not the only two options. The bad news is that the alternative—honoring both our own authentic needs and those of our loved ones—is very challenging.

In fact, feminist psychologist Carol Gilligan states that the central, lifelong task of women's development is learning to care for the self *and* for others. It is a lesson we keep learning, forgetting, relearning—over and over.[15]

Even though I was raised to be a sugar-and-spice girl, I some-how managed to muster the autonomy to earn a PhD at twenty-six. However, when I became a mother at thirty-one, caretaking became the center of my life. By forty, I had grasped the idea that I needed to appear on my own priority list, but usually found ways to take care of myself "on the side" so I could remain focused on my children's well-being.

By fifty, I realized that sacrificing my own welfare and being overly responsible for others was taking a toll on me—and on them. Even so, being aware of my own needs and putting them first was almost impossible initially, especially when mine conflicted with those of a loved one. Life kept sending me learning opportunities though, and by sixty, I was starting to understand that self-care and love of others are not mutually exclusive.

One of these learning moments occurred about ten years ago. My granddaughter Madison (then age nine) called to ask if she and her sister could spend the night with me that weekend. Although I love being with them and almost always jump at the chance, the overnight she suggested coincided with the last day of my thirty-plus-year teaching career and the first day of retirement. It felt really important to me to wake up on the first morning of this new chapter of life alone and undistracted. I wanted and needed to pay attention and to savor the transition.

It was hard to say no, but I knew I had to. I told Madison that I would love for them to come another time soon and that I had made a promise to myself about those two days that I needed to keep. Without hesitation, she said, "OK, Grandma," and I could tell from her tone and timing that she meant it. (Bless her heart.)

A few years later it became apparent that a common culprit in many ensnarements in my life was a fear of being selfish. My therapist suggested spelling the word with a capital *S*, and for some reason, I wanted to add a hyphen: Self-ish. I later discovered that the suffix *-ish* means "belonging to." *Self-ish*: that which belongs to the deep, authentic Self. This is selfishness I can embrace whole-heartedly.[16]

At seventy-two, I am able (sometimes) to be aware of others' needs without ignoring my own, to bear the tension between the two when they conflict, and to choose whichever in that moment holds the greater genuine value. In some moments, I choose my needs (as I did years ago with Madison); in others, I tend to another's need. Sometimes I choose well; other times I make a choice and immediately feel dread, sadness, or anxiety. That is usually a clue that I have made a mistake and need to pay attention—and perhaps change course. Slowly by slowly . . . [17]

Other Authenticity Thieves

There are many other habitual ways of thinking and being that undermine authenticity. For example, blaming other people and circumstances for our unhappiness or irritability interferes with looking at what we ourselves are doing and could do differently in the situation.

Comparing ourselves to others is another obstacle to self-knowledge, whether we pride ourselves on imagined superiority or condemn ourselves for failing to measure up. In either case, such senseless scorekeeping drains energy, separates us from ourselves, and causes disturbances in relationships. Other outward-looking habits are seeking others' approval or recognition, the relentless pursuit of perfection, and the need to be right (and convince others of that). There are likely many other mental shenanigans that lead us away from the truth about ourselves. These are just a few about which I know quite a bit.

Addictions can also distract us from authenticity. The overuse of food, alcohol, or other drugs—as well as compulsive spending, sex, gambling, talking, and helping—are numbing, and they distract us from being aware of our experience and ourselves.

One of the most pernicious and pervasive obstacles to authenticity in our fast-moving and multitasking society is distraction (literally, "to pull apart"). Tablets and smart phones enable us to be in one place physically while our minds are miles away. Personal technology can be enriching when used intentionally, but as a chronic presence, it can separate us from ourselves, from one another, and from the natural world.

For many, multitasking is a way of life (and sometimes death, as in the case of distracted driving). A large number of studies have confirmed that when we do more than one thing at a time, we are actually less efficient and more prone to errors and accidents, and we experience more stress. In dividing our attention, we also rob ourselves of experiencing the intrinsic satisfaction of meeting our authentic needs—being fully engaged in a conversation with a friend, or enjoying the good taste of food when we are really hungry; the pleasure of walking when we need to move, or the delicious sweetness of sleep when we are tired. And our lack of presence and attention has an effect on those we are with (yet not present to), especially young children who need the mirroring of attentive adults.

Tools for Cultivating Authenticity

Paying attention is a vital first step for cultivating authenticity in any stage of life. It is a simple and potent way to become more familiar with the self that is uniquely you.

If you don't already do so, allow yourself ten minutes of quiet solitude each morning and ten minutes at day's end, or pause for a few minutes a few times a day if you prefer. Experiment until you find a rhythm that suits you.

One way to shift from autopilot to awareness is to close your eyes, exhale deeply, and simply notice whatever arises—daydreams, memories, feelings, physical sensations, thoughts—preferably without criticism. (If judgments do arise, notice those and let them go.) Whatever comes holds a clue to a part of yourself that may be trying to get your attention. Just listen.

Note: Paying attention not only fosters authenticity; it also has an added benefit in the winter of life. In her work with elders, Harvard psychologist Ellen Langer has observed that deliberately focusing our attention during the day improves both cognitive and physical health. In her book *Mindfulness*, Langer points out that consciously noting what we are experiencing—

rather than operating on autopilot—enhances cognitive functioning and physical vitality in later life.

Journal writing is one of the best practices I've found for keeping company and staying current with the ever-changing authentic self. If you don't already have one, buy a notebook and try spending fifteen minutes a day writing down your feelings, thoughts, whims, and longings, without censorship. It is especially important to welcome the surprising, peculiar, or disturbing bits of self that find their way into a journal. The purpose of journal keeping is to be yourself freely—not to construct a polished (inauthentic) self. Keep your journal in a private place so you'll feel free to express yourself without censure.

In addition to providing a haven for self-reflection and expression, a journal can also function as a place to work with what you discover about yourself. For example, suppose you become aware of a tendency to judge others and yourself harshly. You might take a journal entry in which the judge was especially harsh, underline the critical comments, and experiment with rewriting each of those from a nonjudgmental, more accepting perspective. A journal can be a safe place in which to experiment with new and awkward parts of the self, to vent emotions that need expressing but are best not shared with another, or to gain clarity about what you're feeling or what you'd really like to do in a given situation, if you dared.

Listening to dreams is another way to tap into the authentic self, according to analytic psychology and many indigenous and spiritual traditions. Dreams contain information about the self that is currently inaccessible to us in waking life. Learning to understand dreams helps us to live in a more aware and authentic way. If this is new territory for you, there are many books that include easy-to-use techniques for understanding and working with dreams, for example Jill Mellick's *The Art of Dreaming* and Robert Johnson's *Inner Work*. (A journal is an ideal place for recording and exploring these night visitors.)

Silence is another powerful ally of Authenticity, as well as other graces like Creativity and Contentment. I highly recommend Anne LeClaire's inspiring and inviting book *Listening Below the Noise*, part memoir, part tutorial in the sister arts of keeping silent and listening deeply. As Parker Palmer suggests in *Let Your Life Speak*, "The soul speaks its truth only under quiet, inviting, trustworthy conditions."[18]

Collaging is a simple, enjoyable way to learn more about the authentic self. Gather materials ahead of time, set aside at least two hours, retreat to a quiet, private, and technology-free space, and enjoy! (See wintersgraces.com/collage for simple instructions and a short list of materials.)

Once your collage is complete, consider the possibility that it contains clues to your deeper longings and values. Like dream symbols, the images that find their way into collages often represent important unacknowledged parts of the self that need attention.

When you're finished, put the collage in a private place where you will see it often but others will not. Spend time with it every few days and notice what surprises, pleases, and disturbs you in this version of yourself.

Daring to Do, Speak, and Think for Yourself. Ursula Le Guin once commented, "There are things that the Old Woman can do, say, and think that the Woman cannot do, say, and think."[19] Take some time to reflect on her words and then make a quick list of what you'd like to do, say, or think that you have not yet allowed yourself. Don't overthink—blurt. (This is a good exercise to do in the privacy of your journal.)

Then reflect on what you've written, noting surprises, themes, and risks that your authentic self might want or need to take. Consider taking one of them (start small, with something that is mildly or moderately frightening).

Practicing Firmness. If standing with yourself in the face of others' doubts and criticism is an area where you need some work, bring to mind a current situation where you are allowing others' opinions to overshadow what you know in your bones. Then imagine what one of the heroines in this chapter's folktales might do (or an audacious, powerful woman in your life, a character from a film or novel, or an assertive heroine like Eleanor Roosevelt or Katharine Hepburn).

Then imagine yourself in the situation, standing up for what you feel, believe, need, or want. According to Carl Jung, the psyche does not discriminate between an outer event and an imagined one, so this is a powerful, risk-free way to develop assertiveness muscles.

Watching Movies. Research in neuroscience on mirror cells reveals that our brains react in a similar way when we have an experience and when we see or hear about someone else having it.[20] Thus, listening to stories and poetry, reading memoirs, and watching plays and movies can affect us profoundly. Consider checking out these films and mini-series that illustrate the powerful push toward authenticity in later life: *Woman in Gold, The Best Exotic Marigold Hotel, Wild Oats, The Lady in the Van, Redwood Highway, Philomena, Grace and Frankie, Last Tango in Halifax,* and *Downton Abbey.*

Shadow Dancing. Bring to mind the three or four people you most admire in the world and write a list of their qualities, the things you most respect about them. (These can be real people, living or dead, or characters from a novel or film.) Do the same with the three to four people you most dislike—what qualities do you find most unpleasant in them?

Sit with your first list and consider the possibility that everything you adore and respect in others is also an unacknowledged part of yourself. How might you go about nurturing (and owning) some of these qualities you admire in others?

Now sit with the second list for a time, trying on the possibility that each of these qualities is also a part of you that you have not yet acknowledged. (What we react to strongly in others is usually charged because it is also a part of us that we have not integrated.) Gently ask yourself, "In what ways am I also . . . ?" Or, "In what ways do I actually wish I were a little more . . . ?"

The purpose is not to feel bad about who you are, but to look truthfully at yourself with curious and kind eyes. Consider how elements of these unappealing qualities might be useful to you and the world. For example, pushiness could be transformed into Necessary Fierceness, and selfishness into loving self-care. According to Jung, all the rejected parts of the self (the Shadow) have redeeming features.

Monotasking. For one day, or even half a day, explore the art of doing one thing at a time with as much awareness as you can. Notice the sensations in your mouth as you brush your teeth; chew slowly and taste the food you eat; stay present and really listen in conversations; and when it's time to wash the dishes, just do that.

Allow yourself to savor being alive, simply doing what you're doing, one thing at a time. Keep all media off, unless at some point you want to engage fully in a telephone call, an Internet search that reflects a genuine interest, or a good movie. When you're done using technology for a specific purpose, turn it off. Notice how you are feeling periodically and at the end of the day or half day.

Meeting Authentic Needs and Wants. Take some time off from responsibilities and obligations and devote yourself to noticing and responding to your authentic needs and longings (start small, with an hour, and work up to a whole day or longer). Sleep when you are tired, get up when rested, eat what you'd really like to eat when you're hungry, keep your own company if you wish, or go somewhere you'd really like to go and enjoy being there. Notice how you're feeling, what you're seeing, hearing, tasting, dreaming.

There are strong cultural warnings (mistaken beliefs) that our bodies and our desires are dangerous and will lead us astray.

However, there is ample evidence that attending to our organism's authentic needs and longings is deeply satisfying and engenders contentment.[21] And joyful people spread joy.

Recommended Resources for Authenticity

Here are some excellent books and two audio series to inspire and nurture authenticity:

Breathnach, Sarah Ban: *Simple Abundance*

Estés, Clarissa Pinkola: *Women Who Run with the Wolves* and her five-part audio series, *The Dangerous Old Woman*

Hollis, James: *Finding Meaning in the Second Half of Life*

Johnson, Robert, and Jerry Ruhl: *Living Your Unlived Life*

Langer, Ellen: *Mindfulness*

LeClaire, Anne: *Listening Below the Noise*

Lindbergh, Anne Morrow: *Gift from the Sea*

Mellick, Jill: *The Art of Dreaming*

Moore, Thomas: *Care of the Soul*

Scott-Maxwell, Florida: *The Measure of My Days*

Woodman, Marion: *The Crown of Age* (audio CD)

2: The Grace of
Self-Transcending Generosity

"Ubuntu [means] . . . my humanity is caught up, inextricably bound up, in yours. We belong in a bundle of life. . . . A person with ubuntu is open and available to others, affirming of others, [and] does not feel threatened when others are able and good, for he or she has a proper self-assurance that comes from knowing that he or she belongs in a greater whole."
—Desmond Tutu, *No Future Without Forgiveness*

A paradox lies at the heart of human development: in the winter of life we become more freely, audaciously, and powerfully ourselves (Authenticity) and at the same time, we grow less concerned with ourselves (Self-Transcending Generosity). A feeling of kinship with other human beings and with Life itself often intensifies with age, and the sense of being a separate, solitary self is muted by a deepening experience of interconnectedness.

As we come to know ourselves as part of a bigger story, self-importance and self-centeredness wane, and a more generous way of being in the world emerges. Our unique, authentic core does not disappear, but in later life we grow more willing to transcend (literally, "to climb over") personal concerns for the sake of something greater.

Many of us experience this expanded Self in moments throughout our lives: as children deeply engrossed in imaginative play, as athletes in moments of "flow," as artists when the muse is working through us, as lovers when the boundary between self and other temporarily dissolves. Similarly, the birth of a baby, the arresting beauty of nature, even deep grief, or the nearness of our own death can rekindle a sense of being part of something greater than ourselves.

Such transcendent or "peak" experiences, as psychologist Abraham Maslow called them, are usually accompanied by feelings of oneness, awe, profound gratitude, and peace. And they tend to become more frequent with age, helping us to sink into a deeper, more interconnected sense of identity.

Humility, Altruism, and Magnanimity

Knowing ourselves as embedded in something beyond the personal self leads to a more generous relationship with the world, one that is rooted in humility and expressed in altruism and magnanimity. These three virtues are the essence of Self-Transcending Generosity, and they encourage the development of other graces as well.

Humility (from the same root as *humus*, meaning "earth") implies having an accurate sense of our value and our place in the world. It is neither over- nor under-valuing ourselves, but being "right-sized," as Rolf Gates puts it in *Meditations from the Mat*. An antidote against pride and egotism, humility emerges as we come to know and accept ourselves as we are (Authenticity) and also recognize that we are neither better nor worse, nor more important, than others. We are each a beautiful singer in Life's Chorus.

Life, in general, and aging, in particular, are humbling experiences, if we allow them to be. Cognitive and physical challenges, the death of friends and family members, and other late-life losses bring us face-to-face with our vulnerability and limitations. With age, we learn that there are some things we simply cannot fix or change. Living through challenges of various kinds, over time, helps soften the rough edges of pride and self-importance.

Knowing ourselves as embedded with other people and species

also fosters an unselfish concern for their welfare and a willingness to extend ourselves on their behalf, without thought of reward or return (*altruism*). Summarizing their own and others' research, psychologist Elizabeth Midlarsky and sociologist Eva Kahana write, "Extreme extensivity of concern [unselfishness or unself-centeredness] becomes increasingly probable as the individual grows older."[1]

Magnanimity (literally, "great soul") means nobility of mind, generosity in overlooking injury or insult, and rising above pettiness or meanness. As we take our personal selves less seriously, there is less need to appear special, protect our image, or have things go the way we think they should (Contentment). Identified with an inclusive Self, we have a broader perspective and thus take offense less easily and forgive more readily. We become more generous in spirit and are better able to live in harmony with others, rather than inadvertently creating discord out of an overly personal sense of identity.

Self-Transcendence in Later Life

The broadening of focus beyond the personal self in later life is a recurring theme in gerontology, human development, psychology, psychiatry, theology, and other fields. One of my favorite descriptions of this trend comes from Richard Rohr's *Falling Upward*. He writes,

> In the second half of life, it is good just to be part of the general dance. We do not have to stand out, make defining moves, or be better than anyone else on the dance floor. Life is more participatory than assertive, and there is no need for strong or further self-definition.[2]

Carl Jung was the first in Western psychology to recognize that in midlife we begin to "outgrow" our ego-based identity and are pulled toward a broader and deeper sense of Self that is uniquely individual but also collective.[3] And Jungian analyst Marion Woodman views the older woman's willingness to transcend her personal agenda on behalf of something more important as a defining characteristic of a mature crone.[4]

Swedish sociologist Lars Tornstam explores the waning of self centeredness in later life and the evolution of a broader, more "cosmic" view of the world in his book *Gerotranscendence*. Many of Tornstam's older subjects described an increased feeling of affinity with other people (including those in past and future generations) and a growing sense of communion with the mystery of life-and-death. Sensing our place in something greater than ourselves, says Tornstam, draws us forward and outward, into a more altruistic relationship with the world.[5]

The 250 Japanese older adults who offered to take the place of young people assigned to clean up nuclear waste after the 2011 earthquake are a powerful example of Self-Transcending Generosity. So are Jimmy and Rosalynn Carter, now in their nineties, who have been working with Habitat for Humanity every year since 1984, helping to build and repair homes and to bring attention to the worldwide need for affordable housing.

A desire to "give back" often intensifies in later life, and communities around the world are enriched by the large numbers of elder volunteers who collect and distribute food to the hungry, tutor children, offer professional or management assistance to non-profits, serve as foster grandparents, raise funds for disaster relief, and otherwise contribute their life experience and skills to the greater human family.

The shift toward a more inclusive identity is a natural trend in later life, but it is not guaranteed. It is more a call that we can answer, resist, or attempt to ignore. And it is a challenge. Developmental psychologist Erik Erikson notes that middle adulthood presents us with a choice: to expand our circle of concern and actively contribute to the broader human family, or to remain primarily focused on our own needs and those of a few select others.

The latter option, Erikson observes, leads to stagnation in midlife and to meaninglessness and despair in the winter of life. On the other hand, contributing to others, especially younger generations (generativity), enhances well-being in later life.[6]

Similarly, psychologist Robert Peck identifies a number of late-life tasks that revolve around the theme of transcendence versus preoccupation. One of these tasks is learning to adjust to physical changes as we age, rather than becoming preoccupied with health problems or physical limitations (body transcendence.)[7] It is easy to fall into what Jean Bolen calls "organ recitals," but chronic complaining about our bodies tends to narrow our focus, to undermine generosity, and to separate us from other people who understandably grow weary of listening to litanies of woe. As Bolen notes, "Whining is conduct unbecoming a crone."[8]

Here is a story from the Kenyah people of Malaysia about a magnanimous old woman who puts the greater good ahead of her own enormous loss and grief. The tale also highlights two traditional roles of the elder: storytelling and the transmitting of values to the young. The story itself is embedded in a short tale-about-the-tale that appears in italics.

Ubong and the Headhunters

It was evening time in the long house of Lepo Tau. The women and children were coming back from bathing in the river carrying on their backs baskets containing water in bamboo tubes.

A few men, who had returned from their farms, were trying to tie their boats at the river banks. They had brought with them some vegetables and a wild boar, which they had caught at their farm. High over the roofs of the house of Lepo Tau, wisps of grey smoke were curling up in the sky.

A few swallows were still busy dipping down over the river, taking their evening meal of insects. Now and again one would dip into the water and out again, leaving behind drops of water like a stream of pearls. On the verandah of the longhouse sat an old woman with silver hair. In the dying light of the day she was busy with her beads, threading them carefully onto a string. She wanted to make a beaded hat to present to her granddaughter who was soon to be married.

A few of the children gathered around the old woman, watching her intently. She looked up from her work, and her face was sorrowful but still kindly, and in her eyes were sorrow and joy mixed together. One of the little children asked her to tell them a story. The old woman put down her beads and the hat she was making, and she told them this story:

Long, long ago, before any of your parents were born, we people of Lepo Tau came and settled on the Baram River. We had to come here from the Usun Apau because of the famine there, and after many wanderings we found this lovely spot at the mouth of the Moh River.

The leader of the people in those days was my husband. He was a very fine warrior called Balan. That year we were just harvesting, and my husband was spending the night in the farm. I stayed at home because we were about to have our first child. Most all the other people were out in the farms.

Suddenly as I sat in the verandah of the house I heard a tremendous noise, and people were shouting, "Ayau! Ayau! Head-hunters! Head-hunters!" Suddenly a host of Bakong people rushed onto the verandah. We were always terrified of the Bakong because they had been our enemies for a long time. I rushed into my room and hid myself in a corner.

The Bakong came and said they were looking for a particular man. "Have you seen him?" I could hear them asking the people outside. No one had seen him. The Bakong then rushed out to the other side of the house brandishing their swords and spears.

I dared not venture out but stayed in my room all night. The next morning, I was waiting for my husband to turn up. He had promised to come back because I was about to give birth. After some time, I heard a few people from the river bank, and I could hear the sounds of mourning. "Who could it be?" I thought.

I rushed out and down the ladder and ran to the river bank,

and there an old man came up to me and said, "I have terrible news for you. Last night the Bakong people killed your husband."

Now, Balan was a very fine man. His hair was sleek black like the back of a snake. He was strong and straight, and his limbs were tough. No one among the whole of the Bakong people dared fight with him, so strong he was. But then I heard the story:

That night my husband was sleeping soundly in a leaf hut far away from the longhouse. Because it was harvest time he was protecting the rice from the hungry squirrels, deer, and the wild boars.

Suddenly out of the jungle and the gloom, a party of Bakong warriors threw down the door of the hut and cut off the head of the sleeping man. For months and months, they had been hunting for a particular man in retaliation for what he had done to them. Unfortunately, they got the wrong man, and the noblest of the Kenyahs, a man who was renowned for peace-keeping, lay a victim of their savage revenge.

There was a great mourning in the house for eight days, and afterwards we buried my husband, and you can see his monument upriver. After some time, my child was born, and he was given the name of Oyau because his father was dead. After a year many people of the house asked me to marry again, but I resolved that I would remain faithful to my dead husband and join him later in Alo Malau.

The Lepo Tau people were filled with hatred for the Bakong people, and they set off up the Moh River and followed the enemy into their own country. Year after year the fighting went on between our two tribes, but I had no thought for revenge.

Every year I thought to myself, why should our people go on fighting like this, killing one another and wasting all their manpower? It was senseless, this eye-for-eye revenge, this never-ending blood feud.

I reminded the people of the great qualities of their dead leader, of his courage, of his prowess at hunting, his pride in his mountain padi field. I used to talk to the young men and tell them to be brave hunters, and to hunt for animals but not for men.

On the wall of my room I kept my husband's sharp parang [a short sword] with a delicately carved hilt, his plumed helmet with its gleaming shower of hornbill feathers, and his string of precious blue beads. I was Balu, a widow, and though free to marry and still young and beautiful, I refused to take anyone in marriage.

After some years I decided on a plan to make peace with the Bakong people. I had heard that a party of Bakong men was coming down the river in a long boat, and our people were getting ready to ambush them. But that night I called a meeting, and because I was a princess I was allowed to speak to them.

"Look here, you people, how foolish you are! All these years you have been fighting with the Bakong people, and they are also Kenyahs. Why should we fight our own kith and kin? Tomorrow when the Bakong people come I am going to invite them up to the house and make a feast and in that way show them that we want to live peacefully with them."

To this all people of Lepo Tau agreed because they too were tired of the endless war and blood feud. The whole night long there was the sound of merriment and festivity in the house. Chickens were killed, wild pigs were roasted, and rice wine was prepared in great earthenware jars.

Early in the morning when the mist was still hanging above the river we could hear the sound of a long boat. The Bakong people were nearing the house of the Lepo Tau people. Just as they were passing, the headman of the Lepo Tau people hailed them and called them to come up.

Shyly the Bakong moored their boats, and they came up to the long gallery of the longhouse. To their astonishment, they were invited to partake of the peace meal. They sat down with their backs to the river. And after they had eaten, the Lepo headman offered them rice wine, and in their songs the Lepo people asked that the Bakong live at peace with them and be friendly with them forever after.

In reply, the headman of the Bakong people offered rice wine to the headman of the Lepo Tau. He asked for mercy, saying that they had done great wrong in killing Balan and that they were brothers. And they promised from henceforth they would no longer go to war with their relatives, the Lepo Tau people. Everyone praised the courage of Balu Ubong, the faithful widow who preached mercy, forgiveness, and love.

The children listened to her story, and as they watched they saw the old woman's eyes grow misty with tears as she remembered her loving husband. From the day of the feast, the Lepo people and the Bakong people have lived peacefully with one another.[9]

Some Questions for Reflection

1. What have been the major losses in your life? How have you responded to them—with a mixture of sorrow and kindness, like Ubong? With anger, blame, and bitterness? Denial and distraction? With depression and despair? Or . . . ?

2. When have you blamed another or sought revenge for a wrong you later learned was unintentional? Have you made sufficient amends? Have you forgiven yourself and the others involved?

3. When have you been punished or blamed for something you did not do, or did by mistake? How did you respond? To what degree have you forgiven those who blamed or accused you?

4. When in your life have you been willing to make a generous gesture of peace toward someone you had seen as an enemy? What was the result?

5. What part of this story speaks most strongly to you, and how is that related to your life, now or in the past? If you were to take to heart the medicine of this story, what shift might you make in your life?

Reflections

What touches me most in this story is Ubong's ability to forgive the senseless murder of her husband, just when she is about to give birth to their first child. What magnanimity, to be able to forgive the men responsible for killing—by mistake—her beloved Balan.

Her terrible loss and immense grief are still apparent in the winter of her life (in her sad but kindly face), yet she has not hardened her heart. At a personal level, she is a grieving Lepo Tau widow, but she also knows herself as a Kenyah and a member of the human family.

Ubong's loss could easily have instilled bitterness and a desire for revenge, but instead it inspires her to a life of peacemaking. She begins by telling stories to the young—a traditional role of the elder—transmitting the values of courage, hard work, and peace to the next generation. In the process, she honors her husband's memory and legacy.

After years of warfare between her people and their neighbors, Ubong's plan for a peace feast is quite risky, and it represents a complete change of direction. Yet it succeeds—in part because the villagers too have grown weary of the killing. As they prepare food and wine for the feast, the sounds of merriment fill the night. Something new is in the air. The next day, the Lepo Tau feed the Bakong people and express their desire for peace, and the Bakong in turn ask for mercy for their mistaken killing of Balan. Both groups promise to live in peace with their relatives, whom they no longer view as enemies. Generosity begets generosity.

There is another seemingly small detail at the beginning of the story that feels important to me: Ubong is beading a hat for her granddaughter who is about to be married. Despite the tragedy that cut short her own marriage and the grief she still feels, Ubong invests her love and hope in future generations.

The Science and Spirituality of Self-Transcendence

Until fairly recently self-transcendence and oneness were regarded as the territory of mystics and spiritual seekers. We are fortunate to be living in a time, though, when many scientists are validating the interconnectedness of life. As naturalist John Muir observed in *My First Summer in the Sierra*, "When we try to pick anything out by itself, we find it hitched to everything else in the universe."[10]

Moving beyond the personal self and recalling our place in a bigger, more inclusive Self is a perennial theme that runs through the world's religions and spiritual traditions.[11] The process is referred to by many names, including *ego transcendence, self-forgetting, cosmic consciousness, spiritual awakening, samadhi (union),* and *the realization of the higher self.* Despite variations in language, the theme is similar: Originally and essentially, we are interconnected in the web of life. For a time, we forget our true identity and unity, and the purpose of life is to wake up and remember who we really are.

For example, the sage Lao-tzu, from the sixth century BC, describes the kindness and contentment that come from remembering our kinship with one another. "Each separate being in the universe returns to the common source. . . . When you realize where you come from, you naturally become tolerant, disinterested, amused, kindhearted as a grandmother, dignified as a king."[12]

According to Oglala Sioux author Ed McGaa, the essence of Native American spirituality is *Mitakuye Oyasin,* which means "we are all related."[13] Within that worldview, all of life is sacred and interdependent. The unique gifts of each person are valued, as is personal action, so long as it does not harm others, Mother Earth, or the Great Spirit. Concern for the whole of life extends forward and backward in time as well. Ancestors are honored, and present decisions are made in light of their potential effects seven generations hence.

Scientists in many fields have begun confirming the oneness of life that spiritual masters have taught for millennia. For example, neuroscientists have discovered that when one person witnesses another's experience, certain "mirror cells" in the same area of the brain are activated in both participant and observer. Dr. Vittorio Gallese points out, "This neural mechanism is involuntary and automatic . . . It seems we're wired to see other people as similar to us, rather than different. At the root, as humans we identify the person we're facing as someone like ourselves."[14] In other words, we are neurologically wired to recognize and respond to one another as kin.

Physicists, too, have confirmed that we live in an essentially interdependent or "entangled" universe. Einstein's observations convinced him that the fundamental truth of existence is relatedness, not separation. In 1972 the *New York Times* published a letter he composed in response to a grieving rabbi who sought his counsel. Einstein writes,

> A human being is a part of the whole, called by us "Universe," a part limited in time and space. He experiences himself, his thoughts and feelings as something separated from the rest—a kind of optical delusion of his consciousness. This delusion is a kind of prison for us, restricting us to our personal desires and to affection for a few persons nearest us. Our task must be to . . . [widen] our circle of compassion to embrace all living creatures and the whole of nature in its beauty.[15]

Astronomers are also finding evidence that we are embedded in a universe more interconnected than previously imagined and that we are all (humans, animals, plants, and stars) made of the same elements. The late Jerry Waxman, an extraordinary astronomy teacher, describes the interconnectedness of life at all levels, from the intracellular to the intergalactic:

> The spectacular truth is—and this is something that your DNA has known all along—the very atoms of your body—

the iron, calcium, phosphorus, carbon, nitrogen, oxygen, on and on—were initially forged in long-dead stars. That is why when you stand outside under a moonless country sky, you feel some ineffable tugging at your innards.[16]

Cultivating Self-Transcending Generosity

The shift from a personality-centered identity to a more inclusive one is a developmental inclination in the winter of life, yet such a fundamental change rarely occurs quickly or smoothly. It challenges the claims of the ego or "little self" and pulls us beyond familiar ways of seeing and being. In addition, this interconnected and interdependent view appears to run counter to much of what twenty-first-century American culture holds dear: independence, self-determination, and individual accomplishment.

But autonomy and interdependence are not really opposites; they are complementary. We are both individuals and part of something larger, and our unique life experience and authentic gifts are what we have to share with the world. Thus, the cultivation of Self-Transcending Generosity entails opening ourselves to experiencing the Self-beyond-ego, continuing to set firm but kind limits on the troublemaking tendencies of the little self, and increasingly using our authentic power and gifts to serve something greater than ourselves.

Nurture the Big Self

The inclusive Self is a perspective and way of being that we return to or rediscover, not something we construct or fully achieve. We can foster the recovery of this Self-beyond-self by taking time out from "the fever of life"[17] and pursuing activities (and inactivity) that broaden our attention beyond the borders of our personal concerns and identity. Savoring the beauty of nature, for example, can put us in touch with the vastness and harmony of the web of life. By simply being quiet and paying attention, the Self-beyond-self becomes a more palpable presence.

The broader vision of the Self-beyond-self is sometimes called *witnessing*. It entails seeing situations in which we're involved from the perspective of a wise onlooker who observes the whole picture, our part as well as others', with compassionate, non-judgmental eyes. When we can allow the clear and kind witness to do our seeing, we deepen our connection to the Self-beyond-self. In the process, our relationships grow more harmonious because our motivation is to understand and live in harmony, not to win or to be right (which are often the ego's misguided motives).

The inclusive Self has its eye on the bigger picture, rather than on our personal desires, preferences, and agendas. Consciously broadening our focus as we move through each day heightens awareness of others who might need kindness or assistance. Giving and doing what we can is a natural response to that awareness, especially in the winter of life when we may move a bit more slowly, have fewer demands on our time, and thus are more likely to notice the suffering of others and to take the time to do what we can in response.

Temper the Little Self

To borrow a metaphor from gardening, the seeds of the Self-beyond-self are planted deep in us from the beginning, and late life provides the sun and the water necessary for their growth. Still, the little self is a perennial presence, like weeds in a garden. As long as they are thinned periodically, weeds can enhance a garden by preventing erosion and providing mulch and shade. And some— like oxalis and wild garlic—have flowers that are quite beautiful. The trick is to keep weeds sufficiently thinned so that they don't consume the bulk of the water and nutrients, or strangle the plants we want to encourage.

Similarly, the little self can serve important day-to-day functions. She is very good at planning and strategizing, for example. As Krishnamurti once quipped, "You need an ego to get to the bus." However, the ego is prone to inflation and other delusions, and needs tempering (literally, "regulating or proper mixing").

Limiting the influence of the little self begins with observing what she does and what happens as a result. Watching the small self is best done with kind and curious eyes, as if she were a child we love who is going through a difficult period and inadvertently causing trouble for herself and others. Conflicts with other people; familiar, tenacious, and unpleasant emotional states; obsessive thinking; and disastrous repetitive patterns of behavior are all rich laboratories for learning about the particular shenanigans of our ego and loosening their grip.

Over and over I learn that all human behavior, regardless of how obnoxious, makes sense in the context of a person's life experience. My own little one is overly sensitive to criticism, afraid of abandonment, and prone to judging herself and others. She takes her mistakes and flaws far too seriously, thinks she is right most of the time (and wants others to agree), and feels overly responsible for the emotional welfare of those she loves. Needless to say, she causes a great deal of grief for me and for others.

Beneath the surface of much of our recurring distress and unhappiness are stories, based on our interpretation of early experience, fueled by subsequent events, and distilled into mantras we unconsciously chant to ourselves. In becoming familiar with the erroneous themes that run through our life story, we can become freer of them over time. We can learn to interrupt a familiar scenario, to see it from a broader perspective, and thus save ourselves and others considerable suffering. The more aware we are of the peculiar mischief of our little self, the better able we are (a least some of the time) to divert her.

My granddaughter Natalie taught me a lesson about the patient work of diversion many years ago. One morning she and her sister and I were walking on the beach and came to a stream, created by recent rains, that was flowing down from the hills, across the beach, and into the ocean. Natalie stopped and began scooping up handfuls of sand and carrying them to the places where small streams were flowing sideways rather than to the sea. Patiently, she patted down the relocated sand, then went for more, apparently determined to block off these small wayward streamlets and encourage them to join the flow toward the ocean.

It was a fairly shallow but substantial creek, and knowing the tendency of water to go where it has flowed before, I was pretty sure her efforts to redirect the stream were doomed. But she was enjoying herself and wanted to keep working, so Maddy and I kept walking the short distance to the end of the beach. When we got back half an hour later, the entire stream was flowing easily to the sea. Natalie's patient scooping and patting had diverted the renegade rivulets.

Whenever we are able to divert the little self in the midst of making trouble, we strengthen the development of the Big Self and reunite ourselves with the larger flow. This is recurring, often difficult, but good and important work, for ourselves and for others. We all benefit each time one of us is willing to move beyond the ego's concerns or distress and to focus instead on what matters in the bigger picture.

Tools for Cultivating Self-Transcending Generosity

Practice Daily. We are blessed to have access to a multitude of practices that help restore awareness of our essential interconnectedness, for example, walking or sitting meditation, inspirational reading, listening to sacred music, or practicing yoga or Tai Chi. Devoting fifteen to thirty minutes each morning (and/or evening) to one of these or another practice is an invaluable way to start and end the day, recalling our place in the great web of life.

Taking time each day to be aware of breathing is a simple yet profound way to experience the interconnectedness of life. As Ram Dass and Mirabia Bush suggest,

> A simple breath meditation can be helpful because it returns us to a basic connection to the world. As we breathe in and out, and bring our awareness gently to our breath, we are experiencing the world coming into us and ourselves going back out into the world. We are reminded in a simple, physical way, that we are not separate from the world but continually interacting with it in the very makeup of our being.[18]

Go Outdoors. One of the most powerful and pleasurable ways to experience being part of the web of life is to spend time in nature. Places of natural beauty restore a sense of perspective, reminding us of the vastness of creation, its exquisite shapes and colors, its steady cycles and surprises, and its varied inhabitants. Each has a place, all are connected, and none is in charge.

Recall Moments of Oneness. Set aside some time to sit quietly and recall a time when you felt at peace or at one with Life. Choose an experience that was especially vivid and allow yourself to go back and remember whatever details you can—what happened, what you saw and heard (and perhaps smelled or tasted), what you felt, and how you were affected at the time and afterward. Such timeless moments are gifts. They are doorways into Oneness and offer important reminders of connectedness when savored afterward.

Express Kinship. Another way to remember our essential oneness is to act as if everyone we meet in the course of a day is a brother or sister (which is true). Extend to friends and strangers alike—

whether they are behaving in ways you like or don't—the same kindness you would to a beloved friend: look into their eyes and smile, nod or say hello (and mean it), and wish them well in your heart. Do this for a week—or a month—and notice what happens in your interactions with others and within yourself.

Walk in the Other's Moccasins. My aunt Verna had a plaque in her entryway that contained a familiar Native American saying: "Don't judge another until you have walked a mile in his moccasins." Verna, who was part Cherokee, lived that credo, and she was one of the most loving people I have known.

The next time you lock horns with someone you find annoying or frustrating, someone you judge or wish would change (especially if this is a person with whom you are frequently in conflict), try taking his or her part in your imagination. How might the situation look through this person's eyes? What might this person's behavior be expressing or trying to achieve, even if it isn't working very well?

Recalling what you know of this person's life experience, how might this present behavior make sense in terms of his or her life story? If this person is a stranger, you might ask yourself: what might make someone act this way? Consider the possibility that he or she is "doing the best with what he or she has been dealt"—as we all are.

Loosen the Grip of Ego. The little self has an exaggerated sense of self-importance and becomes distressed (and distressing) when she doesn't have what she thinks she needs. Fortunately, the ego's upsets offer a chance to observe the little one in action and to loosen her grip on the steering wheel (she is a better passenger than driver).

The next time you are overreacting or are stuck in distress (judging or complaining about another, feeling unduly anxious or offended, envying another's good fortune, being angry about how things are unfolding, or . . .) exhale, take a step back, and see if you can identify the story beneath your reaction. Ask yourself: What, specifically, has set off your little one? What is she telling herself that has her so upset? What is she afraid of, and what does she need from you?

Then look at the situation as the kind witness. From that broader perspective, what is going on for everyone involved? What does each need? Notice the difference in how it feels when the little one is in charge, and when the witness does the seeing. From that inclusive perspective, what might you do to foster harmony in this situation, rather than fear or discord?

Experiment. As you become better acquainted with the particular kinds of suffering your ego tends to stir up, it can be helpful to conduct experiments that give her a chance to experience more inclusive, harmonious ways of being. For example, if she easily slips into needing to be right, invite her to set that aside for a week (or a day) and to listen for the value in others' points of view. When she is tempted to argue that she knows best, urge her to try being quiet instead and see what she can learn.

Any kind of recurring distress can be turned into an experiment (from the root *experiri*, which means "to try")—being depressed, feeling jealous or judgmental of others, or being unduly angry. The key ingredients for an effective experiment are as follows: approach the little one with an invitation (versus condemnation or a demand); suggest a short, manageable timeframe (an hour to a week, depending on the tenacity of the distress); give the ego an alternative focus and task (versus just telling her to stop!); and respond with kind firmness when she reverts to her old tricks (she will) and wants to call the whole thing off (not recommended, though you may need to adjust the experiment in some way).

Notice Effects and Check Motives for Giving. Acts of Self-Transcending Generosity have a clean, good, and right feel to them, even when they involve hardship or risk. On the other hand, giving that is rooted in obligation, self-denial, or compulsion tends to generate feelings of exhaustion or resentment, expectations about how others should respond to our giving, or a sense that there is no room for us in our own life. When your giving is "off" in some way or when others react to your helpfulness with hostility, indifference, or entitlement, it's important to identify what's amiss.

Take some time for yourself, especially if it feels like you can't afford it. Close your eyes and give yourself the gift of a few minutes of breathing deeply and begin to notice the thoughts and feelings that arise, without judging them.

At some point, invite the wise witness to look on the situation that is generating resentment, grief, or overwhelm, and from that perspective try to discern what is going on. Specifically, what is off-kilter? Are some of your authentic needs being sacrificed? Are you giving in a way that does not really serve the other's best interests, or helping more than you can realistically sustain? What can you do to rebalance so that your generosity is unselfish in the best sense of the word?

Sometimes giving and serving are "off" because our motives are unconscious or mixed. Even noble-seeming acts of generosity can be self-serving, motivated by duty or fear; by a desire to appear generous, to feel important, or to avoid the distress in our own life; or by the mistaken belief that it is up to us to make sure everything (and everyone) is all right.

Be honest with yourself: check your motives and notice the effects your giving has on others. How do you feel in the situation, and how do you sense your help is being received? Is it serving the other's highest good, or perhaps inadvertently perpetuating dependency, or the other's addiction to drugs, overspending, or overworking?

If the latter applies, there are twelve-step meetings in communities around the world that can be invaluable (check the web for local Co-dependents Anonymous [CODA] and Al-Anon groups). Excellent, reasonably priced books are available for purchase at most meetings.

Forgive. Drawing inspiration from the widow Ubong in the story above, consider the major losses and disappointments of your life to see whether you are still carrying resentment or hard-heartedness toward others. What would it take for you to be willing to forgive, for your own sake as well as for theirs?

Recommended Resources for Self-Transcending Generosity

Bourgeault, Cynthia: *The Wisdom Jesus*

Carter, Jimmy: *The Virtues of Aging*

Dass, Ram, and Mirabai Bush: *Compassion in Action*

Gates, Rolf: *Meditations from the Mat*

His Holiness the Dali Lama and Desmond Tutu: *The Book of Joy*

Leder, Drew: *Spiritual Passages*

Rohr, Richard: *Falling Upward*

Schachter-Shalomi, Zalman, and Ronald S. Miller: *From Age-ing to Sage-ing*

Schaefer, Carol: *Grandmothers Counsel the World*

Young-Eisendrath, Polly, and Melvin E. Miller: *The Psychology of Mature Spirituality*

3: The Grace of Courage

"Life shrinks or expands in proportion to one's courage."
—Anaïs Nin, *The Diary of Anaïs Nin, Volume 3*

Courage is essentially choosing to move toward fear, rather than running the other way or turning to stone in its presence. The word derives from the French *coeur* (meaning "heart"), which suggests a relationship between the capacity to love and the courageous willingness to do what we must, regardless of the cost to ourselves.

Courage does not imply the absence of fear, but rather responding with integrity in the face of it. A primary virtue in cultures around the world, courage is crucial for living out our deepest values. Without it, our lives (and hearts) shrink, as we pursue instead the well-worn paths of least resistance or of imagined safety.

Courage is strengthened in the winter of life by a number of developmental trends, such as increasing personal power and effectiveness (Authenticity), deepening concern for the well-being of all (Self-Transcending Generosity), an increased capacity to endure uncomfortable emotions such as fear (Contentment), and the flowering of Wisdom (the ability to discern the best course in complex, uncertain, and important matters).

The Many Faces of Courage

The earliest conceptions of courage focused primarily on acts of valor or bravery, especially in combat, but over time philosophers and psychologists have identified several forms of this virtue. The four most common are physical, moral, social, and creative, and many dangerous or difficult situations call forth more than one of these. In addition, a more private, everyday form—sometimes called personal courage—involves meeting ongoing challenges in our own and others' lives, day after day, with wisdom and strength.

Physical Courage

Physical courage means risking injury or even death when something important is at stake, often to protect someone in danger. Declining physical strength, endurance, and speed in late life diminish our physical resources to some degree. However, the internal allies of courage—such as patience, steadfastness, and altruism—are often enhanced, and acts of physical courage still occur in the winter of life.

In *The Heart of Altruism*, Kristen Renwick Monroe tells the remarkable story of Lucille B, a frail grandmother with a heart condition and braces on both her leg and back, who came to the aid of a young woman who was being raped by a large man across the street from her home.[1] Both women survived, though they were seriously injured.

Lucille received an Andrew Carnegie award for her heroism, which made her self-conscious because she saw herself as simply doing what needed to be done. She credits her mother and especially her grandmother for teaching her "to love all humanity . . . to defend people and myself, but mostly to fight against any injustice that was being done."[2]

Personal Courage

Courage means living from love rather than from fear, and every day there are moments of choice when we either respond to what is occurring with fear and avoidance or with commitment and care. For many, the winter of life brings challenges requiring enormous everyday courage—such as caretaking a spouse with dementia;

raising grandchildren whose parents are unable to care for them; or coping with a serious illness of our own. Situations like these call us to respond moment by moment to what is unfolding, keeping our hearts as open as possible, discerning what is needed, doing the best we can, and enduring the anxiety, anger, grief, and other emotions that arise when sustaining courage day after day.

The late Elizabeth Bugental is a beautiful example of personal courage in the winter of life. Elizabeth was my therapist during a painful period in my forties, and I happened to sit next to her twenty years later at an event at the local university. Her husband had recently suffered a stroke that severely affected his memory, and was I moved by the joy with which she spoke of their life together. Even though it was palpable how much she missed the parts of him (and of their life) that were "gone," she also said that every day was different and that they continued to find new ways to love and connect with one another.[3]

Elizabeth later wrote *Love Fills in the Blanks: Paradoxes of Our Final Years*, based on her own and others' experiences of the losses and opportunities that growing old brings. Her life is an exquisite testament to the beauty and power of personal courage and love in the winter of life, and it illustrates how one woman's responding to a painful loss with courage and openheartedness can become a gift to others.

Personal courage can also take the form of the willingness to address—rather than avoid—the wounds in ourselves that in turn wound others. Princeton philosopher and researcher Daniel Putman uses the term "psychological courage" to describe the willingness to confront and work through our destructive habits, addictions, irrational fears and anxieties, and the patterns in our relationships that lead to being emotionally controlled by (or controlling of) others.[4] This is difficult, often painful, yet life-giving work. It seems to me that psychological courage is a key factor in whether we become more rigid, brittle, and defended versions of ourselves as we age, or grow into wiser, more tolerant, and more generous human beings.

It is very human to want to avoid the pain of looking honestly at ourselves by numbing out, denying or minimizing our problems, distracting ourselves, or blaming our distress on others. However, these reactions only perpetuate suffering for ourselves and for those around us. On the other hand, psychological courage means facing, rather than running from, the truth about ourselves, holding ourselves accountable, and dealing with our attitudes and behaviors that harm others and ourselves.

Good friends can assist us in facing the wounded and wounding parts of ourselves—friends who see us clearly and care enough to tell us the truth with kindness. Good psychotherapy can also be invaluable in bolstering psychological courage. And for many, anonymous twelve-step groups provide a safe place to face and speak the truth and to lend others courage and hope as they wrestle with what needs to be addressed in themselves. I've found all three invaluable at different points in my life when I needed to come to terms with something destructive in myself. Through whatever means, in developing the courageous willingness to acknowledge and act on the truth about ourselves, we become freer to live more authentic, fulfilling, and bestowing lives.

Creative Courage

Creative courage involves stepping into new territory and bearing the terror of the unknown. It requires letting go of familiar ways of being and doing and learning to tolerate not knowing. In this sense creativity is not a quality reserved for artists and inventors but is a way of living—and a form of courage—accessible to all of us. Dancer and choreographer Agnes de Mille called it *leaping in the dark*: "Living is a form of not being sure, not knowing what next or how. The moment you know how, you begin to die a little. The artist never entirely knows. We guess. We may be wrong, but we take leap after leap in the dark."[5]

According to gerontologist Gene Cohen, the capacity for creative, courageous vision and action often comes into full flower in the winter of life.[6] The willingness to make creative leaps of all kinds is strengthened by several late-life trends, including the growing sense of mortality that whispers, "If not now, when?" and urges us to jump. Creative Courage is addressed further in the next chapter, The Grace of Creativity.

Here is a story from Senegal, about an old woman who says yes to a summons from a stranger who arrives on her doorstep in the middle of the night. Despite her fear and (literal) trembling, she agrees to walk into the unknown and generously gives of herself when it becomes clear that something important is afoot.

The Midwife of Dakar

Everyone in Dakar knows old Fatu. She is the woman who brings all the children into the world, and there is hardly a black woman who has not needed her help at one time or another when giving birth.

Her cabin was a little outside the town, where nowadays one can see nice modern streets and houses in the fashion of the white man. But at that time, the section was just an isolated place.

One night when Fatu was sleeping, she heard a knock on the door. As she was used to being called in the middle of the night, she thought nothing of it and answered the door, and whom should she see standing there but a big dijinn [genie]!

She was so scared that she wanted to close the door quickly, but the dijinn had foreseen this and seized her hand quickly, pulling her out into the street. He motioned her to follow him, and she did so, trembling all over, not because of the cold but because of her fear. However, she did not dare disobey, for everyone knows that you cannot escape from a dijinn.

So she continued following him through the lonesome roads. Besides, she could soon see that the dijinn did not intend to harm her, and so little by little Fatu began to feel better about the whole adventure. But she could not recognize where she was, though she thought she knew Dakar inside out.

They arrived finally in front of a beautiful palace, bigger and richer than any she had ever seen. Silently she followed the genie through many courts and halls and arrived in a room where on a bed was lying an extraordinarily beautiful woman, surrounded by a crowd of others, all very richly adorned. The queen of the genies was about to give birth, and Fatu now understood why she had been summoned.

Without delay, she started on her work. And when a short time after the little genie was born, Fatu received it and bathed it with great care. She had hardly finished her task and handed the baby over to his smiling mother when everything—palace and people—vanished, and to her great surprise, she found herself no longer in the chamber of the new mother, but in a dark street of Dakar near the old hospital where she had often been before.

She went back home, and, upon entering her cabin, she found the table covered with many coins of silver and gold and a necklace of precious stones. She used the money to live in comfort. As for the necklace, however, she would not part with it. Many people, who had heard the story, offered her a big price for it, but she always refused to sell it, and is probably wearing it to this day, if she is still living on this earth.[7]

Some Questions for Reflection

1. When have you responded willingly to a frightening yet important summons? What has happened as a result?

2. When have you received such a "call" and refused it? What effects has that decision had in your life?

3. When have you experienced an event or encounter that had a numinous or mysterious quality to it? What was it like, how did you respond, and how has it affected your life since?

4. When have you been abundantly rewarded for your participation in an important event or situation? How did you contribute, and what reward(s) did you receive?

5. Is there a priceless necklace in your own life, something you would never give away? What makes it precious; what does it mean to you?

Reflections

The story of Fatu is full of numinous imagery—an enormous, imposing genie; a late-night journey through unfamiliar territory; an exceptionally beautiful queen who is about to give birth; a magnificent royal palace that vanishes into thin air; and the unexplained appearance of a huge pile of treasure in Fatu's simple cabin. All of these are clues that something extraordinary is transpiring.

Understandably, Fatu is initially frightened by the genie, but she summons her courage (physical and creative) and follows the genie into the dark night. As they walk the unfamiliar and deserted streets, Fatu stays alert and aware (she is not blindly following). Paying careful attention, she slowly recognizes that the dijinn does not intend her harm, and she continues to go with him into the unknown.

As soon as Fatu sees the laboring queen, she recognizes why she has been summoned and immediately uses her skills as a midwife to care for the mother and her baby. Midwifery is a traditional role of the older woman, and in many cultures the midwife assists the baby's journey from the womb into the outer world and also the dying person's transition from the seen to the unseen world. It may be that the broom often associated with witches evolved from the midwife's practice of sweeping the threshold at the time of a birth or death, as a cleansing ritual of protection for the newborn or the dying person.

There is another brief but important moment in the story when the royal palace vanishes, and Fatu suddenly finds herself back on familiar ground. For many indigenous peoples, for example the ancient Celts, the veil between the seen and unseen worlds is thought to be particularly thin in certain locations (stone circles and back roads), at certain times of the year (equinoxes, solstices, and quarter days), and at night. That thinness allows for freer flow between the dream world and waking consciousness; between past, present, and future; and between ancestors, the yet unborn, and the living. Fatu's story is an example of a profound though rationally inexplicable experience of crossing the threshold into another world and coming back again.

The riches that she discovers on her table when she returns home suggest that her courage and care have been of great value. She has used her authentic gifts and skills in the service of something important, and she receives both a material reward (silver and gold coins) and a symbolic one.

Fatu discerns the real (non-material) value of the necklace of precious stones. It is a reminder of a powerful, otherworldly experience of courage, trust, and care. Fatu refuses to sell the necklace—even when offered a great deal of money for it—and wears it for the rest of her life. Here she is foreshadowing the Grace of Remembrance, which entails remembering, honoring, and integrating the meaningful experiences of our life in preparation for our death.

Social Courage

Social courage has been described as the willingness to be authentic and vulnerable with another human being, which is the foundation of intimacy. Despite our collective love affair with the idea of being "in love," mature love is hard and important work. It requires courageous authenticity, ongoing forgiveness, and the generous acceptance of another (and ourselves) as we are. Love is a way of being and behaving that we choose, over and over. As the novelist Ursula Le Guin observes, "Love doesn't sit there like a stone, it has to be made, like bread; remade all of the time, made new."[8]

According to many psychologists, the capacity for this kind of authentic, altruistic, and renewing love becomes more common with age and maturity. For example, Kathleen Malley-Morrison (formerly White), a professor of psychology at Boston University, observes that true intimacy (inter-individual love) becomes possible as partners move through earlier stages of relating that are initially self-focused and then role-focused.[9] While age does not guarantee the progression to mature and altruistic love, long years of practice and learning are allies in its development.

Several trends in late-life development help us to move toward a more mature form of love (and the courage it entails) as we age: better acquaintance with our own limitations and foibles and growing tolerance for others' (Authenticity and Compassion), decreasing self-centeredness and a deepening concern for the well-being of others (Self-Transcending Generosity), and a growing capacity for riding the ups, downs, and uncertainties of life with steadiness, humor, and equanimity (Contentment).

Moral Courage

Moral courage is the willingness to stand up for something important, at the risk of ostracism, punishment, or other adverse consequences. It means remaining committed to an important value such as truth, compassion, or justice, even when others are turning a blind eye or refusing to get involved. Moral courage means doing what we can to right a wrong that is causing others to suffer, and it is thus an act of personal integrity and an expression of our connection and responsibility to others.

Las Abuelas de Plaza de Mayo are a moving example of moral

courage during a horrific period in Argentina's history from 1976 to 1983. Each of these grandmothers risked her life to speak out on behalf of the thirty thousand young people, their own and others' children and grandchildren, who were kidnapped by the junta and then murdered or illegally adopted by families who supported the regime, ostensibly to keep the country safe from dissidents and their offspring.

The women's courageous persistence brought about the rescue and return of some children who were taken from their families, the recovery of the remains of many who were killed, and eventually, the prosecution of some of the perpetrators once the constitutional government was reestablished. Although it took decades, the Abuelas' work laid the foundation for the United Nations' 2006 declaration that "Enforced Disappearances" are a crime against humanity and a punishable violation of human rights.[10]

The following folktale from India about an old woman and her son illustrates two different styles of moral courage during another time of injustice and oppression:

The Rope of Ash

Long ago there was a small country called Ajab Desh (Strange Country) that was ruled by a wicked prince, Gajab (Oppression). These were the days of the monarchy, and the people had no option but to obey the Raja, though they had neither affection nor respect for him.

One day the Raja ordered his subjects to take any of their parents who had grown very old and push them down the hill. Such persons, he claimed, were useless and a burden to their families. Although no one liked this order, they had to comply with it. So they threw their old mothers and fathers down the hill. This was a very terrible time in Ajab Desh.

There was one old woman who lived with her only son. When she heard about the Raja's edict, she said to him, "Son, I'll die a natural death very soon. So why kill me now? You could hide me in a cave in the forest and secretly bring me food and water." Her son did as she suggested.

After some time, it so happened that the wicked Raja decided to hold a swaymbara (a contest) to find a suitable husband for his daughter. It was proclaimed that the person who could make a rope of ash and produce it before the Raja would be eligible for being garlanded by the princess and becoming her husband.

Many young men were of course interested in marrying the princess, but all agreed that the task was impossible. When the son narrated the situation to his old mother, she had a solution. "Son," she told him, "on the appointed day, take a rope to the palace. Soak it well in kerosene oil and spread it out to its full length and light one end. Soon the rope will be completely burnt and will turn to ash. This will be the rope of ash."

The old lady's son did as she suggested. On the day of the contest he soaked the rope in kerosene oil and lighted it in the manner advised by his mother. In a moment, everyone present in the darbar (royal court) was beholding a rope of ash. All were surprised, and the princess put the baramala (engagement garland) around the young man's neck.

The Raja asked the boy to tell him how he had come to solve the riddle, and thereupon he narrated the whole story. The Raja listened, and his eyes were opened. He called for the old woman and rewarded her handsomely.

He then passed a decree that none of his subjects should thenceforth kill their aged parents, but rather should serve them with devotion. In due course, the old woman's son ascended to the throne and proved to be a wise ruler.[11]

Some Questions for Reflection

1. What part of this story resonates most strongly for you, and how is that related to your life (now or in the past)?

2. What unjust rules or laws have you felt compelled to follow, even though they violated your values? What effect did your going along have on you and on others?

3. What rules or laws have you dared not to follow because they violated your deepest values? What happened as a result?

4. How have you treated older people in the course of your life? How are you experiencing others treating you now, as you age?

5. When in your life has the wisest and most courageous course involved lying low and waiting patiently?

6. Which is more challenging for you: taking bold and decisive action, or not acting, being patient, and waiting? How so?

7. When have you faced an impossible-seeming task (like making a rope of ash), and how did you respond? Were you able to find a creative solution, like this old woman did? What was it?

8. When have you been able to say something that opened another's eyes? When has someone spoken to you in a way that opened yours?

9. When have you had the courage (like the Raja) to admit that you were mistaken and to right a wrong you once advocated?

10. What bit of medicine might you take from this story to enhance your life and/or others'?

Reflections

At one level, this is a morality tale with a strong message: be kind and generous to your elders. To do otherwise, according to the story, is strange, wicked, and oppressive. This is also the tale of a courageous old woman who, with her son's help, dares to challenge the edict of an oppressive authority in a quiet, patient, yet effective way. It is a fine example of the wise and collaborative nature of courage in later life, and it illustrates the ripple effects of one woman's courage on others.

The old woman asks her son to help her defy a morally egregious law by hiding her away. This is a serious request, especially poignant in that he is her only son, and, if discovered, they both would surely be put to death. As the story unfolds, it becomes clear that her primary concern is not saving her own life but seeing humanity and justice restored for everyone in the kingdom. In asking her son to assist her, she is inviting him to help right a wrong—by risking his life. For me, asking a loved one to take such a risk would require far more courage than taking one that primarily affected myself. Yet it is also clear that her request is an important gift to him: in calling on him, she calls forth the best in him.

It is noteworthy that she requests help, as have other older heroines in previous chapters. They do not demand, harangue, or manipulate. Each simply asks for assistance, and, by example, inspires; others are free to join, or not. This is one of the traditional roles of the elder: transmitting the essential values of a culture by embodying them and pointing to ways that the young might grow into them too, if they are willing.

"The Rope of Ash" also highlights some contrasts between courage in youth and in the winter of life. Unlike young protagonists in more familiar folktales who rely primarily on their physical skills to save the day single-handedly, older heroines draw on their wisdom and creativity. As illustrated in stories from around the world and throughout this book, elders tend to work collaboratively in the face of danger and difficulty.[12]

The ripple effects of the old woman's courageous plan are many: her son is betrothed to the princess, the wicked Raja's eyes are opened, the old woman is brought out of hiding and honored, and the people are instructed thereafter to treat their elders well, which was their inclination all along. And there is a later development: in time, her son becomes a wise ruler. His capacity for wisdom is no surprise. His mother is wise, and to his credit he has consistently recognized and honored her wisdom, even in the face of danger—and all has gone well.

The phrase *in due course* in the last sentence of the story is a reminder that events evolve in their own way, in their own time. One of the gifts of the winter of life is an increasing capacity to wait, to refrain from reacting, to honor life's timing, and to cooperate with—rather than trying to direct—its unfolding.[13]

❧ *Cultivating Courage* ❧

The graces of winter are intertwined with each other, and four have a particular affinity with Courage. The close connection between Self-Transcending Generosity and Courage was explored in the previous chapter, and three other graces are intimately connected to Courage as well: Wisdom (seeing clearly), Contentment (befriending fear), and Authenticity (acknowledging cowardice).

Drawing on Wisdom

Courage is expressed in action, but unless it is rooted in wisdom, it degrades into foolish recklessness, destructive fanaticism, or compulsive, indiscriminant crusading—all of which create far more suffering than they alleviate. Clear seeing is essential in dangerous and difficult situations, and the wise old woman in myth and folklore is known for her ability to see in the dark, or for her triple vision, which enables her to see clearly into the past, the future, and the heart of the present situation.

In order to know whether and how to act, we must first see, as clearly as we can, what is going on, what is at stake, what is most (and less) important, what is likely to happen with and without our involvement, and what the best course of action might be. Yet even when we draw from the well of long years of experience and accumulated understanding, there may be factors at play we cannot see, and our actions may have unintended consequences. Courage means acting in spite of uncertainty, doing our best on behalf of something that is important—knowing that we are not omniscient, nor in control of what will happen next (see the Grace of Wisdom).

Befriending Fear

The cultivation of courage also entails making a friend of fear, for these two are not opposites, but companions. Fear is a natural response to danger and difficulty, and in the face of these, the fast-acting reptilian part of our lower brain triggers an instantaneous fight-or-flight response, often before we are even aware of what is happening. Such reactions have obvious survival value, but fleeing (or fighting) is often not the wisest or the most courageous option. When our car starts to slide on an ice-covered road, for example, the best course is to turn into the skid, even though the "inner reptile" is urging us to fight the slide and turn away from it. Courage is like turning into a skid, toward what frightens us, though fear would have us turn away.

The root meaning of the word *fear* is "to test," and life is a generous provider of challenges that test our mettle. Research suggests that as we age, we develop greater tolerance for fear and other uncomfortable emotions and greater control over our emotional reactions in general (see the Grace of Contentment). The *emotional mastery* of later life is an important ally in learning to face and move through the fear that accompanies challenges of all sizes.

Most of our courageous actions occur in small, ordinary moments when we choose to do the right thing, in spite of fear, doubt, and uncertainty. How we respond to the choices that arise in everyday life becomes the foundation for how we are likely to act when larger difficulties and dangers present themselves.

For example, do we choose to be open and vulnerable with those we love, or try to protect ourselves through blaming, withdrawing, placating, or other defensive patterns? Do we persist in physical exercise, despite discomfort, in order to remain active for as long as we can, or do we give up and tell ourselves it doesn't really matter (when we know that it does)? Do we dare to say the thing that needs to be said, hopefully with clarity and kindness, even though we fear it may cost us dearly—or do we play it safe and keep quiet?

Beginning Where You Are

Sometimes the first step in cultivating courage is the admission of cowardliness (Authenticity). This seeming paradox became clear to me about ten years ago when I found myself thinking about early retirement. The accountant's daughter in me was alarmed by the potential financial implications, but when I was honest with myself, I knew that the job I had loved for decades was no longer a place I wanted to be.

Ironically, I was struggling with this chapter on courage at that time, unable to write because of a vague half-awareness that I was not living very courageously myself. Not knowing what else to do, I found a thin thread of courage, just enough to sit down, to feel what I didn't want to feel, and then to write down whatever came. Instead of a piece on courage, what emerged was a confession of my cowardice.

As often happens when we pay attention and acknowledge where we are, something shifted. Weeks later, on my sixty-second birthday, I filed retirement papers and have never regretted that leap. Over and over I learn that it is far more draining and deadening to avoid the truth than to face and live it.

⫸ *Tools for Cultivating Courage* ⫷

Courage is rooted in awareness, strengthened by practice, fostered by the befriending of fear and uncertainty, and enhanced by the inspiration and company of daring souls. The following tools address these dimensions of courage.

Stay Awake. To stay awake means choosing attentiveness, rather than distracting ourselves with unimportant busyness, ignoring the promptings of our hearts and bodies, or otherwise numbing out—especially when we're in fear or another discomforting state. Without awareness, we don't recognize conflicts, moral dilemmas, and important choices and decisions for what they are. Although subtle and indirect, this is a form of cowardice: the refusal to keep facing and living the truth. Daily meditation, journal writing, walking in nature, and other practices can help to lift the fog of unconsciousness and alert us to those moments when something important is at stake.

Practice. Courage can be viewed as a psychological habit that can be cultivated through practice, just as cowardice is a habit that is strengthened by repetition. As Eleanor Roosevelt points out in *You Learn by Living,* "You gain strength, courage, and confidence by every experience in which you really stop to look fear in the face. . . . *You must do the thing you think you cannot do.*"[14]

If there is something important that you have avoided saying or doing for fear of rocking the boat, being rejected, or looking foolish, consider gathering your courage and doing it anyway. Be as clear and as kind in the process as possible; see what happens.

Explore New Territory. T. S. Eliot once wrote, "Old [people] ought to be explorers."[15] Stay alert to new activities, people, places, ideas, and community projects that call to you. If the cautious, critical chorus starts to sing—*Have you lost your mind? What do you have to offer? At your age?!*—exhale deeply and follow these important tugs of heart, regardless of others' or your own critical opinions.

Celebrate Your Birth Date with a Stretch. In *The Second Half of Life*, Angeles Arrien describes an ancient European courage-building custom that is still practiced in some parts of the Pyrenees mountains in Spain: celebrate your birth date every month for the next year by doing something you have never done before.[16]

What are some of the new edges that call to you that you might dare to explore in the next twelve months on your birth date? Pick one that would be relatively easy and do it the next time your birth date comes around. Consider extending the practice every month for the rest of the year—start with the stretches that generate the least fear and save the scariest ones for later.

Enlist an Ally. Not all courageous acts need be done alone. My granddaughter Natalie and I stumbled into supporting one another through our fears a few years ago when she was spending a weekend with me. I had started swimming in the ocean a couple of weeks earlier and hoped she would join me, but she was nervous about going into the deep, seaweedy water.

The next day she suggested we draw together, and I balked. (I don't know how to draw or paint, even though I've wanted to learn.) I told her I'd be glad to sit with her and write while she drew. She looked at me with her very wise eyes; we both smiled. This time Grandma was scared. So we agreed to support each other.

She coached and encouraged me as I drew. (It was fun, and I actually liked what came out.) And later I kept her company as she found a way to ride the waves, midway between her comfort zone and the deeper water. It was exhilarating for each of us, and it opened up a new dimension in our relationship.

Whom might you invite to join you in mutually stretching your limits?

Reflect on Courage and Its Alternatives. Some say that courage sits near the midpoint on a continuum with recklessness at one end and cowardice at the other. Take some time to reflect on an example of each from your own life—a reckless choice that lacked discernment, a cowardly decision that still has a sting to it, and a wise and courageous choice. What did each experience teach you? What long-term effects can you observe in your life from each?

If one or more of these memories has an unfinished or distressing feel to it, allow yourself to revise or complete it in your imagination. Remember: imagined events can have as much impact as "real" ones.

Consider Current Choices. Spend some time reflecting on some of your recent choices, small and large—what you eat and drink; what you say and don't say; where you are living; how you spend your energy, time, and money; with whom you keep company. Also notice what you are avoiding (those are also choices). Where are you choosing the risky road and where the safe one? How do you feel when you live on the edge? within secure boundaries? Consider the costs of some of your current too-safe choices—what are you losing: self-esteem, sleep, vitality?

The next time you are at a choice point (there are many every day), see if you can discern that still, small voice that lets you know which is the path with heart. Dare to take it and see what happens.

Learn from Others. We are blessed to have access to the writings of many courageous older women (and others) who have dared to face and to listen to themselves, to live by their own lights, and to record their experiences in writing. For example, Florida Scott-Maxwell's late-life memoir, *The Measure of My Days*; May Sarton's late-life journals: *At Seventy: A Journal, After the Stroke, Endgame: A Journal of the Seventy-Ninth Year, Encore: A Journal of the Eightieth Year,* and *At Eighty-Two: A Journal*; and the poetry of Mary Oliver. I also recommend John Welwood's books on the social and personal courage that learning to love another human being entails: *Journey of the Heart* and *Perfect Love, Imperfect Relationships*.

In addition, films with gutsy and inspiring older heroines (and heroes) and supporting characters are increasingly available, and research in psychology and neuroscience suggests that seeing or reading about courage and other virtues in others can inspire similar qualities in ourselves.[17] See especially *Enchanted April* (the courageous shift in the winter of life from a narrow, fear-based existence to a life of love and joy), *Evening* (personal courage and the facing of death), and *Fried Green Tomatoes* and *The Color Purple* (the role of friendship in lending us courage to do and bear what we must).

I also highly recommend *The First Grader* and *The Straight Story*, each based on the life of a courageous older man. In addition, three movies about groups of elders—*Cocoon*, *The Best Exotic Marigold Hotel*, and *Tea with Mussolini*—show a wide range of responses as women and men venture into unknown and uncertain territory of the winter of life.

4: The Grace of Creativity

"Just as aging is a journey and not an end,
creativity is a process not a product."
—Gene Cohen, *The Creative Age*

Creativity is our essence and our birthright, a way of being that every child knows and adults can rediscover. It is often associated with genius and works of art, yet creativity is also a way of living, characterized by curiosity, playfulness, and wholeheartedness—qualities that tend to be at their peak in early childhood and often again in the winter of life.

Whether we're facing a mound of clay, or a dilemma in our personal life or in the larger community, creativity involves seeing things as they are and as they might be. It entails focused attention and effort, as well as the willingness to wonder and meander, to experiment and entertain foolish questions, and to follow wild ideas and irrational hunches without knowing where they will lead.

Creativity means entering unknown territory—without a map—where nothing is certain, anything is possible, and chances are excellent that we will make mistakes and feel utterly bewildered at times. Perhaps most importantly, creativity requires tenacity—the willingness to stay engaged in the process when we are stumped and tempted to quit.

Everyday Creativity

Early studies of creativity focused almost entirely on the extraordinary achievements of exceptional people like Mozart and Einstein, which led to the view that creativity is a rare quality, reserved for a talented few. More recent study has broadened our understanding of creativity to include experiences of discovery and originality that occur in the day-to-day lives of ordinary people.

Coming up with an ingenious solution to an important community problem, making up a simple song to hold the attention of a wriggling grandchild long enough to change his diaper, or pulling together an impromptu feast for an unexpected guest using a motley collection of on-hand ingredients—all of these are examples of what psychologist Ruth Richards calls "everyday creativity."[1] In fact, almost any meaningful activity that involves exploration, discovery, and some kind of expression can be considered creative.

Psychologist Abraham Maslow and others regard creativity as an innately human characteristic,[2] and watching infants and children certainly supports that idea. Dr. Teresa Amabile, director of research at the Harvard Business School, writes, "The kernel of creativity is there in the infant: the desire and drive to explore, to find out about things, to try things out, to experiment with different ways of handling things and looking at things. As they grow older, children begin to create entire universes of reality in their play."[3]

Creativity is primarily associated with imagination, play, and wonder—characteristics of young children and of the open and spontaneous right hemisphere of the brain. Yet the evaluative, order-seeking left-brain also plays a part, especially in fine-tuning. Psychologist and playwright Robert Kastenbaum describes creativity as both an attitude and a process that draws on many modes of being:

Creativity as an attitude asserts, 'This is a fresh moment: I can help bring something new to the world.' Creativity as a process demands, 'Be open to all influences, inner and outer. Experience clearly, keenly, intensely. Now work like a demon! Now step back and inspect like a critic. Now work again!' . . . Creativity is both the instantaneous spark of inspiration and the long, strenuous effort to bring that idea to fulfillment.[4]

The art of creativity lies in the capacity to sense what is needed in a given moment and the willingness to move in that direction, without knowing what the outcome will be.

Late-Life Creativity

Creativity seems to be most at home in the very young and the old. For many of us, the trajectory of creativity across the life span resembles an upside-down bell curve, starting high in infancy and early childhood, descending for decades, rising in middle adulthood, and reaching new heights again in the winter of life. In fact, many have identified the winter of life as a time of optimal creativity. Psychologist Dean Simonton, for example, writes, "Empirical research actually suggests that creative productivity can undergo a substantial renaissance in the final years, especially toward life's close. . . . Some time after the late sixties a resurgence in output often appears . . . [contradicting] the supposed inevitability of the downhill slide."[5]

Gerontologist Gene Cohen concurs. His book *The Creative Age* is filled with examples of creativity in the later lives of public figures like Maria Ann Smith, who developed the Granny Smith apple in her seventh decade, and Anna Mary Robertson Moses, who began her career as a painter at age sixty-eight because her arthritis became too painful for her to continue supporting herself doing embroidery. "Grandma Moses" continued painting until she was 101. Even more inspiring are Cohen's stories of ordinary people whose creativity is expressed in widely varying ways in the winter of life.

Some physical changes in the winter of life such as declining eyesight and hearing may affect some dimensions of creativity, yet it is the nature of the creative spirit to seek and find unusual ways around and through obstacles. Research suggests that cognitive loss in the winter of life is far less pronounced than previously thought, and some late-life cognitive developments actually enhance our capacity for creativity. For example, with age we become more skillful at compensating for our losses and maximizing our strengths when faced with an obstacle or challenge.[6]

Accumulated knowledge and practical intelligence are two other assets in the creative process that tend to increase in the winter of life. And thinking typically becomes more holistic and nuanced (and thus more creative) as we age. For many in later life, reason-based, either/or thinking gives way to post-formal thought, which integrates feeling and thinking and increases our ability to see situations from many perspectives and to entertain multiple solutions to perplexing problems.[7]

Creative Crones in Folklore

The old woman's ability to imagine and implement ingenious solutions to important problems is one of her signature characteristics in folktales around the world. Many stories throughout this book highlight the grandmother's capacity for innovation, especially in times of trouble. Some have appeared already: "The Wise Woman," "Ubong and the Headhunters," and "The Rope of Ash." Another is included in this chapter, and others appear in later ones. The heroines in all of these tales demonstrate the old woman's capacity for creative resourcefulness, and there are some important commonalities in their approaches.

First, each uses ordinary ingredients in fresh ways that bring transformative results. Second, these ingenious old women have great insight into the character of those who are stirring up trouble, and they use that knowledge—aikido-style—so that culprits partic-ipate in their own undoing. These grandmothers do not use force or brute strength, but are mistresses of indirect means, rooted in their wise understanding of the human heart.

In addition, these creative heroines throw themselves wholeheart-edly into their plots, outlandish as they seem at a rational level. They usually involve others in their schemes, rather than saving the day single-handedly. And finally, they don't give up if their original plan starts to unravel. They simply keep thinking on their feet and find yet another way to meet the challenge. They are wonderful models of the art of creatively meeting life as it unfolds, moment by moment.

In the following story from the Ozark Mountains—in local dialect—a wise and wily old woman draws on her astute under-standing of human nature to bring a thief to justice in a most unconventional way.

Poppet Caught a Thief

One time the people that was sleeping in a tavern all got robbed. It looked like somebody must have put powders in the liquor, and stole their stuff while they was asleep.

There wasn't no banks in them days, so travelers had to carry their money in gold. They claimed there was three thousand dol-lars missing, besides four good watches and a snuffbox, which the man says he wouldn't have took a hundred dollars for it.

The fellow that run the tavern would not let nobody leave, nei-ther. "Them valuables must be got back, or else I will wade knee-deep in blood," he says, "because the honor of my house has been throwed in jeopardy!"

The travelers was getting pretty mad, but just then an old woman come along and asks, "What is the matter?" The tavern keeper, he told her, and the old woman says, "My poppet can catch any thief in the world, and it won't take ten minutes!"

She pulled a little wooden doll out of her saddlebag, and rubbed some walnut juice on it, and set it on a stand-table.

"Them travelers can come in here one at a time," she says, "and the rest of us will set just outside the door. Every one of 'em must grab that there poppet and squeeze it. If the man's honest you won't hear a sound, but if he's a thief that poppet will holler like a stuck pig."

The travelers says it is all foolishness, but they will try anything to get away from this lousy tavern. So they went in one after another, but the poppet didn't holler at all.

The old woman looked considerable set back. "Did you all pinch the poppet?" she asked. The travelers all says they squeezed it hard as they could. "Hold out your hands," says the old woman, and she studied each man's fingers mighty careful. Pretty soon she pointed at the traveler that done all the hollering about his snuffbox.

"That's the thief!" she says. The fellow tried to lie out of it, but when they got the rope round his neck he began to holler. "If you turn me loose I will give everything back," says he. "But if you hang me you'll never get a penny because the gold is hid where you couldn't find it in a thousand years."

Well, the tavern keeper was unanimous for hanging him anyhow, but them travelers naturally wanted to get their money back. They promised to put the robber on a good horse and give him three hours' start.

He made everybody swear their right hand on the Book, and then he showed them where the stuff was hid under a woodpile. So pretty soon they turned the son-of-a-bitch loose, and off he went down the road at a dead run. Nobody ever did catch up with him, neither.

Soon as the people got their money and watches, they begun to feel pretty good again. The tavern keeper set up a big dinner, and everybody eat and drunk till they was full as a tick. Pretty soon they raffled off the robber's watch to pay for the dinner, and the man that won the watch give it to the old woman. Finally, a fellow passed the old woman's bonnet around for a silver collection, and then he says, "You can have all this money, if you will tell us how you knowed which one was the thief."

The old woman just grinned at him. "Didn't you hear my poppet holler, when that scoundrel grabbed it?" she asks. The fellow says of course not, and everybody knows a wooden doll can't holler.

"A thief don't know nothin' for sure," says the old woman. "Every one of you honest men squeezed that poppet. But the robber figured there might be a trick to it, so he never touched the poppet. All I done was to look for the fellow that didn't have no walnut juice on his hands."[8]

Some Questions for Reflection

1. What part of this story touches you the most, and how is that connected to your life right now?

2. How comfortable are you in claiming your own gifts, like this old woman who proudly says that she and her "poppet can catch any thief in the world, and it won't take ten minutes"?

3. Where in your life might a bit of creative trickery on your part be "just the ticket"?

4. What has been your best experience of following a far-fetched idea and having it work out well?

5. When in your life has guilt led you to live in fear or isolation, like the thief?

6. If you were to take to heart the medicine of this story, for you, what shift—large or small—would you make in your life?

Reflections

This ordinary, astute old woman exemplifies creativity in the winter of life. In the midst of trouble, she utilizes simple objects (a wooden doll and some walnut juice) in a most unusual way, combines them with her understanding of human emotions (in this case, guilt), and fashions a foolish-seeming yet effective plan for ensnaring a thief.

The first part of the plot is a ruse, but she plays it with such bravado that the men in the bar go along with her seemingly senseless request and squeeze the poppet. When it fails to holler like a stuck pig as she promised, she puts on a puzzled expression—then asks to see their hands. This apparently innocuous request is in fact the real test, and the thief's guilt betrays him.

I find her playfulness throughout the story delightful. Even though she is engaged in serious work (helping to restore justice), she seems to be enjoying herself, making audacious claims about her poppet's abilities and carrying out her preposterous scheme with panache.

Even after justice has been served and the men in the tavern have honored her with gifts, she keeps the game going—perhaps to savor her enjoyment of the experience and their camaraderie a little longer. Rather than immediately revealing how she knew who the thief was, she grins and jokes with them: "Didn't you hear my poppet holler?" Then in the next breath, she is deadly serious and shares some wisdom worthy of remembering: "A thief don't know nothin' for sure."

The end of story highlights the stark contrast between the thief and the rest of the characters. He is isolated, on the run, and living in fear, while the others, having come through an ordeal together, are celebrating their good fortune and being generous with one another. The message is clear: Better to live together with integrity than to try to prosper at another's expense and end up with nothing—and no one.

There is a detail in the story that also strikes me: when the men and the thief are negotiating, he asks that they take an oath on the

Bible that they will keep their end of the bargain. Knowing his own lack of integrity, he needs extra assurance that they will keep their word. There is poignancy in his request that others swear to uphold the rules. His breaking them has made him suspicious—and quite vulnerable.

Creativity and Seeing

Creativity requires both clarity and flexibility of vision—the capacity to see things as they really are and also to envision how they might be. In an essay written at age eighty-four in the last year of his life, Henri Matisse observed,

> Everything that we see in our daily life is more or less distorted by acquired habits . . . The effort to see things without distortion takes something very like courage; and this courage is essential to the artist, who has to look at everything as though he saw it for the first time . . . as he did when he was a child.[9]

Creativity also requires the capacity to shift perspectives, to turn things on their head, to imagine and play with possibilities, and to discover new dimensions, connections, and patterns. Rosabeth Kanter, a professor at the Harvard Business School, says it well: "Creativity is a lot like looking at the world through a kaleidoscope. You look at a set of elements, the same ones everyone else sees, but then reassemble those floating bits and pieces into an enticing new possibility."[10]

Creativity and Passion

Passion is vital to creativity as well; it inspires, stretches, and sustains us. Yo-Yo Ma sees love as a powerful force for unleashing creativity because "If you're passionate about something, then you're more willing to take risks."[11] One of my favorite statements about creating comes from Mozart. When he was four years old, someone asked him how he composed music. He reportedly replied, "I just put together little notes that like each other."

Hungarian psychologist Mihaly Csikszentmihalyi's extensive study of creative artists and scientists led him to conclude:

> Perhaps the most important quality, the one that is most consistently present in all creative individuals, is the ability to enjoy the process of creation for its own sake.
>
> Without this trait poets would give up striving for perfection and would write commercial jingles, economists would work for banks where they would earn at least twice as much as they do at the university, physicists would stop doing basic research and join industrial laboratories where the conditions are better and the expectations more predictable.[12]

According to psychologists Jeanne Nakamura and Mihaly Csikszentmihalyi, vital engagement with something that has passion and meaning is the essence of creativity in the winter of life. In fact, they found that many creatively engaged elders are unable to imagine *not* being involved with that which absorbs them. Whether an older person continues exploring within a lifelong vocation or moves into a new area of passion in late life, the underlying call is the same: to pursue what is meaningful and absorbing for its own sake, apart from other considerations, like reputation, success, or financial gain.[13]

Creativity as a Response to Trouble

Often creativity emerges in response to some kind of trouble. A few years ago, I watched one of my octogenarian neighbors come up with an ingenious way of hauling supplies up to his second-story home.

(The house is built over a garage and only accessible by a long stair-
way that had become increasingly difficult to climb, especially when
carrying heavy loads.)

Mr. Lazarini began looking for a solution by walking around
the house, and when he reached the back, he was inspired. He
found an old wooden box and some rope in his garage, bought
some bits and pieces at the hardware store, and put together a pul-
ley system that enabled him to convey supplies from the family car
up to the second-story deck at the back of the house.

After watching a successful trial run, I made an appreciative
thumbs-up gesture. He laughed and confided, "When you're old,
you've got to get creative!"

Obstacles and challenges often stimulate and encourage creativity, especially in the winter of life as we become more skillful in
working with adversity (see The Grace of Contentment). Dr. Gene
Cohen observes,

> There is no denying that . . . the risk of chronic illness or
> disabilities increases with age. But all around us, throughout
> history and today, there is evidence that the creative spirit
> can find expression despite obstacles, grief, and loss, and
> sometimes even more powerfully in the process. . . . It is no
> romanticization of loss to say that whatever the nature of our
> hardship, in the transition and adjustment it demands there
> is also the potential for creative growth and gain.[14]

Demeaning attitudes toward aging can be an impediment to
creativity—if we buy into them. Robert Kastenbaum points out,
"Perhaps the most daunting obstacle . . . [is] society's rather lazy
belief that we become used up with age, become something less
than ardent spirits that have something significant to express.
'Believe that crap and you're dead!' an elderly poet told me."[15]

We need not buy into such deadening (and inaccurate) notions.
In fact, there is evidence that elders who are creatively engaged with

something they love often become increasingly immune to ageist stereotypes and in some cases overcome age-related losses that could have interfered with their endeavors.[16] Passion is a potent motivator.

Creativity and Her Sister Graces

The Grace of Creativity is supported by other graces of winter, especially Courage, Authenticity, and Self-Transcending Generosity. (The interplay of Creativity with the Graces of Contentment, Simplicity, and Wisdom is addressed in later chapters.)

To create is to step into new territory and bear the terror that accompanies innovation. It means letting go of tried-and-true (and often tired) ways of seeing and doing, and tolerating the anxiety of uncertainty. That takes Courage. Humorist Cynthia Heimel's words capture the essence of creative courage: "When in doubt, make a fool of yourself. There is a microscopically thin line between being brilliantly creative and acting like the most gigantic idiot on earth. So, what the hell, leap!"[17] Creative leaps of all kinds (in art and in the art of living) entail jumping into the unknown—again and again. For many, the awareness of having a limited number of years left increases the willingness to take meaningful risks.

Several dimensions of the Grace of Authenticity also contribute to a creative way of being in the winter of life. The enhanced ability to trust what we know in our bones, the flowering of audacity, the growing ability to stand with ourselves in the face of others' skepticism or criticism, and greater tolerance for our imperfections and mistakes—all of these encourage creativity in later life.

The Grace of Self-Transcending Generosity opens the door to a more-than-personal sense of who we are. Feeling connected to something beyond our personality, we learn, over time, to cooperate with and to trust it. Whether we know that something else as the deep Self, the unconscious, the Muse, or a mystery, creativity requires being open and attentive to it.

Gerontology nurses Priscilla Ebersole and Patricia Hess describe late-life creativity as "a bridge between the growing self and the transcending of self . . . between self-actualization (the reaching of one's highest potential) and the step beyond, to transcend the limitations of ego."[18] In creating, we use the instrument of the self and also allow ourselves to be guided and inspired by something beyond it.

We do not create alone; we are cocreators, really. Creating is like dancing with an unseen partner, infinitely imaginative yet trustworthy. In that dance, we sometimes lead; often we follow. Some composers report experiences of hearing music that they wrote down, rather than created themselves. Paul McCartney described "Yesterday" as a song that was "already all there. Like an egg being laid—not a crack or flaw in it."[19] Beethoven—though deaf—was known to hear entire symphonies in his imagination.

Writers too describe sometimes having a character, poem, or story seem to write itself. When the Canadian novelist Robertson Davies was asked where he got the ideas for his novels, he replied, "I don't 'get' the ideas—they 'get' me."[20]

Benefits of Creative Engagement

Numerous studies in psychology, gerontology, and the arts have shown that late-life engagement with something we love is strongly related to physical health and emotional well-being, a sense of meaning and purpose, and an enhanced capacity to cope effectively with adversity and with aging.

Creativity is pleasurable. It feels good to be engaged with something we love, to discover and share a new way of doing something, to create beauty, to find an unorthodox route around an obstacle, or to address an important need in an unexpected or humorous manner.

And creativity is therapeutic. Engaging in creative expression of all sorts helps release and transform negative emotions, stimulates new learning and discovery, and supports emotional well-being and physical health. Gerontologist and psychiatrist George Vaillant notes that creativity promotes resilience, which he describes as "both the capacity to be bent without breaking and the capacity, once bent, to spring back."[21] At a physical and psychological level, humans are endowed with "self-righting tendencies" that promote healing and recovery from illness, trauma, and other adversity.[22] Creative expression is one of these self-healing mechanisms.

Creativity also encourages the return of a sense of wonder and delight, which is a trend in late-life development. Jungian analyst Allan Chinen writes,

> Creativity and a sense of wonder are two of the most endearing traits in children . . . [and] reclaiming the wonder and creativity of childhood is a task of later life . . . The return of wonder often emerges as a delight in nature . . . [and] enjoyment of the present moment, just as it is . . . The reclamation of childhood delight is actually the fruit of maturation.[23]

Some researchers have looked at creativity broadly as an approach to life and found that a creative outlook is often associated with emotional health and the adjustment to aging. In their research with Israeli elders, for example, Erika Landau and Benjamin Maoz found that an innovative, "what's possible?" attitude, coupled with a willingness to keep growing, supported many elders in venturing into the unknown, continuing to actualize their potential, and experiencing a sense of meaning in their later years.

In contrast, interviews with Landau and Maoz's less creative subjects revealed very different attitudes and experiences. These older adults tended to be "emotionally bound (clinging to life and denying death) . . . sticking to former ways and patterns of rigid behavior, and wanting only to remain embedded in the secure and known."[24]

Dr. Gene Cohen's work as a gerontologist led him to conclude that late-life creativity has a number of benefits for elders as well as those around them. He writes:

> Creativity allows us to alter our experience of problems and sometimes to transcend them . . . We feel better when we are able to view our circumstances with fresh perspective and express ourselves with some creativity. . . . [and that] makes us more emotionally resilient and better able to cope with life's adversity and losses . . . Creative expression typically fosters feelings that can improve outlook and a sense of well-being [which] have a beneficial effect on the functioning of our immune system and our overall health.[25]

Even more importantly, says Cohen, to be creatively engaged in the winter of life serves the whole human family by providing a valuable model of what is possible with age, for younger generations and for society as a whole. "The effect is a boon for [all] generations: the younger adult learns firsthand about achieving a more satisfying aging experience, and the older adult remains engaged in the circle of relationship and emotional intimacy that strengthens connections to others and [the] richness of life."[26]

 ## Cultivating Creativity

Creativity is our essence and our birthright, yet many of us lose touch with the creative spirit in the course of becoming so-called grown-ups. Thankfully, the winter of life is an optimal time to renew our acquaintance with that playful, imaginative part of ourselves. Most of the cultivation tips and tools described below apply to creativity in its broadest sense, as a way of living. A few relate to art-making, an arena rich with possibilities for creativity and play that many of us abandon out of a mistaken idea that art is for artists, but not for the rest of us. Another perspective is that art (literally, "to make special")

is a human activity toward which we are all inclined and that engaging with a user-friendly medium that calls to us can enhance well-being and also contribute to the lives of those we encounter.

Recall Creative Adventures. Bring to mind some of your most enjoyable and fruitful experiences of creativity—as a child and as an adult, with others or alone, when problem-solving, making art, or . . . Savor these experiences of exploration, discovery, and expression now—and when you need an ingenious solution to a daunting challenge.

Remember to Play. Creativity thrives in a climate of playfulness. (Play is engaging in pleasurable activity for its own sake, without agenda.) When we play we are open, curious, and receptive to the unexpected, and we flow with what comes. As Carl Jung discovered, "The creation of something new is not accomplished by the intellect but by the play instinct acting from inner necessity. The creative mind plays with the object it loves."[27]

Every day brings multiple opportunities for creative play, even in the midst of social interactions, personal hygiene, household chores, or volunteer work. To a large extent, the degree of playfulness we bring to any activity is what makes it creative or stale, enjoyable or deadening. Wrapping a gift, for example, can be a creative adventure or a joyless demand—as can walking a dog, or playing in a quartet.

Check out Diane Ackerman's engaging book *Deep Play* for inspiring stories about the extraordinary experience of adult play and the ordinary places it can happen—when bicycling or exploring nature, for example, in the company of animals, and even at work when we are deeply focused and engaged with what we are doing.

Venture Beyond the Familiar. In many ways, the creative process parallels the archetypal journey described by Joseph Campbell in *The Hero With a Thousand Faces*. Both experiences involve leaving the safety and comfort of the known; venturing into unfamiliar territory with its trials, tests, and unexpected allies; discovering something new and valuable; and returning (transformed in some way) to share what has been gained with others. This basic sequence seems to be one that we humans experience throughout life (if we are willing). It is how we create—and how we grow and develop.

Dare to experiment (to try) and see what happens. Try shaking up your surroundings and daily routines—rearrange furniture, take a different route on your daily walk, include beautiful weeds or grasses in a bouquet of flowers, experiment with new combinations of food or clothing, try something you've never done but have longed to do. Moving beyond the familiar heightens awareness, supports cognitive and emotional health, and stimulates creativity.

Creativity thrives on adventure and uncertainty. One of the most enlivening (and terrifying) creative experiences of my life began when a fiddler I was playing Scottish music with suddenly shifted into a fast, wild, and utterly foreign mode. Celtic music is familiar enough that improvising is a joyful stretch, especially with such a good partner. But out of the blue this fiddler began leading us into a kind of fast-paced music I had never played, or even heard. The thought *I can't do this* passed through my mind. But we kept going, and sounds came out of my cello that I don't have the skills to make. It was an ecstatic adventure.

Befriend Mistakes. Creativity entails the ability and willingness to engage with whatever comes, even when it appears to be a mistake. Discouragement (Oh, no!) is a common response to making a mistake, but a more fruitful one is curiosity. (Hmm, now what?) Mistakes are sources of information and potential teachers—if we're willing to learn from them. James Joyce called mistakes "portals of discovery."[28]

The Post-it, for example, was invented by accident when a new high-tack glue recipe failed to hold adequately, and 3M found itself with a supply of apparently unusable, low-tack adhesive. Rather than give up, Dr. Spencer Silver (the creative lead scientist) reframed what might easily have been called a mistake as "a solution without a problem." He invited others to imagine ways that this glue-that-didn't-stay-stuck might be useful. One of his colleagues, Art Fry, tried applying some to his slippery bookmark, and the Post-it was born. Students, librarians, writers, avid readers, and countless others have found myriad uses for this invention that began as an oops.

Remember a time when a mistake you made became an opening, an important step toward a breakthrough, or perhaps even a blessing. What helped to transform that potential disaster into something useful? Recall this story next time you "mess up" and keep playing.

Follow Bliss. My sister discovered a passion (and a remarkable talent) for painting in her mid-sixties. Without any training, she began sketching, then painting; she quickly graduated to recreating masterpieces by Matisse, Van Gogh, and others, and then she moved to original work. I was stunned by her skill, and she confided, a bit shyly, "The brushes kind of tell me what to do to get a certain effect"—a delightful statement, especially given her scientific orientation.

The rekindling of old passions and the discovery of new ones in the winter of life enriches the lives of the impassioned and of those around them. Joy is contagious.

If you don't already have at least one thing that engages and challenges you and brings you joy, find one soon. Notice what you love, remember what delighted you as a child, pay attention to what you dream about, and keep seeking until you find a passion and give yourself to it. It's never too late. For a helpful guide, check out Julia Cameron's *It's Never Too Late to Begin Again: Discovering Creativity and Meaning at Midlife and Beyond.*

Don't Quit; Shift. In her audio series *The Creative Fire*, Jungian analyst Clarissa Pinkola Estés says, "The main trouble people have with creativity is that they stop themselves."[29] Many of us have an image of creativity as uninterrupted flow. And when we hit an inevitable trough in the ebb-and-flow process that creativity is, we are easily derailed, thinking that something is wrong, fearing that we somehow "don't have what it takes." And so we give up.

The next time you're stumped, don't quit; shift gears for a while. Jane Austen was said to play the pianoforte when her writing was stalled. Others knit for a while when stumped, or listen to music, write a letter to a friend, or take a short nap. I usually shift into something familiar and mentally undemanding, like walking, washing the dishes, or pulling weeds, activities that allow my mind to relax and wander—and often to discover something fruitful.

Experiment with ways of backing off a bit that allow you to enter that relaxed, receptive state, rather than giving up.

Think Sideways and Upside Down. The next time you are faced with a challenging situation, rather than trying to find the right answer to the problem, come up with as many possibilities as you can, the more preposterous the better. As Linus Pauling, winner of two Nobel prizes (for Peace and for Chemistry) once said, "If you want to have good ideas you must have many ideas. Most of them will be wrong, and what you have to learn is which ones to throw away."[30]

Ask inviting questions that start with "Maybe . . . ," "What if . . . ," "Why not . . . ," "How could . . . ," or "How else might we . . . ," and see what happens. Let the ideas flow, jot them down, or sketch them—think of ten more solutions and jot those down. Do not edit, censor, or critique; just gather possibilities.

Later, invite your more practical left-brain to see how one of the ideas might be implemented. Or combine bits and pieces from a few of your wild notions and see how that might fly.

Invoke Your Imagination. Get reacquainted with your imagination, that intangible but very real realm of images and intuitions, visited frequently by children, artists, and inventors. Allow yourself to daydream and pay special attention to your reveries before falling asleep and just after waking. Entertain the very real possibility that these—like night dreams—may contain creative hints.

Notice the paintings, the photographs, the lyrics of songs, or the lines of poetry that "grab" you. If a particular image has a strong feel to it, consider playing with it, through drawing, expressing it in dance, writing a poem about it, or using it as a springboard to write a story. Symbols contain meanings that often become clear when we playfully engage with them. Images are doorways to creativity—and they lead us toward wholeness.

Consult Your Nondominant Hand. Many consider our "wrong" hand to be an ambassador from the unconscious, the less socialized and more creative side of ourselves. The next time you are stumped about something, put a pencil in your wilder, less familiar hand and see what this part of yourself has to contribute.

Play with Art Media. First, put aside two deadly notions: that art is about making beauty and that it is only for talented experts, "real artists."

Now, consider playing around with watercolors, charcoal, poetry, clay, beads, fabric, papers, or a musical instrument, focusing on the experience and not on the product. Pick a medium you've been drawn to but haven't dared try and just "mess around." Try all sorts of things with it and see what happens; use your "wrong" hand for a while. When you're deliberately messing around, you really can't mess up. Have fun!

Engaging in art-based activities has beneficial effects on emotional and physical health—and it's enjoyable.[31]

Share Wisely. Be very mindful about whom you let in on your creative pursuits. Creativity, by definition, involves tapping into something new, and humans are generally cautious about the unfamiliar. Furthermore, those whose own creative juices are not flowing tend to react to others' novel ideas with less-than-supportive comments.

Creativity coach Julia Cameron stresses the importance of protecting ourselves from these "poisonous playmates," as she calls them in her book *The Artist's Way*.[32] Only share what you're up to when you want to and with someone you know is 100 percent in your corner. Meanwhile, enjoy the process and be your own cheerleader.

Enjoy Art. Research suggests that elders who engage in the enjoyment of art (whether music, poetry, painting, theater, or other forms) typically experience higher levels of life satisfaction, physical health, sensory competency, and cognitive functioning.[33] Being an appreciator is an undervalued but vital role in the arts, one that often becomes more appealing as we grow older and willingly relinquish center stage (see The Grace of Simplicity).

Many communities have affordable opportunities for enjoying opera and other musical events, theater, poetry, and various visual arts. Consult the entertainment section of your local newspaper or radio station, contact the community service section of your local college, or use the internet to find events that call to you and check them out. Invite a friend to go with you, or go alone (you might meet a new one).

Suggested Resources for Cultivating Creativity

Ackermann, Diane: *Deep Play*

Cameron, Julia: *It's Never Too Late to Begin Again*

Cohen, Gene: *The Creative Age*

Edens, Cooper: *If You're Afraid of the Dark, Remember the Night Rainbow* (a children's book for adults too)

Estés, Clarissa Pinkola: *The Creative Fire* (audio CD)

Fox, John: *Finding What You Didn't Lose*

Goldman, Connie, and Richard Mahler: *Secrets of Becoming a Late Bloomer*

Jamison, Kay Redfield: *Exuberance*

Malchiodi, Cathy: *The Soul's Palette*

Phillips, Jan: *Marry Your Muse*

Richards, Ruth (editor): *Everyday Creativity and New Views of Human Nature*

Sadler, William: *The Third Age*

5: The Grace of Contentment

"Our task is to say a holy yes
to the real things of our life as they exist."
—Natalie Goldberg, *Writing Down the Bones*

Happiness tends to increase with age, and one of the hallmarks of late-life development is the ability to find contentment, regardless of circumstances. Long years of experience and reflection tend to lengthen, broaden, and deepen our perspective, and we become more willing to accept life on its terms, in all its paradoxical complexity and unpredictability. With age, we become more selective about investing ourselves emotionally and more discerning about when to engage and when to let go and let be.

Age-related changes in the brain have a mellowing effect on emotions; negative emotions become more muted, while the capacity for savoring and recalling positive feelings increases. Less reactive under stress, we become mistresses of our emotions, able to navigate life's inevitable ebbs and flows with greater steadiness, equanimity, and humor.

The Psychology of Contentment

Contentment and related subjects such as happiness, positive emotions, life satisfaction, emotional well-being, and emotional intelligence (EQ) are currently the focus of a great deal of research in psychology, neuroscience, and related disciplines. Just a few recent findings are mentioned here, including some rather surprising ones, for example that older people are generally happier than younger ones and that struggling with adversity can contribute to well-being.

Age Is an Ally of Happiness. One of the most heartening discoveries is that happiness tends to increase with age. Several studies, drawing on data from dozens of countries, have confirmed that life satisfaction tends to follow a U-shaped curve across adulthood: contentment is fairly high in young adulthood, slowly drops and hits a low point at about fifty, and then steadily climbs to new heights in later life.[1] Other factors, such as good-enough health, an optimistic outlook, and environmental support play a role in fostering well-being, yet age itself is a friend of contentment. For an excellent presentation on the late-life trend toward happiness, see "Older People Are Happier," a TED Talk by psychologist Laura Carstensen, director of the Stanford Center on Longevity.

Events Play a Small Role, and Adversity Can Be Helpful. "Positive" life events and circumstances appear to have a relatively minor impact on contentment, perhaps as little as 10 percent.[2] Getting a raise or falling in love, for example, can bring a temporary rise in happiness, but the effects are usually short-lived. At the same time, grappling with adversity supports the development of character strengths like equanimity, humility, courage, compassion, and wisdom.[3] And an unchallenged life with too little struggle often leads to a sense of entitlement, low frustration tolerance, and self-centeredness, qualities that undermine contentment and create ripples of misery for others as well.

It's true that intense, traumatic experiences that occur when we are young or without social support can have severe consequences. However, as social psychologist Jonathan Haidt points out, "Suffering is not always bad for all people. There is usually some good mixed in with the bad, and those who can find it have found something precious: a key to [emotional], moral and spiritual development."[4]

Dr. Rachel Remen, whose own response to adversity in her youth has led to a life of wisdom and generosity, observes,

> Most people have come to prefer certain of life's experiences and deny and reject others, unaware of the value of the hidden things that may be wrapped in plain and even ugly paper. In avoiding all pain and seeking comfort at all costs, we may be left without intimacy or compassion . . . In denying our suffering we may never know our strength or our greatness.[5]

Intrinsic Values Matter. A number of studies have revealed that material wealth can actually interfere with happiness, and that the most contented people are motivated by intrinsic values like generosity, rather than the pursuit of fortune or fame. Economists Angus Deaton and Daniel Kahneman point out that while poverty and unhappiness are certainly related, for those with enough, increasing wealth typically means declining happiness.[6]

Summarizing her own and others' findings, psychology professor Sonja Lyubomirsky writes,

> Not only does materialism not bring happiness, it's been shown to be a strong predictor of unhappiness. . . . [It often distracts] people from relatively more meaningful and joyful aspects of their lives, such as nurturing their relationships with family and friends, enjoying the present moment, and contributing to their communities.[7]

In the winter of life, the pursuit of material goals tends to lose its appeal, and intrinsically satisfying values like generosity and compassion become more compelling. Giving ourselves to what matters most and knowing that we are contributing in a meaningful way bring joy and fulfillment. (See the Graces of Simplicity and Remembrance.)

Neuroplasticity. There is evidence that the general level of happiness we experience over the course of a lifetime is relatively stable. Similar to the set point for body weight, some of us tend more toward the curmudgeonly end of the spectrum, while others seem to be genetically predisposed to a more buoyant, optimistic way of being. However, this does not mean that our capacity for contentment is immutably hardwired. Thanks to the courageous pioneering work of UC Berkeley biologist Marian Diamond, we now recognize that the brain has a remarkable, lifelong capacity for change (*neuroplasticity*), despite its tendency to use circuits that are well established.

Psychotherapist Richard O'Connor puts it this way: "A grumpy old man was probably a teenager with a bad attitude; the high school cheerleader is probably a pretty ebullient old lady . . . [However], the new neuroscience is showing us that we can deliberately change the structure of our brains to raise our happiness quotient."[8] Consciously directing our attention toward what we are grateful for (rather than focusing on what annoys us), for example, establishes happiness-enhancing pathways in the brain that are strengthened each time we use them. In this way, we can actively participate in the rewiring of our brains toward greater contentment.

In *Buddha's Brain*, neuropsychologist Rick Hanson points out, "Even fleeting thoughts and feelings can leave lasting marks on your brain . . . What flows through your mind sculpts your brain. Thus, *you can use your mind to change your brain for the better.*"[9] *Buddha's Brain*, written with neurologist Richard Mendius, is an excellent resource, with clear descriptions of how the brain works as well as practical tools for "sculpting" it in the direction of happiness, love, and wisdom.

Contentment in the Winter of Life

The relationship between age and contentment is well-documented, though scientists are still seeking to better understand the reasons for that link. Long years of life experience and reflection play a role in late-life contentment, as do shifts in our perspective and changes in the aging brain that have a calming effect on emotions.

Reflection and the Maturing of Vision

With age, we tend to develop a taste for reflection, which is a prerequisite for contentment. Long years bring a rich store of experiences from which we can learn the art of living, so long as our minds, eyes, and ears stay open, and our hearts remain teachable. Reflection enables us to see more clearly and deeply into life as it is, rather than through the filter of our unexamined opinions, desires, and expectations about how things should be.

From the perspective afforded by many decades, we recognize that the human journey is far more complex, paradoxical, and unpredictable than it may once have seemed. We learn that there are multiple ways of viewing situations, that we do not always know what is right or best, and that actions may not always have the desired effect. Whereas it may once have seemed fairly simple to distinguish good from bad and right from wrong, with age we learn to accept the many shades of gray and the wide array of paradoxes and puzzlements that are the stuff of life.

Such *postoperational thinking* is also characterized by an integration of thinking and feeling as well as the ability to stand back and view situations with greater clarity and equanimity.[10] As we move beyond oversimplified, either-or vision and its inevitable companion, Certainty, we become less reactive and impulsive and more discerning about when to act and when to "let be."[11]

My mother grew more and more content as she aged, and she knew a lot about letting be. (She was also gusty and could be quite a force.) About two years before her death, I was visiting one day and asked how she was doing. Instead of her usual response ("wonderful" or "really good,") she said, "Pretty good." When I urged her to tell me more, she said, "There are some things going on around here that I don't much like."

When I asked her what things, she paused and said with a

shy smile, "I don't remember." We both laughed, and then I asked what she did when there was something going on that she didn't like. She thought for a moment and said, "Well, first I see if there's anything I can do about it, and if there is, I do it. And if there isn't, I let it go." Years later, I realized she was passing on a wonderful recipe for contentment.

Emotional Climate of Later Life

Despite the inevitable losses of late life, emotions like sadness and anger become more muted and less frequent with age, while the capacity for joy, delight, wonder, and gratitude often deepens. One reason for this shift is the tendency for the emotion-processing centers of the brain (the amygdalae) to become less reactive with age, especially to negative emotional stimuli.

In one study, for example, psychologist Mara Mather and her associates showed younger and older adults both negative and positive imagery and noticed significant differences between the two age groups, in terms of brain activity, emotional experience, and recall. Brain scans revealed that elders' amygdalae were less responsive to negative stimuli than to positive stimuli. In addition, older participants reported fewer negative emotions during the process and were more likely to recall positive imagery afterward, compared to younger participants.[12]

In later life, we develop what some gerontologists call *emotional mastery*: the ability to recognize and regulate our emotions and to express them in nonharming ways. Our responses to other people and to life events tend to mature and become more adaptive, flexible, and kind. With age, for example, we are less likely under stress to blame or turn against others and more likely to try to understand and find meaning or humor in the situation. Summarizing a number of studies with adults over sixty-five, psychology professor Dacher Keltner notes, "With age people can more readily move in and out of different emotional states . . . [and] report experiencing more freedom and control during emotional experiences."[13]

Emotional mastery begins with the acknowledgment of our feelings, even, and perhaps especially, the less pleasant ones. For it is the distressing emotions that have the greatest potential for teaching us what we need to understand. Over time, observing and being honest with ourselves about our feelings brings greater awareness of the patterns of thought and feeling that lead to contentment (like forgiveness and humor) and those that usually lead to misery (like self-righteousness and impatience). If we allow our emotional "guests" to be our teachers and our guides, as the Sufi poet Rumi suggests in "The Guest House," we become more discerning about which feelings to acknowledge and let go of, and which to express, and how and to whom to express them.

The following well-known story, probably Cherokee in origin, illustrates the emotional mastery that often develops in the winter of life: One evening after a fierce battle in which most of his people have been killed, an old man tells his grandson, "There are two wolves fighting within me. One is full of anger and wants revenge; the other is full of sorrow and grieves for all the lives that have been lost today." The boy is silent for a time and then asks, "Grandfather, which wolf will win?" And the old man replies, "The one that I feed."

A few years ago, I witnessed a friend stop herself in the middle of an emotional storm, step back, and acknowledge how she was contributing to her own suffering. We are both blessed to be part of a women's group that's been meeting for forty-eight years, and she'd been sharing how angry she'd been for the past week or two, at virtually everyone who'd crossed her path, from annoying drivers to family members.

Then she suddenly stopped recounting the events that had set her off and confessed, "I realize that I like being righteously indignant." The truth of that statement hung in the air; some of us nodded. We also know the delicious but deadly rush of intensity that can accompany righteous anger—and how much suffering it usually brings.

The willingness to look inward and be honest with ourselves, as my friend did, makes the difference between continuing to be caught in an emotional storm and being able to move through it. As psychologist Daniel Goleman explains, "The design of the brain means that we very often have little or no control over *when* we are swept by emotion, nor over *what* emotion it will be. But we can have some say in *how long* the emotion will last."[14] As we become more familiar with the terrain of our own heart—as we get to know the slippery places and the ground that feels good under our feet—sometimes we can intervene and disperse a gathering storm before it sweeps us away.

Being mistresses of our emotions means that we do the best we can, moment by moment, in choosing which wolves to feed and which to acknowledge and send on their way. Emotional mastery is a commitment, not a quality we acquire all at once. Age and practice can help us to grow more discerning about when and how to express emotions in ways that are authentic, appropriate, and minimally harmful to others and ourselves.

Here is a story from the Tamil people of India about a poor old widow living in miserable circumstances. Her suffering is relieved when she allows herself to express her anger and sorrow in a creative, nonharming way.

Tell It to the Walls

A poor widow lived with her two sons and two daughters-in-law. All four of them scolded and ill-treated her all day. She had no one to whom she could turn and tell her woes. As she kept all her woes to herself, she grew fatter and fatter. Her sons and daughters-in-law now found this a matter for ridicule. They mocked her for growing fatter by the day and asked her to eat less.

One day, when everyone in the house had gone out somewhere, she wandered away from home in sheer misery and found herself walking outside town. There she saw a deserted old house. It was all in ruins and had no roof. She went in and suddenly felt lonelier and more miserable than ever. She found she couldn't bear to keep her miseries to herself any longer. She had to tell someone.

So she told all her tales of grievance against her first son to the wall in front of her. As she finished, the wall collapsed under the weight of her woes and crashed to the ground in a heap. Her body grew lighter as well.

Then she turned to the second wall and told it all her grievances against her first son's wife. Down came that wall, and she grew lighter still.

She brought down the third wall with her tales against her second son, and the remaining fourth wall, too, with her complaints against her second daughter-in-law.

Standing in the ruins, with bricks and rubble all around her, she felt lighter in mood and lighter in body as well. She looked at herself and found that she had actually lost all the weight she had gained in her wretchedness.

Then she went home.[15]

Some Questions for Reflection

1. What part of this story speaks most strongly to you, and how is that connected to your life?

2. How do you find emotional equilibrium in the midst of distress?

3. When have you been the object of ridicule? How did you respond? Have you forgiven your tormentors?

4. When have you been guilty of ridiculing others? What motivated your mistreatment of them? Have you made amends? forgiven yourself?

5. When have you used food in order not to feel your feelings? What ripple effects does this form of self-protection have?

6. In what other ways do you attempt to buffer yourself against unwanted emotions? Compulsive busyness or shopping, alcohol or other drug use, overindulgence in entertainment, or . . . ? What are the costs of these forms of avoidance?

7. When have you noticed feeling lighter after expressing anger and/or sadness, and when have you felt worse afterward? What makes the difference?

8. Are there grievances in your present life you need to express? How might you do that in a way that does not harm others or yourself?

9. If you were to take to heart the medicine of this story, for you, what shift—large or small—would you make in your life?

Reflections

The old woman in this folktale may well be in one of those situations that Reinhold Niebuhr describes in the beginning of his well-known prayer: "God, grant us grace to accept with serenity the things that cannot be changed."[16] Given the time and place in which the story is set, it seems unlikely that she could simply move out and find new living arrangements. She is embedded in a traditional, hierarchical society, and she is old, female, widowed, and poor and thus dependent on her sons and their wives for survival. They take care of her physical needs, but at great emotional cost to her.

In the beginning of the story, the old mother copes with her growing unhappiness by overeating, a common response for women, especially when angry or depressed. Sadly, this attempt at self-protection or soothing is almost always a form of self-sabotage as well, creating even more suffering (potential health problems as well as shame and self-loathing).

Our heroine discovers a way out of her abject misery: she tells the truth about what she is feeling in a way that unburdens her own heart but does not worsen the situation. As she dares to acknowledge what is in her mind and heart, she can feel herself growing lighter, and she keeps going until all her grievances are expressed (literally, "squeezed or pressed out," from the same root as *espresso*). She has been sitting on a great deal; the weight of her woes is enough to bring down four stone walls!

Then she went home. There is a bittersweet poignancy in this last sentence; it's not a tidy, happily-ever-after ending. We are left to imagine what happens once this heroine gets back home. My sense is that the old woman who returns may well be a different person than the one who left that morning in such misery. And that may alter the family system, as it often does when one person makes an internal shift, even if others are not privy to it.

It is possible that her sons and daughters-in-law may sense a difference in her. She might seem stronger, less defenseless, and that could result in their treating her better—or not. What is most important is that she has come home to herself and established herself as the mistress of her own emotions. Regardless of what her family members do and don't do in the future, she belongs to herself again and need not internalize their treatment or their view of her. And if she starts to forget her value again, she now has a remedy.

Befriending Adversity

Another dimension of contentment that often ripens in the winter of life is the willingness to accept and learn from adversity. When we are facedown in the muck of misery, it is quite human to want it to be over as soon as possible. From the perspective afforded by long years and the maturing of vision, however, the distinction between good and bad experiences tends to soften, as it does with other apparent opposites.

From the long view, it is clear that sometimes getting something we want comes at an unexpectedly high price. And sometimes a disaster leads to a blessing beyond our imagining. Adversity can be a teacher and a guide, if we are willing to look and learn, and elders are usually more willing pupils. The word *adversity* comes from the Latin *adversus*, which means "turned against." Situations that run counter to what we desire, hope, or expect can challenge and stretch us in directions we may not want to go but that may ultimately benefit us and the world.

Psychologists Laura King and Joshua Hicks describe how the growing acceptance in later life that we are all "marked" for suffering paradoxically strengthens the capacity for contentment:

> The very experiences that mark us may become a source of strength and play a role in the creation of a different and more integrated self. . . . The humble, courageous admission that we are all marked is the first step toward [emotional] maturity. . . . Happiness in this context may well be a richer, more durable experience . . . more bittersweet, involving the recognition of legitimate loss and [human] fragility . . . The mature person is not "sadder but wiser"—but rather, wise and still inspired and fulfilled—and ultimately happy.[17]

The root of the word *suffering* means "to allow," and paradoxically our capacity for contentment is directly related to our willingness to allow ourselves to suffer. In accepting adversity and learning to work with it, we open ourselves to the gifts that may lie within and on the other side of suffering. Older adults tend to take setbacks more in stride and are generally more skilled at finding silver linings than are younger ones. And they are more apt to respond to difficult situations creatively and with good humor, like the heroine in the following story from England. Despite her material poverty, this ebullient, resilient old woman meets a series of losses with good humor and gratitude.

The Hedley Kow

There was once an old woman, who earned a poor living by going on errands and such like for the farmers' wives round the village where she lived. It wasn't much she earned by it; but with a plate of meat at one house, and a cup of tea at another, she made shift to get on somehow, and always looked as cheerful as if she hadn't a want in the world.

Well, one summer evening as she was trotting away homewards, she came upon a big black pot lying at the side of the road.

"Now *that*," said she, stopping to look at it, "would be just the very thing for me if I had anything to put into it! But who can have left it here?" And she looked round about, as if the person it belonged to must be not far off. But she could see no one.

"Maybe it'll have a hole in it," she said thoughtfully. "Ay, that'll be why they've left it lying, hinny. But then it'd do fine to put a flower in for the window; I'm thinking I'll just take it home anyways." And she bent her stiff old back, and lifted the lid to look inside.

"Mercy me!" she cried, and jumped back to the other side of the road. "*If it isn't full of gold PIECES!*"

For a while she could do nothing but walk round and round her treasure, admiring the yellow and gold and wondering at her good luck, and saying to herself about every two minutes, "Well, I *do* be feeling rich and grand!"

But presently she began to think how she could best take it home with her; and she couldn't see any other way than by fastening one end of her shawl to it, and so dragging it after her along the road.

"It'll certainly be soon dark," she said to herself, "and folk'll not see what I'm bringing home with me, and so I'll have all the night to myself to think what I'll do with it. I could buy a grand house and all, and live like the Queen herself, and not do a stroke of work all day, but just sit by the fire with a cup of tea; or maybe

I'll give it to the priest to keep for me, and get a piece as I'm wanting; or maybe I'll just bury it in a hole at the garden-foot, and put a bit on the chimney teapot and the spoons—for ornament, like. Ah! I feel so grand, I don't know myself rightly!"

And by this time, being already rather tired with dragging such a heavy weight after her, she stopped to rest for a minute, turning to make sure that her treasure was safe.

But when she looked at it, it wasn't a pot of gold at all, but a great lump of shining silver.

She stared at it, and rubbed her eyes and stared at it again; but she couldn't make it look like anything but a great lump of silver. "I'd have sworn it was a pot of gold," she said at last, "but I reckon I must have been dreaming. Ay, now, that's a change for the better; it'll be far less trouble to look after, and none so easily stolen. Yon gold pieces would have been a sight of bother to keep 'em safe. Ay, I'm well quit of them; and with my bonny lump I'm as rich as rich!"

And she set of homewards again, cheerfully planning all the grand things she was going to do with her lump of silver. It wasn't very long, however, before she got tired again and stopped once more to rest for a minute or two.

Again she turned to look at her treasure, and as soon as she set eyes on it she cried out in astonishment. "Oh my!" said she, "now it's a lump o' iron! Well, that beats all; and it's just real convenient! I can sell it as *easy* as *easy*, and get a lot o' penny pieces for it. Ay, hinny, and it's much handier than a lot of yer gold and silver as'd have kept me from sleeping o' nights thinking the neighbors were robbing me—an' it's a real good thing to have by you in a house. Ye niver can tell what ye mightn't use it for, an' it'll sell—ay, for a real lot. Rich? I'll be just *rolling*."

And on she trotted again chuckling to herself, till presently she glanced over her shoulder, "just to make sure it was there still," as she said to herself.

"Ey, my!" she cried as soon as she saw it. "If it hasn't gone and tuned itself into a great stone this time! Now, how could it have known that I was just *terrible* wanting something to hold my door open with? Ay, if that isn't a good change! Hinny, it's a fine thing to have such good luck."

And, all in a hurry to see how the stone would look in its corner by her door, she trotted off down the hill, and stopped at the foot, beside her own little gate.

When she had unlatched it, she turned to unfasten her shawl from the stone, which this time seemed to lie unchanged and peaceably on the path beside her. There was still plenty of light, and she could see the stone quite plainly as she bent her stiff back over it, to untie the shawl end.

All of a sudden, it seemed to give a jump and a squeal, and it grew in a moment as big as a great horse. Then it threw down four lanky legs, and shook out two long ears, flourished a tail, and went off kicking its feet in the air, and laughing like a naughty mocking boy. The old woman started after it, till it was fairly out of sight.

"WELL!" she said at last. "I *do* be the luckiest body hereabouts! Fancy me seeing the Hedley Kow all to myself, and making so free with it too! I can tell you, I *do* feel that GRAND . . ."

And she went into her cottage and sat down by the fire to think over her good luck.[18]

Some Questions for Reflection

1. What part of this story stands out for you, and how is that related to your life?

2. How skillful are you at remaining cheerful when your resources—financial and otherwise—are low?

3. What have been the major losses of your life, and how have you responded to them?

4. What current loss or disappointment in your life might you be able to "reframe" as a change for the better or a potential blessing in disguise?

5. How often do you take the time to sit down and count your blessings? And if, right now, you were to make a list of the things for which you are grateful, what would it include?

6. If you were to take to heart what is, for you, the message or medicine of this story, what change—large or small—might you make in your life?

Reflections

The first time I came across this story, I thought the heroine was a bit over-the-top. After living with the tale for a few years though, I've come to appreciate what a fine embodiment of the Grace of Contentment this old woman is.

Despite her material poverty, she manages somehow to get by and always looks cheerful, as if she hasn't a care in the world. As the story unfolds, through loss upon loss, she remains optimistic and grateful for what she has, and she meets each diminishment with good humor. Rather than bemoaning the loss and comparing her present lot with what she once had, she imagines the benefit of what now exists. She is masterful at finding the blessings that lie hidden in adversity.

In the end, she is left with nothing—no thing—yet she is delighted by her brief encounter with the Hedley Kow, who appears magically out of the large stone—and then disappears. It might seem that she has now lost everything, but her focus is on enjoying what she has experienced.

The last thing we hear (so typical of this contented old woman) is that she sits down by the fire to think over her good luck. She is blessed with a capacity for savoring simple and magical moments and by her willingness to meet the changing circumstances of her life with flexibility and gratitude.

⟫⟫⟩ Cultivating Contentment ⟨⟨⟨

Contentment can be enhanced in a number of ways, by nurturing her allies (savoring, gratitude, and humor); by acknowledging and working free of the patterns of thinking and feeling that feed the wolves of discontent; and by learning to work with adversity.

Savoring the Good

Psychologists and neuroscientists have discovered that positive emotions have a number of beneficial effects. They promote flexibility in thinking and problem-solving, they counteract the effects of negative emotions, they enhance psychological resilience and physical well-being, and they trigger upward spirals of contentment.[19]

Probably the single most important thing we can do to shift the brain toward contentment is to notice the small experiences of joy, delight, and affection that occur every day and to savor them fully. Over time, basking in positive experiences as they happen and recalling them afterward gradually shifts the brain in the direction of greater happiness.

Pause and fully enjoy moments of happiness as they happen each day. It is so easy to rush through them, or not to notice them at all. The longer we hold a positive emotional experience in our awareness, the stronger its neurological effect, in the moment and in memory.[20] And fortunately, savoring joy and simple pleasures is an inclination as we age. (See the Grace of Simplicity.)

Recalling positive emotional experiences is also helpful in counteracting the effects of negative emotions. The next time you're aware of lingering anger, depression, or anxiety, bring to mind an experience that evoked strong feelings of love, joy, delight, or contentment, and bathe in it for twenty seconds or more. Each time we experience positive emotions in real time or in memory, we strengthen happiness-enhancing pathways in the brain.

Expressing Gratitude

Gratitude is a potent ally of contentment. Over time, the simple practice of noticing each day what we are grateful for can turn a grumbling or anxious heart into a joyful one.

For three weeks, write down ten things for which you are grateful at the end of each day, preferably new ones every night. As you recall the day's blessings, let yourself reexperience them briefly, and then jot them down in a notebook. After twenty-one days, take stock of how you are feeling and living your life. If this practice agrees with you, consider continuing it, especially in difficult times.

Laughing with Ourselves and Each Other

Nonaggressive humor—especially the ability to laugh at ourselves and our foibles—often increases with age and is a good friend of contentment. And scientists have found that both laughter and smiling have physical and emotional benefits for ourselves and for others.[21]

Some years ago, while editing this particular chapter, I was ironically grumpier than I could remember being in a long time. Everything annoyed me—the relentless spring wind, the huge number of fruitless and misdirected phone calls it was taking to get my garbage collected and internet provider changed, even the overwhelming number of gatherings I'd agreed to attend for friends and family who were retiring, graduating, or celebrating milestone birthdays. (The latter was an especially ridiculous source of grumpiness, but there it was.)

When my friend Ellen called from New York and asked how I was, I blurted, "I'm writing about contentment and I'm pissed at everything!" We had a good laugh. Acknowledging the truth to a friend and laughing at myself helped bring me out of my sideways state, back into flowing with life. Laughter helped me see that everything I had been railing against was quite unimportant and that the blessings in my life at that time far outweighed the annoyances on which I'd been focusing.

The next time you notice yourself complaining or find yourself in a grump or funk, annoyed with the world and most everything in it, take a step back and see if you can find something humorous (ironic, paradoxical, ridiculous, or ludicrous) in your circumstances. Have a good laugh.

Taming the Wolves of Discontent

Much of our discontent is of our own making, rooted in mistaken attitudes, limiting beliefs, and hurtful habits of mind and heart, especially our insistence (usually unstated, of course) that life should go according to our plans and desires. With reflection and a large dose of psychological courage, we can learn to recognize the particular seeds of our discontent, especially in the winter of life. Rabbi Abraham Heschel observes, "The years of old age . . . are indeed formative years, rich in possibilities to unlearn the follies of a lifetime, to see through inbred self-deceptions, to deepen understanding and compassion, to widen the horizons of honesty, to redefine the sense of fairness."[22]

While our particular mix of follies and self-deceptions is unique, here are some fairly common notions that invariably lead to unhappiness:

- Believing we are unworthy of happiness
- Thinking we are entitled to happiness and feeling disappointed or angry when things don't go as we think they should
- Blaming outer events and other people for our discontent rather than being accountable for our own emotions
- Comparing ourselves to others
- Needing to be right (and making others wrong)
- Worrying about the future
- Hanging on to the past and refusing to let go of what no longer is; being unwilling to forgive others (and ourselves)
- Longing for what isn't and complaining about what is
- Being so preoccupied with our own desires, goals, and plans that we fail to recognize what is going on around us

As we grow familiar with our particular inner troublemakers (the thoughts, emotional patterns, and reactive behaviors that create disharmony and dissention within and around us), we are freer to choose, at least some of the time, not to feed those wolves of discontent. We become better at saying to ourselves, "Don't go there," thus interrupting the chain reaction of thought and emotion that we know from experience leads to unhappiness. Even when we fall into an old pattern, we can shorten the duration of misery by acknowledging where we are caught and making a choice to stop feeding that particular wolf.

Spend some time reflecting on the litanies of discontent that visit you most frequently: worrying, envying, fuming, complaining, despairing, comparing, condemning, feeling overwhelmed, or . . . When one of them comes calling, instead of following it down an emotional rabbit hole, see if you can simply name it—"judging" or "worrying," for example—and let it pass. Even better, see if you can send a little kindness or even love toward it. (Positive emotions are a powerful tool for undoing lingering negative emotions.) Remember: every time you interrupt an old pattern of discontent, you are changing the circuitry of your brain.

If the litany persists—some are quite tenacious!—spend some time listening to it. What is Worry so frightened of? What is it that Complaining really wants? What does Self-Loathing need from you? See if you can bring to mind—briefly—previous experiences of these patterns in order to get a sense of their origins. (The more we learn about these recurring patterns, the less hold they have over us.)

Tenacious troublemakers are like nightmares or the children of distracted parents: they have information we are not hearing, so they up the ante to get our attention. Take to heart any messages you receive in your imagination from these distressing (and distressed) visitors. (It is sometimes helpful to put a pen in your nondominant hand when asking a particular troublemaking gift-bearer what she needs.)

Releasing Emotions in Nonharming Ways

One dimension of being mistresses of our emotions is the ability to express feelings in ways that are both effective and nonharming. Playing with art media can be an excellent way to release pent-up emotions or to express feelings that are difficult to share. Here is an exercise a student once taught me for expressing painful emotions in a safe way:

Take a piece of paper (large or small), some paints, and a paintbrush (or some colored markers), and write what you are feeling in big letters across the top of the page. Turn the paper in another direction, take another color, and write some more. Keep rotating the paper and changing colors—experiment with writing in circles and waves, on the diagonal, however you wish. In time, you'll notice the page filling up; keep painting until you've expressed everything you need to.

It's fine to paint or write over other words; in fact, that's encouraged. In the end, you'll have a sheet of paper, full of color and lines that are no longer distinguishable as words. You'll have moved the emotions out of your body onto the safety of the page, where they lie hidden in plain view. You may want to hang your painting on the wall, tear it up, or burn it. It's up to you.

This exercise helped me through one of the most painful and frightening periods of my life. I made time to paint every morning for two weeks, starting with my fears for a loved one and gradually finding myself painting prayers for his well-being instead. The papers were not only healing for me but also beautiful, and I ended up using them as wrapping paper at Christmas that year. (By that time, thankfully, the danger had passed.)

The body can also be an invaluable ally in releasing disturbing mental and emotional "baggage." Engaging in physical activity like walking, swimming, or biking is an excellent way to release emotions, while at the same time taking care of your health. Here are some other suggestions for enlisting the assistance of your body in reestablishing emotional equilibrium:

Symbolic movements and gestures can be powerful releasers, for example, raising your shoulders as you inhale and then lowering them as you exhale deeply (and noisily), letting go of whatever is distressing you. Making fists as you inhale and opening your hands as you lower them and exhale is another way to release troubling emotions. Be sure to end on an exhale.

Even household chores like sweeping, emptying the garbage, clearing away clutter, washing dishes or windows, pruning, weeding with vigor, or beating a rug can help carry away persistent unwanted inner "guests." Use your imagination and picture these activities as symbolically loosening, gathering up, and disposing of distressing thoughts and feelings. Then recall a moment when you felt especially content and bathe in that memory for several breaths.

Learning from Adversity

One of the most powerful tools for cultivating contentment is learning to remain open in the face of suffering, rather than closing down or attempting to run from it. As Buddhist teacher and author Pema Chödrön writes in *When Things Fall Apart*: "Life is a good teacher and a good friend. . . . Every day we are given many opportunities to open up or shut down . . . Most of us don't take these situations as teachings. We automatically hate them [and] run like crazy . . . Every moment is a teacher."[23]

As I've aged it's become clear that the most difficult and painful experiences of my life have been among the most important: excruciating isolation in adolescence, the sudden and early death of my father, a shattering betrayal, the near loss of my sons at a young age, witnessing the suffering of beloved children (and being unable to intervene effectively), and my mother's fading into dementia.

Each of these pushed me to question and reevaluate almost everything, taught me painful yet invaluable lessons, and forced me to discover parts of myself that might not have developed otherwise. At the time, some of these situations were more painful and frightening than I thought I could bear. At this point though, I can see with gratitude the gifts that Suffering brought in her wake: a larger store of patience and strength, greater connectedness to and compassion for others, wiser understanding of the world and the human heart, and renewed gratitude for the vast, beautiful mystery that is life.

The next time you are in the grip of suffering, see if you can allow yourself to move toward it and stay with it. Feel your emotions, notice your thoughts, pay attention to the sensations in your body—and observe how all of these change from moment to moment, in intensity and in quality. When a wave of sorrow, anger, or anxiety comes over you, be gentle with yourself and stay as present and aware as you can. It is often the case that we find islands of peace, even of joy, in the midst of pain.

In the grip of suffering it may also be helpful to remember times when seemingly hopeless situations resolved themselves in unexpected ways.

Spend some time remembering a loss that led to new discoveries, suffering that contained a life-altering lesson, disappointment that turned out to be a blessing in disguise, or a situation that unexpectedly took a turn for the better. Dwell on these memories when fear or despair come calling. Be open to surprising developments in your current struggles.

Use whatever tools you have at your disposal to go into—rather than flee from—what is troubling you. The willingness to embrace the flow of life, as it is, benefits others as well because when our hearts are content, we respond to the world with greater kindness and understanding. We are less contentious. Even in the midst of stress and sorrow, acceptance helps us to meet other people and situations with an open heart.

Recommended Resources on Contentment

Boorstein, Sylvia: *Happiness Is an Inside Job*

Carstensen, Laura: *A Long Bright Future* and her April 2009 TED Talk, "Older People Are Happier"

Chödrön, Pema: *When Things Fall Apart*

Goleman, Daniel: *Emotional Intelligence*

Haidt, Jonathan: *The Happiness Hypothesis*

Hanson, Rick, and Richard Mendius: *Buddha's Brain*

His Holiness the Dalai Lama and Desmond Tutu: *The Book of Joy*

Johnson, Robert, and Jerry Ruhl: *Contentment*

Keltner, Dacher: *Born to Be Good*

King, Laura A., and Joshua A. Hicks: "Whatever Happened to 'What Might Have Been'?"

Lyubomirsky, Sonja: *The How of Happiness*

Salzberg, Sharon: *Lovingkindness*

I also recommend four movies that illustrate moving through suffering toward contentment in the winter of life: *Enchanted April* (Joan Plowright's character); *St. Vincent* (Bill Murray's character); *The Best Exotic Marigold Hotel* and the sequel, *The Second Best Exotic Marigold Hotel*. (Several characters in these last two films reveal the possibility of late-life contentment in the face of adversity, and also show how defending ourselves against suffering can imprison us in bitterness).

6: The Grace of Compassion

*"Compassion in action is paradoxical and
mysterious. . . . It is joyful in the midst of suffering and
hopeful in the face of overwhelming odds. . . .
It is done for others, but it nurtures the self."*
—Ram Dass and Mirabai Bush,
Compassion in Action

Compassion (literally, "to suffer with") is a state of openheartedness
that allows us to sense another's suffering and to respond with
kindness and generosity. Compassion begins with self-acceptance
(Authenticity) and the growing recognition of our kinship with all of
life (Self-Transcending Generosity). It is supported by the Graces of
Contentment and Courage and is inseparable from Wisdom, which is
the capacity to discern how best to respond in important, emotionally
complex situations.

Compassion as Virtue and Necessity

For thousands of years in cultures around the world, compassion
has been considered the highest expression of our humanity.[1] From
her extensive study of the world's religions, British author Karen
Armstrong concludes, "The religious traditions were in unanimous
agreement. The one and only test of a valid religious idea, doctri-
nal statement, spiritual experience, or devotional practice was that it

must lead directly to practical compassion . . . [making] you kinder, more empathetic, and . . . [more likely] to express this sympathy in concrete acts of loving-kindness."[2]

Lovingkindness (*metta*) and compassion (*karuna*) hold a particularly important place in Buddhism and are two of four sublime states of mind, along with joy for others' happiness (*mudita*), and equanimity (*upekkha*). The Dalai Lama describes love and compassion as the remedy for both internal distress and outer conflict. "Compassion is not something childish or sentimental . . . No matter how much violence or how many bad things we have to go through, I believe that the ultimate solution to our conflicts, both internal and external, lies in returning to our basic underlying human nature which is gentle and compassionate."[3]

Of course, returning to that deeper, kinder essence requires enormous discipline and practice. However, at this point in history when kindness and compassion seem to be at such a low ebb, deepening our capacity for openheartedness (especially toward those we are tempted to call enemies) seems more essential than ever, for our own well-being and for the sake of the human family.

We are fortunate to be living in an era when scientists in a variety of fields are engaged in studying compassion and its effects on physical and emotional well-being and on relationships between individuals, groups, and nations. Their work is demonstrating what spiritual teachers of the world have known for millennia: that we are all connected (our brains are wired to respond to the suffering of others) and that the cultivation of compassion through meditation and other practices enhances health, well-being, and the quality of relationships.

In *The Compassionate Instinct*, Dacher Keltner, Jason Marsh, and Jeremy Adam Smith summarize the findings of a wide range of recent studies of compassion in neuroscience, evolution, psychology, and other fields:

> Neuroscience suggests that . . . kindness really is its own reward. Moreover, kindness is contagious: research finds

that when we offer modest expressions of gratitude—the simple "thank you," smile, or warm gaze—we prompt other people to reciprocate the kindness toward us and toward others. . . . Research suggests that compassionate behavior not only exemplifies a good, moral way to live, but carries great emotional and physical health benefits for compassionate people, their families, and their communities. . . . Behaviors like compassion and kindness are actually conducive to human survival—and essential to human flourishing.[4]

Compassion in Later Life

Despite the wealth of recent research on compassion, its relationship to age, thus far, has received relatively little attention.[5] However, many qualities associated with other graces (such as self-acceptance, humility, altruism, forgiveness, emotional mastery, and empathy) are essential dimensions of compassion as well. In that sense, the Grace of Compassion can be seen as a natural outgrowth of the late-life gifts of Authenticity, Self-Transcending Generosity, Contentment, Courage, and Wisdom.

The Grace of Authenticity brings greater awareness and acceptance of ourselves as we are, including our limitations and vulnerabilities. As we learn to treat our imperfect selves with more tenderness, we are inclined to be kinder toward others as well. Buddhist teacher Pema Chödrön explains, "Having compassion starts and ends with having compassion for all those unwanted parts of ourselves, all those imperfections that we don't even want to look at . . . As we learn to have compassion for ourselves, the circle of compassion for others . . . becomes wider."[6]

The Grace of Self-Transcending Generosity. As we come to sense ourselves as embedded in a greater Self, our relationships with others take on qualities of kinship: humility, altruism, forgiveness, magnanimity, and unselfishness. Knowing ourselves as one with other people and creatures, we become more tenderhearted toward them, as we would be toward a beloved child, imperfections and all. Ram Dass and Mirabai Bush describe beautifully the relationship between compassion and interconnectedness:

> When we experience the pain of others in our own blood and muscle, we are feeling compassion. It begins as gentle love and acceptance of ourselves, and it extends to include our family and friends and, eventually, all beings, those we know and those we do not, as well as all of nature—rocks and raccoons and stars and water . . . Although the suffering of others may not be our fault, it *is* our responsibility, not in a heavy sense . . . but in a natural way, as if we were all part of the same body.[7]

The Grace of Contentment. The muting of negative emotions in later life, the broadening of our perspective, and the growing capacity to respond to stress and conflict with kindness, patience, and empathy are dimensions of Contentment that are essential elements of Compassion as well. Emotional maturity and mastery enable us to navigate the negative emotions that surround suffering, to see into the heart of another's distress, and to sense what might help to ease it. The Graces of Contentment and Compassion resemble breathing. Contentment, like inhaling, fills us with empathy, bathes us in well-being, and softens our responses to others, even in difficult situations. Compassion, like an exhale, extends those same qualities of kindness, patience, and understanding toward others.

The Grace of Courage. It seems to me that every act of compassion requires courage. In choosing to open our hearts in the face of others' suffering, we make ourselves vulnerable—to their pain, to our own emotions, to the situation, and to the unknown. Daring to look and be moved by another, rather than averting our eyes to preserve our own comfort, is both compassionate and courageous.

So often our lack of kindness toward another's struggles is rooted in the fear that we won't know what to say or do in response. Compassion is the willingness to find out by daring to be present. It means caring more about the well-being of another than our own potential discomfort. It's been my experience that when I am willing to stay open and present with another in her suffering, it usually becomes clear what is needed. And those encounters almost always bless both of us in some way.

My friend Judy recently told me a story about an experience of mutual blessing she'd had the night before. She'd pulled into a gas station on her way home from an all-day meeting with quite a bit of extra food in her car, including some chocolate cupcakes. She noticed a poor-looking man standing nearby. Part of her wanted to play it safe and look away, but she felt touched by him and walked over and asked if he liked chocolate. When he said that he did, she offered him the cupcakes. His face lit up as he told her, "It's my birthday today."

Knowing Judy, it is easy to imagine the mutual smiles of warmth that passed between them at that point. Later, as she was filling her tank and he sat eating the cupcakes, she realized that he probably needed the cheese and bread in her car far more than she did. She went over again to ask if he wanted them. As she handed him the second round of food, they looked into one another's eyes, both of them moved to tears.

The Grace of Wisdom. Compassion also entails discernment, the ability to see clearly what is happening, what is needed, what is possible, and what is not. Sometimes wise and openhearted seeing inspires overt action; at other times, it may not. Yet even a nod, a warm gaze, or a smile can be a form of compassion. Circumstances may limit what we can do in response to another, but as a quality of heart, compassion is limitless.

Here is an Eskimo[8] tale about an old woman who is the only one in a village able to see past her neighbor's gruff exterior and perceive his broken heart. He is so unpleasant and full of rage that most people avoid him, for fear he might kill them. Yet in her compassionate wisdom the old woman senses the root of his pain as well as what might ease his suffering. Her response to him reflects many elements of compassion: courage, openheartedness, empathy, respect for the other, wise discernment, inspiration, and reciprocity.

The Running Stick

Long ago, in the village of Na-ki-a-ki-a-mute, there lived a strong man, or chief, with his wife, to whom he was very devoted. They had no children, but among their neighbors was a little girl who lived in a tiny house with her grandmother. These two were very poor, but the chief was rich, and the chief's wife loved the little girl and had her with her often. Indeed, the child used to come every day to fetch water for the chief's wife, from the water hole through the ice in the river nearby.

One day the man went off hunting, and when he came back with a fine fat seal for their food his wife was gone. He called and called her, but she did not answer. Then he went to all his neighbors seeking her, but no one had seen her, and no trace of her could be found anywhere. There was not even a footprint to show which direction she had gone.

The poor man was nearly crazy with grief and anger, for he felt sure someone must have taken his wife away from him. He became fierce and sullen, brooding over his troubles and loneliness, and would speak to no one. In fact, no one dared come near him for fear of being killed. All day long he would sit out in front of his house with his big bow and quiver full of arrows, watching; at night he could not sleep, nor did he eat.

One day the old grandmother said to the little girl, "I am sorry for that poor man; he is so unhappy. You go to him and ask him to come and eat with us. His wife loved you. He will not hurt you. Try to bring him back with you."

Very timidly, the little girl obeyed, for in her heart she was afraid to go. When she got near the chief's house she stopped and felt like turning back, for he sat there looking so fierce and gloomy that she was frightened. But when he saw the child standing there he motioned for her to come. Then she no longer felt afraid, but went and sat beside him, and told him what her grandmother had said.

The chief said nothing, but when she slipped her little hand in his, he got up and went with her to her home, where her grandmother had already cooked him a fine supper of reindeer meat. The poor man had not eaten for so long that he was starving, and when he finished all the meat the old woman had, he sent the little girl to his own house to get some more.

As soon as the little one had gone out of the room, the grandmother said to him, "I sent for you because you have been kind to us, and I believe I can help you find your wife. You must make a good strong staff of driftwood, then take this bunch of charms and tie it firmly to the stick." She gave him a bunch of little charms—ivory animals and faces and some tufts of feathers from sea birds.

Next, she said he must set the stick upright in the ground, in front of his house, very firmly, so that the wind could not blow it over. When he had done this, he should go to bed and sleep. In the morning he must examine the stick carefully, and go in the direction in which the stick leaned. Whenever he stopped for the night he must set the stick in the same way, and in the morning the stick would point the direction he must follow to find his wife. "If you obey my instructions," said she, "the stick will lead you straight to your wife."

Then the little girl came in with some more reindeer meat, and the man ate until he was satisfied, and then went home. As soon as he reached his house, he made a fine staff, tied the charms to it, and planted it firmly in the ground before the door. Then he went in and, rolling himself up in a big bearskin, fell asleep.

He woke in the morning feeling well rested and more like himself than at any time since his wife's disappearance. It was late, and the sun had already risen. He hurried out anxiously to look at his stick. It was bent directly toward the North, so he pulled it up and started on his journey, with the staff moving along before him.

For two days and two nights he traveled without rest, having a hard time keeping up with that stick, which hopped along in front of him. Then, being tired, he stuck the staff into the ground and went to sleep. When he woke, the stick was again pointing North. This time it leaned over more than before.

For three days and nights he traveled, then he slept, and in the morning his faithful staff was bending way over, still toward the North. "My wife cannot be very far away," he thought.

That night he slept again, and when he awoke, the staff had leaned so far over that the tip almost touched the ground; so he felt sure he must be near his journey's end. About noon, when the sun hung very round and very red, low down in the sky, he came to a huge snow house, the biggest house he had ever seen. Right by the house stood four posts close together, and on those posts was hung the skin of an enormous bird.

Hiding himself among some willow bushes, he watched to see what would happen. Pretty soon a very tall man came out of the house and went to the posts. Climbing up on them, he took the skin, put it on, and flew away over the sea. When the bird was out of sight, our friend took his faithful staff and went into the house. There he found his wife, who was very happy to see him. "I knew you would come and find me," she said. "That terrible big bird carried me away in his claws; that is why you could not find any footprints in the snow."

Her husband wanted her to come home with him at once, but she told him that it would be better if she could first see the bird-man, who would come back soon again. Her plan was to send the birdman on some far, distant flight, so that they might get away during his absence. She gave her husband some food, and he went back to his hiding place to wait for the birdman to come and go.

After a short time, the bird came back with a walrus in one

claw and a seal in the other. Flying to the rack, he took off the bird skin, hung it up, and went into the house. When he came in, he found the woman crying.

"What do you want?" he said.

"I want a white whale and a humpback whale. I don't want any seal. I am tired of seal and walrus meat. Boo-hoo!" and she howled and wailed dismally.

"Only be quiet," said the birdman, "and I will get you what you want." And he came out again and, putting on his bird skin, once more flew out over the sea.

When the bird was out of sight, the woman ran from the house to her husband, who put her on his back and started for home as fast as he could go. He was the swiftest runner in his village and covered the ground pretty fast; but, after all, legs are not wings. It was not long before they met the birdman coming back with a whale in each of his talons. When he saw the man carrying the woman away on his back, the bird was very angry, and circled about the air over their heads, calling out to them. "I shall kill you. First, however, I am going to take these two whales home, then I shall come back and kill you." And he flew away.

The man ran as fast as he could, but just as they reached the banks of a big river the bird came in sight. The man and his wife dug a cave in the riverbank and hid in it while the bird flew by looking for them. Nowhere could the big bird find those two people, although he was sure they must be hiding somewhere nearby.

Suddenly he circled about and flew down to the water. "I shall set my great wing across the river like a dam, and the water will rise and drown them," he cried. So he stretched his great wing across the river, and the water rose over the wing and crept nearer and nearer to where the man and his wife were hidden.

The two poor people were in despair. They thought that surely they would be drowned, when suddenly the man remembered his father, who was a witch doctor, and some magic words came to his mind:

"Klu-a-luk.

"Mul-a-luk.

"Puk-a-luk.

"Freeze up hard,

"Or you must run dry."

He said these words over three times aloud. At that moment, the water of the river began to freeze. (It was the month called *Naz-ze-rak-sek* by the Eskimo, which means "October.") At last the river froze so hard and solid that the bird's wing was frozen fast into the ice, and he could not pull it out. Then the husband killed the wicked bird and, plucking out one of the long feathers from its wing for a charm, took his wife safely home without any further trouble.

They brought the old grandmother and the little girl to live with them, and they were all happy the whole winter long with the meat of the big bird for food.[9]

Some Questions for Reflection

1. What part of this story stands out for you, and how is that related to your life?

2. When have you been "nearly crazy with grief and anger"? What helped you move through that experience?

3. When in your life have you persevered in a frightening task because it was important to do, as the granddaughter does when she invites the chief to supper?

4. When in your life have you experienced being "guided," as the chief is by his staff? What guided you, and what was that experience like?

5. Whom in your life have you been able to count on, in the way the chief's wife knew without question that he would find her? Who can count on you, no matter what?

6. If you were to take to heart the medicine of this story, for you, what action—large or small—would you take in your life?

Reflections

The grandmother in this story is a wonderful embodiment of compassion, and she illustrates each of the characteristics of compassionate love described by Dr. Lynn Underwood in her cross-national study of suffering and compassion: free choice; heartfelt response; fundamental valuing of the other person; accurate understanding of the situation, the other, and oneself; and openness/receptivity.[10]

The old woman senses the chief's suffering beneath his rage and chooses to extend herself to him, despite his gruff demeanor (*free choice*). Her neighbors, on the other hand, are afraid of him and choose to keep their distance.

In opening her heart to his suffering (*heartfelt response*), the old woman is able to see deeply into the chief's situation, to sense what might ease his suffering, and to identify what she might do to help (*accurate understanding*).

After feeding the chief, the old woman gives him a place to start: making a strong staff out of driftwood. The fact that she has him carve the staff (rather than giving him one) suggests her respect for him and her ability to see and encourage his resourcefulness, even in his weakened state (*fundamental valuing of the other*). She then gives him some charms and bird feathers to tie on the stick, reflecting her accurate sense of the root of the problem and the "medicine" he will need to find his wife and bring her home. The grandmother does what she can to help and leaves the rest to the chief—and to Fate (*openness and receptivity*).

Her plan has a grace to it, as evidenced by the ease with which it unfolds and by its mutually beneficial conclusion. It is an inspired mix of her kind heart and wise discernment, his resources and abilities, the healing power of love and of nature, and the ongoing unfolding of Life itself. The old woman clearly understands that relieving the chief's suffering is not all up to her; she plays her part, the chief plays his, and Life plays its part.

Symbols

There are three symbols in this story that are worth exploring: the driftwood staff, the river, and the birdman.

Driftwood. The chief's staff is made of driftwood—a stick that has been detached from a tree, immersed in water for a period of time (tossed about, softened, and smoothed), and eventually brought back to land and put to good use. In the loss of his wife and in his journey to find her, the chief undergoes a similar process: separation, ordeal, transformation, and bountiful return. As mentioned in the Grace of Courage, this is an archetypal pattern, reflected in initiation rites around the world, in myths and folktales, in drama and film, and in our lives, each time we find a way through a life-altering challenge.

Mythologist Joseph Campbell describes this quintessentially human narrative in this way: "A hero ventures forth from the world of common day into a region of supernatural wonder: fabulous forces are there encountered and a decisive victory is won: the hero comes back from this mysterious adventure with the power to bestow boons on his fellow man."[11]

The River. Important events in many folktales take place near rivers, which are sources of life and abundance. However, when someone tries to use the water of life for their own gain and treats others with cruelty instead of compassion, water invariably becomes an agent of destruction, through flooding or, in this case, freezing.

Water is also strongly associated with emotion, with tears and sweat, and with the deepest layers of the heart or soul. In *The Water of Life*, mythologist Michael Meade points out that the willingness to experience painful emotions is the key to being fully alive and fully human:

> Denying the importance of one's inner life and the emotions that flow through it tend to numb a person in this world and turn everything in the inner world to stone. . . . The pain remains but becomes buried in the soul. . . . The Water of Life awaits in the garden at the center of the soul, but a person must pass through an emotional zone to reach it. . . . Each passage to the Water of Life requires a breaking through something that has become fixated in the mind or hardened in the heart.[12]

The chief's response to the loss of his wife is a poignant example of how the attempt to protect ourselves against pain hardens us and separates us from life. The chief allows his heart to begin to soften again when he accepts the little girl's hand and her grandmother's invitation of nourishment. In contrast, the birdman remains isolated and hard-hearted throughout the story. His attempt to drown the chief and his wife by damming the river leads instead to his own poetically icy death.

The Birdman. This small man disguised as an enormous bird, for me, symbolizes pretense, selfishness, domination, and greed, though birds generally represent more positive traits, such as freedom, perspective, and the realm of spirit.[13] The behavior and the fate of the birdman in this tale show how a life based on self-interest and greed, rather than compassion and generosity, is misguided and ultimately self-destructive.

The chief takes one of the birdman's long wing feathers as a charm, and, according to Joseph Campbell, the hero usually returns home with something that has the potential for transforming the world. Feathers are often used in shamanic healing, and the chief's journey has reconnected him with that dimension of his life—and his father's life.

The last thing we hear is that the two families (which now live as one) survive the entire winter on the meat of the birdman. What was destructive—once confronted and subdued—has become a source of nourishment. And so it is each time we dare to move, with kindness, toward the hardened places in ourselves or in another.

Cultivating Compassion

Start with Yourself

There are a number of paradoxes that run through the Grace of Compassion, and one of these is that while compassion is a natural expression of our deepest nature (the inclusive or Big Self), it is also very hard work, especially when the person in need of kindness is oneself. As meditation teacher Jack Kornfield writes, "One of the greatest blocks to lovingkindness is our own sense of unworthiness. If we leave ourselves out of the circle of love and compassion, we have misunderstood."[14] The consensus of psychologists as well as spiritual teachers is that compassion for others must begin with kindness toward our imperfect selves and our own suffering. Otherwise our responses to others' struggles easily become tinged with impatience, resentment, righteousness, pity, self-importance, expectations for some kind of return, or other undoers of compassion.

A few years ago, I was giving myself a hard time for having knees that were aging much more quickly than the rest of me. I'd adjusted to not dancing, but when it became necessary to hold on to railings to go up and down stairs, I began to feel depressed and angry. And then one day—perhaps because I was writing about compassion at the time—I began to sense another voice, a kinder one, like a friend concerned for my well-being rather than a critical judge impatient with my limitations. And that change in perspective enabled me, in time, to see more clearly what was happening (I'd given up and was really unhappy) and what might help (exercising every day, regardless of how I felt, and making an appointment with an orthopedist to see whether it was time for the knee replacements I'd been resisting).

Softening my heart toward my body's limitations and vulnerabilities encouraged me to take better care of myself. Bike riding and going to the doctor became acts of love, rather than exercises in futility. And once again, I learned that kindness toward myself spills over into kindness toward others.

The next time you notice that you're looking at yourself with critical eyes and a hardened heart, stop, close your eyes, and breathe deeply into your heart. Then imagine sending kindness toward whatever you are experiencing— the inner critic and also whatever she is condemning. (It sometimes helps me to imagine that these are children fighting, both beloved and both needing kindness and care from me.)

Or invite the Kind Witness to look at the situation inside you (see The Grace of Self-Transcending Generosity). From her broad, wise, and loving perspective, what is going on, what is needed, and what might you do to be kind to yourself? Consider doing it, as you would for a dear friend.

Because compassion for others is rooted in kindness toward ourselves, it may be helpful to revisit some of the tools described in the Grace of Authenticity (especially Paying Attention, Silence, Meeting Authentic Needs, *and* Shadow Dancing*).*

By enhancing our emotional well-being, the Grace of Contentment strengthens our capacity for being kind to others. Thus, reviewing some of the tools in that chapter may also be helpful, particularly Savoring the Good, Taming the Wolves of Discontent, Releasing Emotions in Nonharming Ways, *and* Learning from Adversity.

Practice Lovingkindness

Deepening our capacity for compassion is probably the single most important thing that we can do for our own and others' well-being, and several studies have revealed that lovingkindness (LKM) and other forms of meditation stimulate areas of the brain associated with kindness, empathy, and concern for others, and lead to more compassionate behavior toward those who are suffering.[15]

The basic idea of LKM is to become quiet and then to send wishes for health, happiness, and peace toward all beings—loved ones, strangers, those we find difficult to love, and ourselves. Basic instructions are available online at https://jackkornfield.com/meditation-on-lovingkindness/ as well as at http://www.mettainstitute.org/mettameditation.html. Sharon Salzberg's *Lovingkindness* and Jack Kornfield's *The Art of Forgiveness, Lovingkindness, and Peace* are wonderful resources.

One of the beauties of lovingkindness meditation, according to some teachers, is that it is adaptable and can be practiced in various ways and places. Sharon Salzberg calls meditation "the ultimate mobile device; you can use it anywhere, anytime, unobtrusively."[16] For years, a mail carrier in our area (now retired) made a daily practice of sending kind wishes toward each of her customers as she put mail in their boxes.

Every day, life presents each of us with opportunities for sending good wishes toward people we hear or read about, toward those whose paths we cross, toward those we know, and toward ourselves. It may be helpful to start with someone who has loved and blessed you in your life, and slowly work toward sending kindness to those you find hard to love—your least favorite politician, for example, the driver speeding through an intersection, or someone who is causing others to suffer in some way. This is a tall order, but it is a learnable skill that benefits others as well as ourselves.

If you don't already have a practice for nurturing compassion, find a meditation teacher or a class, check out the sources and instructions above, or begin practicing on your own. When resistance arises—"this isn't doing any good" or "he doesn't deserve kindness"—let it go and continue sending kindness.

Because compassion arises from remembering our kinship with others, it may be useful to revisit some of the tools described in the Grace of Self-Transcending Generosity (especially Practice Daily, Walk in the Other's Moccasins, Notice Effects and Check Motives, *and* Forgive*).*

Stay Present

One of the most essential and most difficult aspects of compassion is that it requires us to remain present in the face of suffering, whether our own or another's. There is a strong desire in all of us to run from pain, to go numb, or to look the other way, yet compassion means caring enough to take in what is happening, to feel it, and then to respond as best we can. Being present and openhearted in the presence of suffering can be frightening, but it may be the greatest gift we can give another person.

I once learned a profound lesson from a man who was standing on a corner holding a sign that read: "Thank you. Anything Will Help." He moved me, and, thinking I had a few dollars to share, I pulled my car over and discovered only thirty-six cents in my wallet. I gave it to him rather sheepishly and told him I'd thought I had more to give him. He smiled at me with kind eyes and said, "It all helps—what matters is you stopped." Then he told me, "The hardest thing about being out here is most people look away." I have never forgotten his words.

The next time you find yourself turning away from another's (or your own) suffering, pause and see if you can discern what is so disturbing to you. What are you afraid would happen if you dared to be open and present in the situation? The purpose of this exercise is not to berate yourself but to reconsider: is it really necessary to protect your heart right now? If not, try staying open and see what happens.

Keep It Simple

A central theme in compassion literature, expressed by psychologists, educators, mystics, and activists alike, is the powerful impact that small, simple acts of kindness can have. In fact, the grand gestures of giving are often more an expression of our own need for recognition or approval than a selfless desire for another's well-being.

Educator and activist Marian Wright Edelman notes: "We must not, in trying to think about how we can make a big difference, ignore the small daily differences we can make which, over time, add up to big differences that we often cannot foresee."[17] Consider trying this simple but potent practice for cultivating compassion that Jungian analyst Robert Johnson and coauthor Jerry Ruhl suggest: "Simply look for an opportunity each day to tend to the needs of someone in a human way. Small acts of kindness are best for cultivating the gift of compassion."[18]

Serve in Winter

In late life, many of us feel a deep need to give back and do what we can to ease the suffering of the world in some way. Open hearts and willing hands are needed everywhere: in our families, our neighborhoods, and our communities; in places of extreme suffering around the world; and in the natural world that holds us all in her embrace.

We all have gifts that could be of benefit to others: reading to children, delivering meals to those who are ill and isolated, picking up garbage on walking trails or at the seashore, praying each morning for peace or for those who suffer. Check out these two inspiring books: *The Virtues of Aging* by Jimmy Carter (which focuses on serving in the winter of life) and *Compassion in Action: Setting Out on the Path of Service* by Ram Dass and Mirabai Bush (quoted earlier in this chapter). Both contain soulful stories, great wisdom, and practical information about being of service in this beautiful and battered world.

Recommended Readings on Compassion

Armstrong, Karen: *Twelve Steps to a Compassionate Life*

Chödrön, Pema: *When Things Fall Apart*

Dass, Ram, and Mirabai Bush: *Compassion in Action*

His Holiness the Dalai Lama and Desmond Tutu: *The Book of Joy*

Keltner, Dacher, Jason Marsh, and Jeremy Adam Smith: *The Compassionate Instinct*

Kornfield, Jack: *The Art of Forgiveness, Lovingkindness, and Peace*

Salzberg, Sharon: *Lovingkindness*

7: The Grace of Necessary Fierceness

"When a woman is at home in her wildness,
rooted in her instincts, and attuned to the
voice of her deepest knowing, she is a formidable
presence . . . [and] thunders after injustice."
—Clarissa Pinkola Estés,
Women Who Run with the Wolves

Necessary Fierceness is the willingness to be ferocious when the stakes are high and when gentler, subtler methods prove insufficient. Motivated by concern for the greater good and akin to "tough love," Necessary Fierceness is not vengeance, violence, or raw rage. Nor is it the wanton destruction of innocent people for a cause, no matter how holy. Rather, it is a blend of anger's heat and discerning restraint that is sometimes necessary to stop a bully in his tracks, to restore justice, to set a necessary limit, or to teach an unwelcome but essential lesson.

Reclaiming Fierceness

Many of Winter's Graces, such as Courage and Compassion, are valued in cultures around the world. Fierceness, on the other hand, is not generally perceived as a virtue, especially in women. The word *fierce*—like *feral*—comes from the Latin *ferus*, meaning "wild and untamed." Fierceness, then, is an expression of wildness—that natural, undomesticated core of us who knows what she knows and does what she must. In her extraordinary book *Women Who Run with the Wolves*, Jungian analyst Clarissa Pinkola Estés describes the Wild Woman within each of us as the source of our power and integrity who thunders in the face of injustice. Thundering wildness—not cruelty or violence—is the essence of Necessary Fierceness.

Most women raised in the 1950s and earlier received strong messages that ferociousness is thoroughly unsuitable for females. "Sugar and spice and everything nice—that's what little girls are made of," an old nursery rhyme advised. Most folktales popular at the time also discouraged the development of female fierceness. Stories like Snow White featured young heroines in distress, gallant young men who came to their rescue, and ugly hags, intent on destroying young protagonists for their own selfish ends. These tales conveyed clear messages about men's power and competence, young women's weakness and ineptitude, and old women's repulsiveness and cruelty.[1]

In recent years scholars have begun retrieving other folktales with competent, brave young heroines and wise, powerful, sometimes-fierce old women.[2] These stories place the wicked witch tales in an expanded historical and cultural context, making it clear that the witches and hags of our childhood represent a distorted, lopsided form of the sometimes-fierce Old Woman, who has held a place of honor in world mythology and folklore throughout much of human history.

A Brief History of Feminine Fierceness

Fierceness was an important aspect of the ancient Goddess, worshipped in matriarchal societies around the world until about 3000 BCE. Ferocious and also nurturing, beautiful and ugly, young and old, she created and destroyed life, taught and tested human beings, and protected and punished them, as needed.

Necessary Warriors

Some ancient fierce goddesses were created for the express purpose of defeating power-mad gods or humans. For example, when the Buffalo Demon Mahishasura was on a murderous rampage, threatening to destroy the earth, the heavens, and the netherworld, the Hindu gods brought forth Durga, The Invincible, to subdue him.

Also known as Durgatinashini (The One who Eliminates Suffering), Durga used a range of weapons to defeat Mahishasura, including a sword, a thunderbolt, a lotus bud, and a conch shell in which the sacred sound of Om resonates—each of these was a gift from one of the gods. Her story is an example of the balanced, creative, purposeful use of fierceness in the face of senseless destruction.[3]

Similarly, the Egyptian goddess Sechmet was called into existence when humans began misusing their power to try to overthrow the gods. Ferocious as a lioness, the powerful Sechmet slaughtered those who were threatening the divine order, tearing apart their bodies and drinking their blood.

However, dangerously drunk on blood and her own rage, Sechmet came close to annihilating humankind altogether. At that point the gods tricked her into drinking a blood-like liquid that contained powerful mind-calming herbs, which put an end to her rampage.[4] Sechmet's story contains an important reminder that the heat of fierceness can become an all-consuming wildfire unless tended with care and consciousness.

Mothers of Life and Death

Other fierce goddesses were understood as mothers of both life and death. Presiding over the endless cycles of birth, death, and rebirth, they brought forth life, sustained it, and, at the appointed time, ended it, thus setting the stage for new life.

Coatlique, for example, was worshipped in ancient Mexico as the Mother of Life and of Death. She is most often portrayed as an old woman wearing a garland of hearts and hands and a skirt of swinging serpents and skulls, yet as Mother of Life she was also honored with the first flowers of spring each year.

Similarly, Asase-Yaa is revered for giving birth to humanity and for reclaiming her children at life's end. Even today, many in West Africa still worship Old Woman Earth as womb and tomb. She is the source of all life, the place to which her children return at death, and the womb from which they are later reborn.

As the midwife of life and death, the ancient Thracian goddess Hecate also played a variety of vital roles in birth, death, and in between. Often accompanied by a three-headed dog (or having three heads herself), her images range from moderately to intensely fierce. She is often depicted holding a torch, the key to the under-world, and a knife, for cutting away the false or superfluous.

More powerful than all the Olympian gods, Hecate swept the threshold to protect the newborn and accompanied each person to the underworld at the time of death. She typically appeared on back roads, especially where three paths met, holding a lantern or torch for lost travelers. She also sat alongside kings as they rendered judgment and assisted mortals and lesser deities who were unjustly caught in the crossfire of inter-deity conflict. In her varied roles, Hecate exemplifies purposeful fierceness coexisting with protective-ness, guidance, and wisdom.

Maiden–Mother–Crone

According to some scholars, the Goddess in old Europe and Brit-ain was often worshipped as a trinity, with each aspect reflecting a phase of the moon and a season of a woman's life. The Maiden, as waxing moon, represents innocence, new beginnings, youth-ful enthusiasm, and birth. The Mother, as full moon, symbolizes ripeness, fertility, sexuality, and fulfillment. The Crone, as waning moon, embodies wisdom, repose, and endings. Hers is the fierce and necessary face of death. The Triple Goddess was revered in all her aspects, each one regarded as sacred and essential in the unbroken cycles of nature.

In *The Language of the Goddess*, archaeologist Marija Gimbutas points out that in mythology, the Crone often shape-shifts into the Maiden, suggesting that the old woman represents both death and regeneration. These unending cycles of life-death-rebirth can be found throughout nature. In a sunflower, for instance, the sprouting, growing, and budding plant can be seen as the Maiden, and the full-blooming flower as the Mother. The Crone represents the dying flower and the "deadhead" that shelters the seeds of the next round of life through the winter until they are ready to be released into the earth in spring. Like the Mothers of Life and Death, the Crone embodies both endings and new beginnings.

The Fates are one form of the triple goddess found in Slavic, Scandinavian, and Mediterranean mythologies. In ancient Greece, for example, the Moirae were three white-robed sisters, each of whom played a vital part in human destiny. Clotho—The Spinner—bore the distaff and spun the thread of life. Lachesis—The Measurer—took the thread from the distaff and allotted each human a given number of years. The fiercest task fell to the oldest, Atropos—The Inevitable—who snipped the thread of life at the prescribed time.

Ancient fierce goddesses like Atropos, Hecate, and Asase-Yaa were multi-faceted and played vital and varied roles—creating, nurturing, testing, teaching, destroying, and transforming. Not selfishly or wantonly destructive, each became an instrument of fierceness when needed. For detailed accounts of how the old woman, whose fierceness was tempered by wisdom, compassion, and concern for the greater good, morphed into the ugly, self-serving, terrifying witch, see Demetra George's *Mysteries of the Dark Moon*, Barbara Walker's *The Crone*, Marija Gimbutas's *The Language of the Goddess*, and *The Goddess Trilogy* from the National Film Board of Canada.[5]

Fierceness in Winter

Humankind has long looked to its elders to provide the fierceness that is necessary to guide the young into adulthood, to restore justice, to protect the innocent, to offer correction when needed, and to tend the dying. These are not easy roles, nor popular ones, and they require qualities of character that typically flower in the winter of life, such as wise discernment and the courageous willingness to do what must be done for the greater good, despite the cost to oneself.

In many Native American tribes, old women have the final say in important and difficult matters. For example, if the Grandmothers determine that a chief is not serving the tribe well, they give the word, and he steps aside.[6] Saying no to the status quo is one form of Necessary Fierceness.

Another way to think about Necessary Fierceness is to liken it to being a wise warrior. We tend to associate warrior-ness with young men rather than old women, but at a psychological level, we all have warrior potential within us. It is either conscious and thus available to be used effectively, or it is unconscious, which is far more dangerous.

In its most primitive form, the warrior archetype epitomizes the underbelly of power and aggression: it is self-serving, ruthless, and obsessed with winning. Wise warriors, on the other hand, according to Jungian analyst Carol Pearson, are respected "for their toughness and for their intelligent assessment of people and situations, so they can fight when fighting is called for and seek compromise when that is possible."[7] A wise warrior is engaged in the world, yet detached enough to be able to discern the best course without bias. And she is willing to be fierce when necessary on behalf of those who are suffering.

In her TED Talk, Stanford psychologist Laura Carstensen points out that the one exception to the general mellowing of emotions in later life is the elder's response to injustice and the suffering it causes others.[8] Psychiatrist Jean Bolen concurs:

> Wrongdoing that provokes mother-bear fierceness is almost always both a betrayal of trust and an exploitation of others. . . . In the third phase of her life, [a woman] becomes angry at what she is seeing beyond her personal situation. Her anger may be directed at injustice, stupidity,

narcissism, addictions, carelessness, and cruelty that affect others that are disempowered, or at social evils that institutions and politicians are ignoring. . . . Women who reach the point of enough is enough *and have wisdom, compassion and humor* [italics mine] are formidable forces for change.[9]

The italicized caveat in the preceding paragraph is vitally important because without the tempering effects of wisdom and other qualities, fierceness can easily become destructive, rather than life-giving. A good friend in her seventies (I'll call her "Rachel") recently shared a difficult experience that exemplifies the blend of courage, compassion, and wisdom that necessary fierceness entails.

Over a period of months, three young women had come to Rachel separately, each conflicted or otherwise distressed about her sexual involvement with the leader of their spiritual community. Some of these liaisons overlapped in time, and the leader had insisted that each keep her relationship with him secret. (Similar incidents, decades before, had occurred and ostensibly been dealt with by the co-leader of the group, who had since died.) When it became clear that the leader was continuing to misuse his position to pursue affairs with students, Rachel knew she needed to do something.

She spoke to the teacher privately first and urged him to get counseling, but his initial response was denial. Then he admitted some of the involvements, but he blamed the students for seducing him. He expressed no remorse, no sense of wrongdoing, and no intention to alter his life in any way. At that point, Rachel felt a moral responsibility to inform the community about his behavior so that further incidents might be prevented.

I was impressed by her courage and also by her obvious compassion for the leader, as well as for the women who had come to her for support. Once the information became public, reactions were strong and varied. Many in the community expressed relief and gratitude that the truth had come out (some of them had known about one or another of the affairs). A few others defended the leader, insisted on his innocence, and attacked Rachel for making trouble. Some of the accusations were vicious, and Rachel's response was a beautiful example of necessary fierceness: a mix of kind forbearance and a firm refusal to deny what she knew to be true.

Rachel knew that she needed to break the silence, and communication is more open as a result. Months later, events are still unfolding, and the outcome is uncertain, as it always is when we dare to say what must be said without knowing where it will lead.

Here is a story from Iceland, in which the old woman's capacity for necessary fierceness is starkly apparent. It is reminiscent of the myths of Durga and Sechmet, in that a powerful force is moving toward senseless destruction and must be stopped. This heroine understands what must be done, though it will horrify everyone. When the time is ripe, she enlists the help of her son in an act that is as fierce as it is necessary. The example here is extreme, but the story illustrates the collaborative courage of later life as well as the differences between necessary fierceness and vengeance.

The Son of the Goblin

The farm Bakki (now called Prestbakki, in Hrutafjordur) once stood farther north than it does now. The reason for its being moved from its ancient to its present position is as follows:

It happened that a certain farmer's son courted the daughter of the priest who lived in Bakki. The priest refused the young man's offer, which grieved the suitor so sorely that he fell sick and died and was buried at the church near the priest's house. These events had happened in summer.

The winter following, people noticed a certain strangeness in the demeanor of the priest's daughter, for which they could not account. One evening it happened that her foster-mother, an old and wise woman, went out to the churchyard with her knitting, as it was warm enough, and the moon had but few clouds to wade through.

Some time before this, the old woman's foster-child had told her that since his death her lover had often been to see her, and that she found herself now with child. The ghost had assured the young woman that her infant would prove an ill-fated one. So, the unfortunate girl had asked the old woman to try to prevent further visits from her ghostly lover. It was for this purpose that the good woman had gone to the churchyard.

She went to the grave of the young man, which was yawning wide open, and threw her ball of yarn down into it. Having done so she sat down on its edge to knit. There she sat until the ghost came. At once he begged her to take up her ball of yarn so that he might enter his coffin and take his rest.

But the old woman said, "I have no mind to do so, unless you tell me what you do out of your grave at night."

He answered, "I visit the priest's daughter, for she has no means of preventing my doing so. Ere long she will be delivered of a boy."

Then the old woman said, "Tell me this boy's fate."

"His fate," replied the ghost, "is that he will be a priest at Bakki. The first time he pronounces the blessing from the altar, the church with all its congregation will sink down to hell. And then my vengeance will be complete, for the injury the priest did me in not allowing me to marry his daughter during my lifetime."

"Your prophesy is, indeed, a great one, if it meets with a fulfillment," answered the old woman, "but are there no means by which so horrible a curse can be prevented?"

The ghost replied, "The only means are for someone to stab the priest the moment he begins to pronounce the blessing, but I do not fancy that anybody will undertake that task."

When she had gathered this information, the old woman said to him, "Go now into your grave and be sure never again to come out of it." After this, the old woman drew up her ball of yarn, and the corpse leaped into the grave, over which the earth closed itself.

Then she recited some magic spells over the grave, which bound the corpse in its last rest forever. Then, she returned home, telling no one what had passed between her and the goblin-lover.

Some time afterwards, the girl was delivered of a fine and healthy boy, who was brought up at Bakki by his mother and his grandfather (though the latter did not know who the father was). In his early youth, people saw that the boy excelled beyond all his companions both in mind and body. And when his education was complete, and he had arrived at the proper age, he became his grandfather's curate.

Now the old woman saw that something must be done to prevent the approaching disaster, so she went to her son, who was a man of great courage and one who did not shrink from trifles. She told him the whole story of the interview with the ghost and begged him to stab the young priest just as he began to pronounce his blessing from the altar. The old woman promised that she would bear all the consequences of the deed.

Initially, the young man was very unwilling to do what his mother asked, but she pressed him with earnest entreaties, for the sake of the whole village. And at last he made the promise she required and confirmed it with an oath.

At length, the day came when the young curate was to perform service for the first time. The large congregation assembled in the church and was impressed by his eloquence and sweet voice. But when the youth stood at the altar and raised his hands for the benediction, the old woman signed to her son, who rushed forward and stabbed him, so that he fell dead on the spot.

Horror-struck, many rushed forward and seized the murderer. But those who went to the altar to raise the priest found nothing of him except the top bone of his neck, which lay where he had been standing.

Everyone now saw that what had happened was no everyday murder, and that a goblin was involved. The old woman, standing in the midst of them, told them the whole story. When they had heard it, they recovered from their panic and thanked her for her foresight, and her son for his quickness and courage.

They then perceived that the east end of the church had sunk down a little into the ground because the goblin-priest had had time to pronounce the first few syllables of the blessing. After this, the farm of Bakki was so haunted by goblins that it was removed from its old to its present location.[10]

Some Questions for Reflection

1. What part of this story speaks most strongly to you, and how is that related to your life?

2. When has someone tormented you for refusing to go along with what he or she asked of you? How did you respond?

3. In what ways have you tormented someone who prevented you from having what you wanted? What happened to him or her and to you as a result?

4. How able are you, like the old woman, not to talk about something you know, but simply to hold it in your heart until the time is ripe for speaking or acting?

5. When/where in your life has it been necessary to confront a well-liked person who had the appearance of goodness but a destructive hidden agenda? How did you handle that situation?

6. When/where in your life have you experienced a curse disguised as a blessing? Or delivered a blessing that was really a curse?

7. Have there been circumstances that have led you to relocate because a place/situation felt too full of goblins? How ghost-free has your new location proved to be?

8. If you were to take to heart the medicine of this story, what action might you take in your life?

Reflections

I debated whether to include this intense story, but there is much to be learned from it. This old woman is a fine embodiment of fierceness tempered with compassion and wisdom. She demonstrates the grandmother's capacity to listen carefully to others' suffering, to consider a situation from many perspectives, to take time to see clearly what must be done, and then to act on behalf of the greater good regardless of the cost to herself.

She responds to the haunted young woman by first seeking out the ghost on his turf. She tosses a ball of yarn into his grave and then sits down to knit. Initially these acts seem odd and pointless, but they reflect the grandmother's courage and composure and her familiarity with the other world. The old woman does not use her knowledge and power to shame, blame, or coerce the ghost. Instead, she engages him in conversation, asking him questions about what he does at night, what the fate of the demon child will be, and how the curse might be averted.

Clearly, she is seeking information for the good of the village, but she also gives the ghost a chance to tell his story. She listens calmly, without judgment or reaction, even though he is intent on destroying the whole village because of his grievance toward the young woman's father. Once the old woman obtains the information she needs, she removes the ball of yarn, lets the ghost back into his grave to rest, and then seals it, for his sake and everyone else's.

The old woman waits—for twenty years at least—not telling anyone about her conversation with the ghost, or the destruction he has planned. She does not attempt to control fate, to change the course of events by reporting the demon priest or warning the villagers. In her wisdom, the old woman understands that forces far greater than herself are at work and that she must wait and watch until the time for action arrives.

The grandmother's plan is extreme—involving the killing of a priest—yet it is the only way the village can be saved from destruction. The old woman enlists the help of her son and makes it clear that she will bear full responsibility for the killing, in case the plan should fail. As events unfold though, extreme fierceness was in fact necessary, and the village is saved from annihilation.

This story offers an excellent contrast between necessary fierceness and vengeance, as embodied by the old woman and the ghost. The grandmother is motivated by concern for others; the ghost, by a personal vendetta. She is mistress of her emotions, able to sit calmly in a graveyard knitting and to listen to a ghost describe a heinous plot, without reactivity. In contrast, he is so mired in his anger and hatred that he plans to destroy an entire village because he was denied the hand of a woman he wished to marry.

The old woman is clear, is focused on what must be done, and is willing to bear the consequences of her actions in order to save others. The ghost is self-righteous to the point of delusion, and his son becomes a pawn in his vendetta. This is a chilling illustration of how hatred, tightly and righteously held, can affect (and infect) subsequent generations.

The Foundation of Fierceness

I think of Necessary Fierceness as the cayenne pepper of Winter's Graces. Used with care, it can provide a needed "kick." Without the balancing effects of other ingredients, it burns. Seven Graces of Winter are involved in the skillful use of Necessary Fierceness, beginning with the foundational Graces of Authenticity and Self-Transcending Generosity. As we come to know and accept ourselves as we are, we are better able to perceive other people and situations as they really are. Increasing assertiveness and the refining of authentic power give us the ability to trust our own knowing, to set important limits, to stand up for what matters, and to take effective action, despite others' disapproval. The Grace of Self-Transcending Generosity brings a deep sense of oneness with all of life and helps us to see beyond the motivations of the little self and to act on behalf of the greater good.

Courage also plays a vital role in Necessary Fierceness, enabling us to place love ahead of fear and to do what is needed, regardless of the cost to ourselves. In fact, fierceness can be seen as an extreme form of courage in dire circumstances. The Grace of Contentment brings emotional mastery: the capacity to tolerate a wide range of emotions and to channel rather than vent them. Instead of mindlessly reacting or taking sides in the face of suffering or injustice, as mistresses of our emotions we can pause, look at the situation from many perspectives, understand its complexity, and then begin to see what is needed.

The Tempering of Fierceness

Temperance—restraint, or moderation in action, thought, or feeling—is considered a virtue or core value across time and cultures,[11] and it is essential for the wise and effective use of ferociousness. As Carol Tavris notes in her book *Anger: The Misunderstood Emotion*, "The moral use of anger, I believe, requires an awareness of choice and an embrace of reason. It is knowing when to become angry— 'this is wrong; this I will protest'—and when to make peace; when to take action and when to be silent."[12] The Graces of Compassion, Creativity, and Wisdom temper the fire of fierceness, bringing balance and refinement and offsetting the tendency for fierceness to devolve into self-righteousness, vengeance, or violence.

The Grace of Compassion provides a necessary counterpoint to fierceness because taking a stand on behalf of a just cause can easily degrade into a hard-hearted stance against those on the other side of the aisle, the street, or the border. Without compassion for everyone involved, advocates quickly turn into adversaries. It is very easy to slide into blaming, taking sides against some as we defend others, or becoming attached to being right and winning, all of which inflame rather than alleviate conflict.

Hard as it is to do in the face of suffering, remaining respectful and openhearted toward everyone involved, especially those with whom we disagree, is vital if fierceness is to be effective and healing. Having compassion for victims and perpetrators alike helps us move beyond the desire to condemn and punish and to work toward justice, forgiveness, and healing for all. The Grace of Compassion tempers fierceness with humility and tolerance, reminding us that we all know what it is to suffer—and to inflict suffering. As Kathleen Fischer writes in *Transforming Fire*, "Part of forgiveness is the realization of our capacity to wound . . . [and] our common humanity."[13]

In *The Stoning of Soraya M.*, a fine and very disturbing Iranian film, an older woman exemplifies the tempering of outrage and fierceness with compassion. The woman's niece has been falsely accused of infidelity and is about to be stoned to death. She risks her life trying to save Soraya, speaking the truth to those in power, appealing to their goodness, challenging them publicly, even throwing herself in the line of fire and offering to take the place of the young mother—all to no avail. Afterward, at great risk, she makes sure that the world hears this (true) story.

Remarkably, despite her passionate fight for justice, her heart does not harden. When she speaks to the mayor, an old friend who allowed this travesty to occur, her compassion for him is palpable: "May God forgive you for what you did today." She points directly at his duplicity and cowardice, and yet she wishes him forgiveness. That kind of openheartedness enables fierceness, like a laser, to heal as it cuts.

Finally, the Graces of Creativity and Wisdom add breadth, depth, clarity, and freshness of vision that enable us to see whether fierceness is actually needed and in what form. Creativity stretches our perspective beyond entrenched ways of thinking and seeing. Especially in highly charged or polarized situations where great suffering is present, curiosity and "suppleness of mind," as my friend Robin used to call it, help us to walk patiently around a problem and look at it from many points of view. The willingness to consider the unlikely and improbable often leads to an unexpected solution that turns out to be exactly what is needed.

Perhaps most important of all, necessary fierceness requires wisdom, the capacity to sense the best course of action in important and complex matters. Paradoxically, such discernment is the product of both involvement and detachment: engaged concern for the suffering of others coupled with a detached ability to see the situation in all its complexity and to discover a life-serving way to address it.

Cultivating Necessary Fierceness

Necessary Fierceness is a challenging grace for many women because it brings us face-to-face with qualities that run counter to our early conditioning as nurturing caregivers. Despite the feminist revolution, in our heart of hearts, many of us remain ambivalent about the seemingly unholy trinity of power, anger, and aggression, upon which fierceness depends. Re-visioning these three is a necessary first step in cultivating this Grace.

Re-visioning Power

The Grace of Authenticity includes a discussion of the true meaning of power (the potential for effectiveness) and its refinement in late life (p. 24). Necessary Fierceness is not possible without access to our genuine emotions and authentic power.

Reclaiming Anger

Anger is a common, complicated, and urgent emotion, and it's tangled up with frightening misconceptions, especially for womankind. Thankfully, researchers are challenging many of these mistaken ideas, demonstrating that anger is a natural response to a perceived violation of oneself or others and is not necessarily linked to violence and destruction. In fact, it can serve positive social functions. As sociologist Christa Reiser points out,

> Because anger is potentially so constructive, we cannot afford to leave it alone, to not teach others ways to deal with it constructively. Only then can it realize its positive functions: to serve as a warning, energize us for action, motivate us to understand others' feelings, and work toward justice.[14]

Research also suggests that ideas about acceptable and unacceptable expressions of anger vary across cultures and across gender, race, and class lines as well. For women of color in this society, for example, provocations for anger are more frequent and prohibitions against its expression more stringent.[15] In *Sister Outsider*, Audre Lorde describes the "symphony of anger" that women of color in America experience growing up in a society that silences and demeans them.

> I say *symphony* rather than *cacophony* because we have had to orchestrate those furies so that they do not tear us apart. We have had to learn to move through them and use them for strength and force within our daily lives. . . . How to train that anger with accuracy rather than deny it has been one of the major tasks of my life.[16]

Anger is a signal that something is amiss, as its etymology suggests. *Anger* shares a root with *anguish* and refers to distress that is related to constriction or tightness. Anger can be useful in our relationships with one another and in the larger world. It can move us into action on behalf of something important, and it can wreak havoc. Carol Tavris describes anger's potential as a force for both "good and evil":

> I have watched people use anger, in the name of emotional liberation, to erode affection and trust, whittle away their spirits in bitterness and revenge, diminish their dignity in years of spiteful hatred. And I watch with admiration those who use anger to probe for truth, who challenge and change the complacent injustices of life, who take an unpopular position center stage while others say "shhhh" from the wings.[17]

A healthy relationship to anger is essential for Necessary Fierceness. These four books offer guidance on learning to recognize, temper, and harness anger, without being consumed by it: Kathleen Fischer's *Transforming Fire: Women Using Anger Creatively*, Carol Tavris's *Anger: The Misunderstood Emotion*, Harriet Lerner's *The Dance of Anger: A Woman's Guide to Changing the Patterns of Intimate Relationships* (especially chapters one and nine), and Clarissa Pinkola Estés's *Women Who Run with the Wolves: Myths and Stories of the Wild Woman Archetype* (especially Chapter 12).

Reconsidering Aggression

Of these three qualities—power, anger, and aggression—the last may have the worst reputation. Variously defined as an unprovoked attack or invasion, an intentional action aimed at hurting or destroying another, and hostile or destructive behavior or actions, aggression would appear to have no place in a book about late-life gifts and graces. However, its root meaning—like power and anger—suggests otherwise. *Aggression* comes from two Latin roots, *ad* ("to") and *gradi* ("step"), which suggests moving toward, not inflicting harm.

In psychology, most studies of aggression have focused on its destructive effects. However, psychiatrist Frederick "Fritz" Perls observed that aggression is a biological function that plays a necessary role in humans' ability to digest food, assimilate experience, and live in balance and harmony with the world. In *Ego, Hunger, and Aggression* he makes some instructive distinctions between *annihilation* (whose aim is to eradicate something altogether), *destruction* (whose aim is the elimination of an existing structure, but not its essence), and *aggression* (whose aim is "to get hold of" something for the purpose of assimilation and growth). Looked at in this way, aggression serves an important function.

Anne Campbell, a psychologist and criminologist, observes that women are typically less comfortable with aggression than men are. In *Men, Women, and Aggression*, she reports that women tend to view their own aggressiveness as a failure to control their anger and thus feel guilty or ashamed afterward. Men, on the other hand, perceive aggression as "a legitimate means of assuming authority over the disruptive and frightening forces of the world around them."[18] Rather than guilt or shame, they generally report feeling calm after being aggressive, their power and self-esteem restored.

Practicing Restraint

If anger is the fire that fuels fierceness, restraint is the virtue that refines it into a force that brings healing rather than more suffering. Restraint means being thoughtful and disciplined about our speech and actions, rather than giving into the heat of the moment and striking out at those who are causing others to suffer.

In *Refuge*, author and conservationist Terry Tempest Williams tells a story of rage and restraint that occurred when she discovered that a nearby bird sanctuary had been completely and deliberately destroyed. "I knew rage," she writes. "It was fire in my stomach with no place to go." At the same time she recognized the importance of restraint—"the steel partition between a rational mind and a violent one."[19]

Witnessing injustice and senseless suffering can ignite fury and rage in our bodies that could easily lead to violent retaliation, were it not for that steel partition and our willingness to honor it. Restraint is the ability to pause—to not lash out—and to allow our anger to be transformed into what Williams calls "sacred rage," which is a powerful and effective force for justice.

In a similar vein, nonviolent activist Barbara Deming emphasizes the importance of transforming raw, unhealthy anger, which she calls "affliction," into healthy anger that is sometimes essential for effective action. In *We Cannot Live Without Our Lives*, she writes:

> If we are willing to confront our most seemingly personal angers, in their raw state, and take upon ourselves the task of translating this raw anger into the disciplined anger of the search for [just] change, we will find ourselves in a position to speak much more persuasively.[20]

To work effectively for justice requires meeting those we oppose with a combination of powerful assertiveness and respect, says Deming. "We can put *more* pressure on the antagonist for whom we show human concern."[21] In addition to its non-harming effectiveness, nonviolence has another obvious advantage: unlike violent speech and action, which add fuel to fire, peaceful resistance breaks the cycle of violence and retaliation so prevalent in the world.

Tools for Cultivating Necessary Fierceness

Befriending the Wild Woman. For a real treat—and an excellent tutorial in retrieving, nurturing, and honoring your fiercely authentic, natural, and undomesticated soul—read or listen to *Women Who Run with the Wolves* by Clarissa Pinkola Estés.

Remembering. Take some time to reflect on some of your best and worst experiences of anger—whether you were angry or were the recipient of another's anger. When has it been an effective fuel or tool, and when has it caused harm to others or yourself? What seems to make the difference?

Honoring the Wise Warrior. Using clay, paint, fabric, metal, driftwood, or other materials, spend some time creating an image or a figure of a wise and compassionate warrior to support you when something important needs your fierce attention. For inspiration (and a simple pattern), check out Nancy Blair's *Amulets of the Goddess* (pp. 67–72), which contains instructions for creating a doll to represent the transformation of anger into power.

Releasing Anger. The next time you're furious, for your own sake and others' sake, acknowledge and then release your fury in a non-harming way. De-fused anger is a far more useful and effective fuel than raw rage. My friend Bruce used to write ferocious, uncensored letters when he was angry, which he then ripped up or burned, rather than sending. For other ideas, see *Releasing Emotions in Nonharming Ways* (p. 130).

Tempering Fierceness. In tribal cultures, elders use their considerable power to bless others and "almost never" to curse them, according to Malidoma Somé in *The Healing Wisdom of Africa*. It is entirely possible to be fiercely determined and at the same time to be compassionate and respectful. And the combination is almost always more effective than raw rage.

Anger can be very helpful in getting us to the point of "enough is enough." How we express/harness that anger determines whether it reduces suffering in the world or inadvertently increases it. A little fierceness goes a long way. Before acting with ferocity, pause and take time to:

- Assess the situation from many points of view
- Actively seek to understand the validity of each viewpoint, not just the one with which you feel the most sympathy
- Check your motives, judgments, and possible projections (In what ways are you like those you would oppose?)
- Entertain unlikely and improbable approaches, including non-action, at least for a time
- Keep your sense of humor handy (laughter—especially at ourselves—can be a good de-fuser)
- Keep your heart, mind, ears, and eyes open as you speak and take action—notice the ripples of what you are saying and doing and make adjustments as needed
- Keep seeking solutions that are healing for everyone involved

If you find yourself called upon to act in an entrenched, highly polarized situation, you may find the literature on nonviolent resistance and restorative justice helpful.[22]

Embracing the Other. Many women raised to be "good girls" have a huge investment in being seen as nice, supportive, and agreeable. As a result, we may become cut off from other equally important qualities, like fierceness, power, mischievousness, intractability, selectivity, disagreeableness, and the capacity for setting limits, saying no, and making important kinds of trouble.

Spend time cultivating one or two of these "bad girl" qualities using some of the tools described in earlier chapters (poetry, written dialogues, collage, etc.). Write a story about a fiercely formidable heroine and see where it takes you. "Once upon a time there was a fierce and formidable woman . . ." Read books and watch movies with powerful, determined heroines, like Fried Green Tomatoes *and* Tea with Mussolini.

On the other hand, some women enter the second half of life with easy access to their fury and fierceness. Many experienced or witnessed injustice as children and became staunch advocates of the underdog by calling out those they see as perpetrators. They are courageous and loyal, outspoken, honest, and direct—and sometimes unnecessarily brutal. Their words can bring clarity and truth to a situation; they can also injure others and rupture relationships. For women on this end of the fierceness continuum, those in whom rage and fury flow easily and regularly, restraint is especially important. Here are a few suggestions:

Slow down. Avoid flaming emails (they travel entirely too fast), impulsive texts and phone calls, and precipitous actions. Pausing to reflect on your reactions, to separate the personal from the bigger picture, and to consider options and possible outcomes enhances effectiveness. If your plan is a good and necessary act of fierceness, it will still feel appropriate in a day or two.

Check your motives. Before speaking or acting, ask the deepest, stillest, clearest part of yourself questions like these: *What is really going on with me? What has me so upset? When have I felt like this before? What thoughts are fueling my emotional reactions? Who is behind my rage: my ego, genuine concern for the greater good, or . . . ?* Take your time with this process—motives are not always immediately clear and are often mixed.

Vent in a safe place. Letting off steam in the pages of a journal, growling and/or stomping in a private place, or painting on a large sheet of paper using bold strokes and intense colors are good ways to release anger. They may also help clarify what has triggered your ire. Sometimes anger is personal and transient and simply needs to be acknowledged and allowed to pass through.

At other times, anger is a signal that something is indeed "rotten in Denmark," and fierce action on behalf of others who are suffering may be necessary. Take a hint from Hamlet and Sechmet though: ferociousness can be consuming. Necessary Fierceness requires the discipline of staying aware and honest with yourself about your motives and your impact.

Heeding the Cries of the World. Almost everywhere we look there are people suffering, situations crying out for wise and compassionate mediation, and just causes in need of effective and tenacious champions.

Consider the world, both local and large, and notice what calls out to you. Where have things gone too far in the wrong direction? Where are people and other species in distress? Which form of suffering are you most drawn to help alleviate: homeless families, isolated elders, exploited children, an endangered species, or . . . ? Use your indignation as fuel, and then act with wisdom, compassion, creativity, and (when necessary) fierceness.

Being Fierce with Ourselves. There is a saying in analytic psychology, "as without, so within." It means that what we react to in the outer world is often a reflection of something we are not paying attention to within ourselves.

When I'm angry or otherwise upset about another person or situation, I've learned to ask myself, *What is my relationship to this quality/theme?* Much as I resist doing this, asking the question usually clarifies some of my own unfinished business that needs attention. We are much cleaner agents of influence and change when we keep our own house in order. This is a lifelong endeavor, and it can save us (and others) a lot of grief.

The next time anger or another distressing emotion keeps buzzing around in your psyche, gather your psychological courage and ask yourself: what about me, in this regard? Be fiercely honest yet compassionate with yourself and take care of your business before attending to someone else's.

Recommended Readings on Fierceness

Estés, Clarissa Pinkola: *Women Who Run with the Wolves*

Fischer, Kathleen: *Transforming Fire*

George, Demetra: *Mysteries of the Dark Moon*

Tavris, Carol: *Anger*

8: The Grace of Simplicity

"'Tis the gift to be simple, 'tis the gift to be free.
'Tis the gift to come down where we ought to be . . ."
—Joseph Brackett, "Simple Gifts" (Shaker hymn)

My friend Robin appeared in a dream of mine a few years ago, carrying a lantern, which she showed me was both a winnowing device and a source of light. At the time, she had generously been editing some of the earlier chapters of this book, and the dream seemed an apt metaphor for what she had been doing: pruning away the unnecessary and, in the process, shining more light on the essential.

Robin's motto as an editor was "less is more," and that was how she lived—with great intention, devotion, and simplicity. It occurred to me later that the winnowing lantern she carried was also a wonderful image for the Grace of Simplicity—the natural inclination in the winter of life to focus on what matters most and to let go of the rest.

Several late-life trends move us toward simplification—physical energy wanes somewhat; the nearness of death and the preciousness of life become more palpable; appearances, achievement, and acquiring tend to lose their appeal; and it becomes increasingly important to devote the time and energy we have to what is most meaningful. In winter, we become like winnowers—from the same root as *wind*—sifting through possessions, roles, activities, relationships, and commitments, and allowing nonessentials to be carried away.

Focusing on the Meaningful

How we each spend the last season of our "one wild and precious life,"[1] matters. The nearness of death ups the ante, often bringing startling clarity about what is essential and what is not, what is true for us and what is not, what we must see and feel and say and do, and what can and must be let go.

Gerontologists and developmental psychologists have observed that older adults typically become more selective about the people and activities with which they engage, in order to allow time and energy for what genuinely matters.[2] For some, spending time with grandchildren is a primary focus; for others, working on behalf of an important social or environmental cause. Still others feel a sense of urgency to attend to a long-deferred dream—to learn to paint or play a musical instrument, to visit old friends, or to spend more time in quiet solitude. Many elders continue working, often in a more selective way, focused on aspects of their work that are most compelling or rewarding. Those fortunate enough to retire have the added blessing of more time to devote to what calls them most deeply. However, the inclination to attend to meaningful priorities, whatever they may be, is a developmental trend, regardless.

Paring Down/Relinquishing

In the winter of life, we become more aware that we can no longer "do it all." Our energy and our time on this earth are limited, and we must let go of what is no longer meaningful in order to free ourselves to pursue what is. It is no accident that in myth and folklore, it is most often the old woman who is called upon to cut away or burn up the superfluous, inauthentic, and unimportant. The crone's courage, fierceness, and wisdom enable her to discern what is life-giving and what is not, and to allow what must die, to die.

In *Vital Involvement in Old Age*, Joan and Erik Erikson and coauthor Helen Kivnick point out, "Old age is necessarily a time of relinquishing—of giving up old friends, old roles, earlier work that was once meaningful, and even possessions that belong to a previous stage of life and are now an impediment to . . . resiliency and freedom."[3]

Jungian analysts Marion Woodman and Jean Bolen both describe the older woman's inclination to pare down her life and to let go of material possessions and involvements that no longer express her deepest values.[4] Relinquishing relationships can be especially difficult, requiring both courageous clarity and kindness. Bolen writes,

> Wise crones know that their time and energy are precious. *Whatever you do takes from what you otherwise could have done.* If the truth is that it is time to end some relationships in order to have time for yourself and for those people in your life who [most] matter, this truth needs to be faced and the intention . . . has to be acted upon [with clarity and kindness].[5]

Often, paring down means letting go of life's center stage and being content to play supporting roles, as needed. Personal ambition tends to wane as we age, and contributing to the well-being of future generations becomes increasingly important. The old woman may be called upon to take charge in some situations, but often she makes a cameo appearance and then steps aside so that the young may learn how to be the heroines and heroes of the future.

Here is a story from the Netherlands about an old woman with simple needs who travels lightly through life. She exemplifies the "detached engagement with life" that Erik Erikson identifies as an elder virtue—helping a family in distress, and then going on her way when her work is done.

The Haunted House

Not so long ago a haunted house stood near Dokkum. Every night, on the stroke of twelve, there was a most terrible noise in one of its bedrooms. No one would sleep in that room, and all the furniture had been removed, except for an old bed. The people who lived in the house had tried to find out what caused the unearthly noise, but since no one was brave enough to stay in the room at night, it remained a mystery.

One evening, when it had been raining for a week, a little old woman came to the door. The trees were dripping, the streets were flooded, and water ran in a swift stream down the road. The leaden skies seemed to have endless rain left in them. The fields had begun to look like lakes, and it was difficult to get about.

The poor woman was soaked to the skin. The rain dripped from her hair to her shoulders. Her shoes squished with water. She had tried to put her skirt over her head as a kind of umbrella, but that was soaked, too. She was timid about knocking on the door, but she thought, "The people who live here can only tell me to go away—that's the worst they can do."

But to her amazement the maid who answered the door asked her to step inside. A couple of children peered curiously at her from the other end of the hall. She beckoned to them to come nearer, for she loved children, but they turned away and ran.

An old gentleman came out of the dining room. "Would you like to spend the night here, little lady?" he asked.

"Oh, yes, please, mijnheer [my lord]."

"And you're not afraid?"

"Why should I be afraid?"

"Would you care to sleep in a haunted room? It's the only one that isn't occupied."

"In any room, mijnheer, even if there were a dozen ghosts."

He looked at her sharply. "Well, come along with me."

As she walked beside him, the little old lady looked back and saw the trail of water she was leaving. "It's a pity to drip all over your nice floor," she apologized.

"Think nothing of it," he said. "If you're willing to spend the night in the haunted room, I'll be most grateful. Then, perhaps, we'll come to the end of this mystery."

There was nothing special about the room, except that it was furnished only with the old bed. The walls were thick, and the sill under the window was wide. The old gentleman sat on it and looked at his guest thoughtfully.

"Are you sure you are not afraid?"

"If mijnheer had been walking in the rain as long as I have been, he wouldn't be afraid either. I am far too tired to be afraid." She watched the water dripping from her clothing to the floor.

He said, "I suppose you'd like to go right to bed?"

"If mijnheer would send me a towel so that I can dry myself I would be grateful. Then I shall sleep in that beautiful bed."

"*One* towel!" cried the old gentleman. "I'll have them bring you ten!"

When she had dried herself the old woman climbed into bed and fell asleep at once, despite the sound of the rain pounding on the roof. She slept right around the clock. And when she awoke in the early morning, the door was opening slowly, and a little girl was peering around it.

"Come in, little one!"

"Are you the rain-lady?"

"Why, what a nice name you've thought up for me! And what's your name, my dear?"

"Annetje."

"And how old are you?"

"Four, and next week I have a birthday." The little girl looked at the rain-lady. "Why aren't you dripping anymore?"

"I slept between dry sheets, and I don't want even to think about rain!"

They heard a loud noise in the hall. Annejte looked frightened. "Oh, that's Grandfather. He said I must never come into this room."

The old woman had forgotten all about the ghost; she decided that she had better go at once. She dressed hastily and slipped quietly downstairs. As she was opening the outer door, she remembered that she had not thanked her host for his kindness.

When she found him, he shook his head. "Do you mean you would have gone away without telling me what happened in that room during the night?"

"Happened?" she said. "Nothing happened. I slept."

"Didn't the ghost appear? Why, in my room, I heard the horrible racket at midnight!"

The woman said, "Would you like me to stay in the haunted room another night? This time I'll try to keep awake to see if the ghost comes."

"That would be fine." He called to one of the maids, "See that our guest has everything she wants."

That night the old woman went to bed early so that she could get her sleep before midnight. Suddenly she woke and sat up in bed. It was pitch black outside, but in the room there was a dim blue light. Where did it come from? Should she call her host?

Near the window a figure was walking back and forth. She could hear the footsteps as measured as those of a sentry. But she felt no fear. Peering out between the bed curtains, she called, "Who are you?"

The ghost came toward her and held out his hand in front of her face. "Go back to sleep!" he ordered.

The old woman sighed and settled her nightcap on her head. "Well, if you say so, I'll go back to sleep, but hurry up with whatever you're doing, will you?"

"Hmmm!" the ghost said. "You don't seem to be afraid of me!"

She lay down again and pretended to sleep, but she kept her eyes half open. And whenever the ghost looked toward her she almost closed them. She could see him well enough between her narrowed lids. He was tall and thin and wore a dirty cap on his sparse hair and dilapidated slippers on his feet. His trousers were ragged, and there were big slits in his coat; there was a sparkling of dust on his shoulders.

All at once, with frightening speed, he leaped onto the wide windowsill. He dug his fingernails into the wood and lay there howling. The rain-lady sat up again, but a little more cautiously than the first time.

With one bound, the ghost sprang toward the bed, and she barely had time to throw herself down again, pretending to snore, before she felt his eyes boring into her. He shook his fist at her, and his fingers rattled like dry bones. Now the old woman was really frightened. She could almost feel his hands around her throat, and she heard his voice in her ear saying, "Lie still, and see nothing!"

As soon as he turned back to the window, she raised herself on one elbow and parted the bed curtains. She saw the ghost take some carpenter's tools from his pocket—a hammer, a file, and a small saw. He began to work on the windowsill, ripping out the woodwork beneath it.

Just as he tore the last board loose, a torrent of golden ducats poured onto the floor in a clinking stream. The ghost squatted and pulled more coins, of gold and silver, from a hollow place in the wall. Then he began to put the coins in piles, counting, counting, in a hoarse voice.

The little old woman hardly dared breathe, but she soon saw that his mind was only on his money. Suddenly, the clock in the hall began to strike. The ghost leaped up, flung the coins back, helter-skelter, into the hole beneath the window sill, replaced the boards, and on the last stroke of midnight, he disappeared into thin air.

The woman wondered if she had dreamed what she had seen. She lay wide-awake, listening to the rain that was still falling in the dark skies, and waited for morning. As soon as it was light, she dressed and crept downstairs. A sleepy maidservant met her in the hall.

"Was the ghost there?" the girl asked.

"Yes. Tell your master to get up. There is a fortune in that room."

Soon all the family had gathered around her. "Tell us what happened!" they cried. But when she told them they could not believe it.

"Go and look," she urged. "You will find riches there you never dreamed of!"

Even so they would not take her word for it until they had pried up the windowsill. Then a great gasp went up, for the money fell out in a seemingly endless stream. It covered the floor.

When the stream of coins finally stopped, the old woman said, "But where did all these coins come from? How did they get here?"

The grandfather was the only one who could answer her. He said, "In this house, long ago, there lived a miser. His neighbors did not know much about him, but they did know that he was a mean and selfish man. He drove the poor from his door rather than give them a crust. One time he even sold the home of one of his debtors just because he wanted more money.

"When he died there was no one to mourn him. Not a penny was found in the house, so he was buried in a pauper's grave. People wondered what had happened to all the money he must have had. In the great carved chests, they found only cast-off clothing.

"No one ever thought of a hiding place. Who would have imagined that money could be hidden under a windowsill? That was probably why the miser's ghost came back to this room every night. His punishment must have been to count the coins over and over again, as he had done in his lifetime, until by some chance, they were found by living people.

"Now," the old man concluded, "I am sure he will never come back."

"Do you really think so?" the little old woman said. "Then I am glad that I was able to lay the ghost."

"Yes," he said, "and for that reason, and to show our gratitude, I invite you to stay with us always."

She shook her head. "What would I do here? No, I must go as I came." She pulled her skirt over her head again and, without another word, went out into the rain.

The rain poured off the roof and the wind drove it in gusts down the road. The children ran to the door, calling after the woman, "Come back, rain-lady! Come back!" But she did not seem to hear them and disappeared into the mists.[6]

Some Questions for Reflection

1. What stands out for you in this tale, and how is that related to your life?

2. When have you been encouraged by the realization that the worst that could happen is that you would be told no?

3. When have you experienced reaching toward a child in love and had him or her turn away? How did you feel? respond?

4. When have you persisted in a task in spite of being terrified? What fueled your courage and resolve?

5. When in your life have you been focused solely on money, and what was that like?

6. When have you said no to a tempting offer that did not reflect your deepest priorities? What was that experience like?

7. When have you said yes to such an offer, and what happened as a result?

8. If you were to take to heart the medicine of this story, what shift might you make in your life?

Reflections

The rain-lady in this folktale illustrates several dimensions of the Grace of Simplicity—moderate needs, dedication to what matters most, and the ability to say no to what does not.

She is staying with an affluent family but asks only for what she needs—a place to sleep for the night and a single towel. Her host offers her ten towels and later "everything she wants." Despite his generosity, she does not ask for extra towels, warm food, hot tea, a bath, or dry clothes—all of which would have been reasonable requests and most likely granted.

This old woman is devoted to her priorities, yet she allows them to shift with changing circumstances. Her initial concern is finding shelter from the storm for the night, and she is willing to risk rejection and to stay in a haunted room in exchange for a dry place to sleep. Later, when she sees how distressed the family is about the frightening sounds the ghost makes at night, she offers to stay another night to solve the mystery.

Once she has succeeded she takes her leave, declining the family's invitation to remain. Her priorities lie elsewhere. She does not ask them for an umbrella, food for the road, or a lift home in a cozy carriage. She simply pulls her skirt over her head, leaving just as she arrived—doing what she must and making do with what she has.

The story contains another element of simplicity as well: valuing the quality of life more than material wealth. A seemingly endless supply of gold is uncovered, but very little is made of that in the narrative. The family is focused on being free of the ghost (not on the treasure that is now theirs). And the grandfather expresses the family's gratitude with a heartfelt offer—not a monetary reward, but a home and a family with whom the rain-lady could share the rest of her life. The old woman is pleased to have helped restore tranquility to their home, but their kind invitation does not suit her—and she knows it. (She says, "What would I do here? No, I must go as I came.")

The contrasts between the old woman and the miserly ghost teach some important lessons about simplicity, contentment, and generosity on the one hand and greed and suffering on the other. The ghost is the epitome of selfishness: completely consumed by his money, unable to enjoy what he has yet wanting more, indifferent to the needs of others, and utterly isolated in his life and even after death. Although he has great wealth, he takes no pleasure in it. He is a poignant embodiment of Dante's image of the greedy in *The Divine Comedy*. Cursed with grotesquely long arms, the greedy sit in hell at a lavish banquet unable to feed themselves and starving in the presence of abundance because they will not feed one another.

In contrast to the greedy ghost, the old woman is kind and generous throughout the story. She apologizes for dripping water on her host's floor, she is concerned that her soaking clothes not soil the beautiful bed they offer her, and she is kind to the children even though they run away from her initially. And when it becomes apparent that the family is still uneasy about the night noises, she generously offers to stay a second night to solve the mystery so they can live in peace. As this story demonstrates, the Grace of Simplicity keeps us focused on what really matters. It lightens our load and frees us to do what we must and to help others when we can.

Savoring and Delight

As we simplify our lives, relinquishing the nonessential and focusing on what matters most, we renew our acquaintance with the wonder, delight, and timelessness of early childhood. We become recipients of one of the sweetest gifts of late life: savoring.

Young children and elders are a bit like vacationers who are captivated by the sights and sounds of a new place when they first arrive and are again more attentive as their departure approaches. In her nineties, Helen Nearing, who lived a very simple life for almost fifty years in rural New England, describes her deepening capacity for savoring and delight as she aged: "The sea, a lake, all become as in childhood, magical and a great wonder: then seen for the first time, now perhaps for the last. Music, bird songs, the wind, the waves—one listens to tones with deeper delight and appreciation [in old age]."[7]

I once heard Marion Woodman—a Canadian Jungian analyst and a wise and wonderful winter's woman—tell a story that captures the essence of late-life simplicity and delight. In her eighties at the time, she described how much she was enjoying being in her kitchen each morning, washing dishes, singing old hymns, and savoring the early hours. "It's like every day is Sunday," she said with delight. A moment later, with a twinkle in her eye, she quipped, "I do know that every day isn't Sunday!"[8]

In her late-life memoir, Florida Scott-Maxwell describes the delight she experienced savoring ordinary moments in the winter of her life:

> Now each extra day is a gift. An extra day in which I may gain some new understanding, see a beauty, feel love, or know the richness of watching my youngest great grandson express his every like and dislike with force and sweetness. . . . Who knows, it may matter deeply how we end so mysterious a thing as living . . . I've taken a long time to feel it as very truth: The last years may matter most.[9]

Letting Go and Preparing for Death

The Grace of Simplicity deepens our capacity for relinquishment and thus helps prepare us for the final surrender into death. Psychologist Robert Peck describes late life as a time of progressively letting go of limiting dimensions of our identity, beginning with the roles we have played in our careers and families in earlier seasons of life. As we release our attachment to social standing and past accomplishments, we are free to discover and develop dimensions of ourselves beyond the borders of earlier roles.

Similarly, as we learn to work with and accept the limitations and losses of our aging bodies, we recognize that there is more to us than our physicality. Finally, says Peck, we transcend the ego, the limited sense of a personal, isolated self. This surrendering allows us to participate fully in life, and at the same time to come to terms with our own death. He writes,

> The constructive way of living the late years might be . . . to live so generously and unselfishly that the prospect of personal death—the night of the ego, it might be called—looks and feels less important than the secure knowledge that one has built for a broader, longer future . . . through children, through contributions to the culture, through friendships . . . [which go] beyond the limit of [one's] own [skin and life]."[10]

The fear of death typically wanes in the winter of life, and many have noted the paradox that befriending death brings us more fully into life. As social visionary Duane Elgin explains,

> Death, then, is an uncompromising friend that brings us back to the reality of life. . . . In consciously honoring the fact of our physical death, we are thereby empowered to penetrate through the social pretense, ostentation, and confusion that normally obscure our sense of what is truly significant. An awareness of death is an ally for infusing our lives with a sense of immediacy, perspective, and proportion. In acknowledging the reality of death, we can more fully appreciate our gift of life.[11]

Simplicity and Her Sister Graces

Simplicity is intertwined with several other Graces of Winter. It is inseparable from Contentment and is a further expression of Authenticity and of Self-Transcending Generosity. Simplicity draws strength from the Graces of Courage and Necessary Fierceness and is closely linked to Creativity as well.

Contentment is the capacity to find happiness regardless of circumstances, and Simplicity teaches us the art of being content with having enough. These two graces are virtually inseparable. To those of us accustomed to too much, however, a simple life may sound more like misery and deprivation than happiness. One of the earliest proponents of the simple life, the Roman philosopher Seneca (4 BC to 65 AD) addresses this common and enduring misconception: "It is not the [person] who has too little, but the [one] who craves more, that is poor."[12]

Naturalness, a lack of pretense or guile, and directness of expression are dimensions of Simplicity that are also friends of Authenticity. As our mortality becomes a more palpable reality, there is an increased sense of urgency to honor what truly matters and to let go of nonessentials, pretensions, social position, and other "trappings."

Sunset Story is a fine documentary with touching examples of late-life simplicity and naturalness. The setting is a residential home for elderly activists, and the primary protagonists are two very different women who forge a deep friendship in their eighties and nineties. They illustrate many dimensions of the Graces of Authenticity and Simplicity: their lack of pretentiousness, the direct simplicity of their speech, the devotion of their energy to what matters most, their capacity to say no to what they do not value, and their gracious acceptance of death. It's well worth seeing.

Material simplicity is often prompted by a heightened awareness of the interconnectedness of life and the recognition that our decisions and behaviors impact others. Giving away what we do not need, doing without unnecessary luxuries, and considering the needs of others and the health of the environment when making decisions are expressions of Simplicity as well as Self-Transcending Generosity.

In a culture where the acquisition of material possessions plays such a central role in economics, social status, self-image, and daily life, and where distraction, rushing, multi-tasking, and constant stimulation are the norm, living simply is neither simple nor easy. In fact, it often feels like trying to walk against a rushing tide. It takes great Courage and sometimes Fierceness to live simply in the midst of extravagance and too-much-ness, to say no to invitations and involvements that distract us from what we most value, or to allow ourselves to be unreachable by text, phone, or email for periods of time so that we can focus and attend to our most pressing concerns.

Simplicity also draws on Creativity because living simply is an ongoing process requiring flexibility, ingenuity, permission to change our mind, and the willingness to keep experimenting. Duane Elgin writes,

> This [simple] way of life is not a static condition to be achieved, but an ever-changing balance that must be continuously and consciously made real. . . . How we simplify is a very personal affair. . . . We each know where our lives are unnecessarily complicated. We are all painfully aware of the clutter and pretense that weigh upon us and make our passage through the world more cumbersome and awkward.[13]

Cultivating Simplicity

Simplicity is a fluid grace. It assumes a unique form in each person's life, and its expressions may change radically over time. We alone know what is most important to us and what we can do without. And what enlivens us at one time may become a burden at another—and vice versa. Regardless of the various and ever-changing forms it may take, the Grace of Simplicity typically entails these three dimensions: living our priorities, relinquishing nonessentials, and savoring the present moment. Here are some tips and tools for cultivating each of these.

Slowing down is an essential first step in nurturing simplicity. There can be tremendous joy in allowing ourselves to move at our own pace, rather than hurrying from place to place. Age tends to slow us down a bit, which can make us more attentive to what is happening around and within us.

Moving slowly encourages us to pause and savor the present moment—to taste the apple we are eating, hear the sound of the rain on the roof, or enjoy the glee of children climbing trees or wading through puddles after a big rain. Even so-called ordinary moments become extraordinary when we move slowly enough to notice and appreciate them. In *Graceful Simplicity*, Jerome Segal describes the beneficial effects of moving through life at a slower, more human pace:

> The time we give to things reflects our values. When everything is rushed, then everything has been devalued . . . To live gracefully is to live within flowing rhythms at a human pace . . . There is time to pay respect to the value of what you do, to the worth of those you care for, and to the possessions you own. Gracefulness is not possible when life is frenetic, when we are harried, or suffer from overload, time crunch, and a vast multiplicity of commitments and pressures.[14]

Carl Honoré's *In Praise of Slowness* is a fine book about the high cost of chronic hurrying and the benefits of moving through life at a more human pace. It is a personal account of one man's discovery of what musicians call *tempo giusto*—"the right speed"—and also a highly readable history of humankind's relationship to time and the emergence of Slow and other deceleration movements around the world.

When you find yourself mindlessly hurrying through the day, exhale, slow down, and notice what is going on within and around you. Savor sights, sounds, and smells and enjoy the gift of being alive. Use this or another decelerating practice as often as you need it. Over time, moving slowly begins to feel natural, and it is infinitely more satisfying than rushing.

Clearing clutter is another crucial dimension of simplicity, and its fruits include order, calm, harmony, and beauty. Decluttering is essentially allowing ourselves to live with the things that we really need or value (the necessary, the beautiful, and the meaningful) and to let go of everything else.

Many of us acquire so many possessions in the course of our lives that we become burdened by the constant need for cleaning, maintaining, repairing, storing, and moving them around in order to make room for more. It is easy to become, as Frank Lloyd Wright puts it, "little more than janitors of [our] possessions."[15] Many elders report that they are motivated to let go of unimportant things before they die, so that their children do not inherit the burden of sorting through their clutter.

It takes courage and trust to give away what we do not need (but fear we might someday) and what we do not value, especially gifts from loved ones. Decluttering is a gift of lightness, peace, and freedom to ourselves (and to our loved ones who will survive us), and it puts things back in circulation that others might need or would cherish.

A number of helpful books offer tips for clearing clutter and strategies for keeping our lives clutter-free, for example, Marie Kondo's *The Life-Changing Magic of Tidying Up*, Elaine St. James's

196 * Winter's Graces

Simplify Your Life (pp. 10–13); Cecile Andrews's *The Circle of Simplicity* (pp. 37–39); and Sarah Ban Breathnach's *Simple Abundance*, especially the meditations for May.

The internet is also awash in information on decluttering. Simplicity tip: be selective in what you download/print. When you have enough information to get started, stop collecting. Only acquire more if and when you need it.

Clarifying genuine priorities is essential to living a simple life focused on what matters most to us, and it can be a challenge—especially for those who have lived full and busy lives, for those whose first inclination is to say yes to invitations and requests, and for those who tend to put others' needs ahead of their own. Having all three of these tendencies—and yearning for a simpler life—has required that I learn to distinguish between yes and YES, between what I would like to do and what I MUST do.

Traffic lights became a useful metaphor. I was pretty good at saying no to red lights (things I really did not want to do), but yellow lights (things about which I had mixed feelings) were a bigger challenge. At a certain point, I realized I simply did not have energy for yellows anymore. In fact, there are so many greens, so many appealing pulls on my time and energy, that I've had to create a fourth category—flashing greens. These are my current priorities, the YESes—like writing this book—that I know I must attend to, even on days when I'm tempted to distract myself with something else.

Consider your own priorities at this point in time. If you were entirely free to devote yourself to those few things that matter most to you, what would they be? How much of your time and attention do you give these flashing green lights?

Saying NO to distractions and nonessentials is central to living simply and may sometimes require harnessing the Graces of Courage
and Necessary Fierceness. It takes clarity, commitment, and courage to say no to the things that pull us apart (the root meaning of
distraction), especially when others are invested in our saying yes.
Something I have learned repeatedly in recent years, directly and
from observing others, is that when we dare to admit and honor the
authentic no's in our life, that often opens the space for someone else
to come forward for whom that task is a YES and a potential source
of fulfillment.

Here's an example: At a meeting of the Shirleys (named for a
vital, vibrant woman in her eighties), three of us witnessed our friend
Dena give herself permission not to continue spearheading an annual
fundraiser in our local community. The cause is very worthy, and her
talents as an organizer have proved invaluable in past years, yet there
were other commitments that she felt a growing need to honor.

She is wise enough to know that she can't do it all, but she was
having trouble freeing herself from this task. After describing the
dilemma, she began to laugh as she realized that the pull to stay
involved was rooted in the illusion that to continue would make
her a better person. (It is clear to all of us that she is wonderful,
either way.)

Identifying the (often unreasonable) thoughts that keep us from
honoring the authentic no's in our life, as Dena did, can be helpful
when we find ourselves struggling to relinquish something we want
and need to let go of. At the root of most reluctance is fear—that we
will be judged or rejected, that others will be disappointed, or that
something terrible will happen if we say no. In truth, when we over-
ride our deepest priorities, bad things do happen: our actions easily
become tainted with resentment, we are usually less effective, and
we inadvertently become sources of suffering.

A friend once told me that in a Tibetan Buddhist community
of which she is a part, volunteers are encouraged only to serve in

ways that bring them joy. For me, anticipatory dread (rather than joy) is an important signal that I'm about to embark on something that is not really a priority, or that I'm taking on too much.

When you become aware that you are grumpy, joyless, chronically exhausted, or resentful, take an inventory. Jot down where and how you have been spending your time lately—include appointments, meetings, and social events, solitary pursuits, and internal activities as well— meditating, planning, worrying, replaying events, second-guessing yourself, judging others, etc.

Go back over the list and put a check by each item that brings you joy, put a minus by every item that robs you of joy, and leave the rest blank. Then consider the possibility of letting go of some of those minus entries. Of course, there will be some that are joyless but important any- way—like going to the dentist. But for the most part, when we are joy- ful, we spread joy; and when miserable, misery. Dare to imagine what you would really like to release in order to devote your time and energy to what is most important.

Pausing to savor the present moment is a delicious practice that slows us down; brings us into the present; lowers stress; heightens aware- ness and aliveness; enhances our capacity for enjoyment; and fosters gratitude, simplicity, and contentment. Versions of this tool appear in many chapters because this tiny shift in attention can mean the difference between rushing through life and living it fully.

The next time you realize you're barreling through life or walking around on autopilot, bring your attention back to the present and pay attention to what is going on—the sensations in your body, your breath; the sights, sounds, and smells around you.

When you notice something beautiful—birds singing, the movement of clouds across the sky, the sound of music, a line of poetry, the smell of sweet peas, the taste of a pear, someone smiling or being kind to someone else—let yourself really savor the experience, as you might have done as a young child when the world was fresh and new and you lived in timeless time.

Being in nature can teach us a great deal about simplicity. Nature is also the best schoolhouse I know for immersing ourselves in beauty, for encouraging us to move slowly and with awareness, and for instructing us in the endless and graceful cycles of birth-death-rebirth that are the stuff of life.

Cultural anthropologist Angeles Arrien writes,

> In our later years, there is a deep desire to simplify our lives and to return to the enjoyment of our childhood explorations of the natural world. We recognize that it feeds our souls. . . . The desire to replenish, rebalance, and come into inner harmony and natural rhythm is a universal longing that spans time and traditions. We can nourish it in nature."[16]

Rural and wilderness areas are places we can often find and bathe in quietness. And in cities, parks provide open space that invites our eyes to relax and take in the beauty of trees, flowers, fountains, or bodies of water. Gardens are also places where we can contact the simple beauty of nature, whether a large plot or even a compact container garden on a terrace in the middle of the city.

Take yourself into nature each day; see what happens.

Economy of speech is another dimension of simplicity. I am blessed to have a few people in my life—all of them daily practitioners of some sort of meditation or prayer—who have taught me, by example, a great deal about simple speech. Here are some things I've learned from observing them:

• *Listen more, talk less.* Focus more on understanding than on being understood (or being right!). Don't interrupt or finish people's sentences. Pause before speaking and ask yourself: Is what I have to say clear, is it honest, is it kind, and is it necessary to say right now? If not, stay quiet and see what happens.

- *When you do speak, be descriptive, not judgmental.* Accusing, "loaded" language tends to clutter communication and often derails it. Speak as you would like others to speak to you.

- *Keep it simple*; fewer words generally have more impact.

For more on "how to talk about things that really matter," check out *The Tao of Conversation* by Michael Kahn.

Mindful consuming (of material goods, media, technology, and energy) is integral to living simply and deliberately. The goal is not austerity or deprivation but rather the genuine satisfaction and aliveness that comes from living intentionally from the inside out—as opposed to being driven by unconscious needs or the suggestions of advertising. As psychologist and author Thomas Moore observes, "Simplicity doesn't mean meagerness but rather a certain kind of richness, the fullness that appears when we stop stuffing the world with things . . . . You can't force simplicity; but you can invite it in by finding as much richness as possible in the few things at hand."[17]

In a similar vein, Duane Elgin points out that simple living enhances aliveness, while mindless consumption burdens us:

> To live simply . . . means to encounter life more directly, fully, and wholeheartedly. . . . We need little when we are directly in touch with life. . . . When we remove ourselves from direct and wholehearted participation in life, emptiness and boredom creep in . . . [and] we search for something or someone that will alleviate our gnawing dissatisfaction. . . . If we fully appreciate [all] that life offers us in each moment, then we feel less desire for material luxuries that contribute little to our well-being and . . . deprive those in genuine need.[18]

I highly recommend three books for further discussion of mindful consuming (and other dimensions of simplicity): Cecile Andrews's *The Circle of Simplicity*, Jerome Segal's *Graceful Simplicity*, and Duane Elgin's *Voluntary Simplicity*.

Silence and monotasking, two important allies of Simplicity, are addressed in earlier chapters: *Silence* (p. 43) and *Monotasking* (p. 45).

9: The Grace of Remembrance

"We make meaning by moving back and forth
between the remembered past, the experienced present,
and the expected future."
—William Randall and Gary Kenyon,
Ordinary Wisdom

In the winter of life, the approach of death is more palpable, and the need to know that our lives have had meaning and value becomes more pressing. Early memories, even long-forgotten ones, return naturally in dreams, in wakefulness, and in those states of reverie that lie between the two, providing the material we each need to complete our life. Coming to terms with the life we have lived—accepting it and ourselves as good enough—enables us to live more fully and freely in the present and to look toward the future, even toward death, with greater equanimity.

The Grace of Remembrance extends beyond one's own life as well. It brings the recognition that each person's life story is a precious version of the human drama that began long before his or her birth and will continue into an unforeseeable future. In Remembrance, we honor our ancestors whose lives made our lives possible. And as elders we contribute to the future by sharing with younger generations the wisdom, strength, and hope that long years of experience and reflection can bestow.

Revisiting the people and scenes of the past that come calling allows us to savor and be grateful for the blessings we've known.

Disturbing memories can be a gift of another sort, offering the chance to work through lingering guilt, grief, and other unfinished business. The life review helps prepare us for death, yet it has profound benefits for living too, enhancing psychological well-being, deepening our store of wisdom, and enriching the legacies we have to share with younger members of the human family.

Remembrance in Late Life

Gerontologist Robert Butler was the first to describe the importance of the late-life inclination to review and reflect on one's life. Prior to the 1960s, reminiscence was viewed as an unhealthy preoccupation that led to elders "living in the past" and losing touch with the world. However, Butler observed that recollecting and working through memories is vitally important both for the quality of life and the preparation for death:

> [Through reminiscence] reconsideration of previous experiences and their meanings occurs, often with concomitant revised or expanded understanding. Such reorganization of past experience may provide a more valid picture, giving new and significant meaning to one's life; it may also prepare one for death, mitigating one's fears.[1]

In their study of elders, Erik and Joan Erikson and coauthor Helen Kivnick also found that "old age is a time for remembering and weaving together many disparate elements and for integrating these incongruities into a comprehensive whole."[2]

The life review leads toward cohesiveness, yet the process takes time and usually entails a great deal of meandering. As gerontologist and psychotherapist Marc Kaminsky points out, for most older people the life review is "not composed of an orderly progression of memories, organized into a coherent narrative . . . Life reviews are largely quiltwork affairs, a matter of bits and pieces all stitched together according to a not very readily visible pattern."[3] In the midst of what may seem to be random and unrelated memories, however, certain themes recur over time and begin to reveal an underlying pattern of meaning.

Looking back does not always result in meaningful integration and wisdom, however. Psychiatrist Arthur McMahon and psychologist Paul Rhudick found that some older adults dwell nostalgically on the past as a way to avoid facing present problems, or use their (selective) memories to justify themselves, their past actions, and their present circumstances.

However, their best-adjusted subjects—whom McMahon and Rhudick describe as *storytellers*—"recount past exploits and experiences with obvious pleasure, in a manner which is both entertaining and informative. They seem to have little need to depreciate the present or glorify the past, but they do reminisce actively."[4] These older people exemplify how remembering and sharing our life stories can be a gift to ourselves and to others.

Welcoming Memories and Emotions

The flow of memories in late life occurs naturally, yet a constructive life review depends on our welcoming—not minimizing, distorting, or dismissing—the people and events of our lives that present themselves for recollection. Memories are messengers, much like dreams. They usually point to something important, and they come in the service of wholeness and well-being. Each memory is an opportunity to relive and better understand our lives and ourselves. Attending to memories and experiencing the emotions they evoke is important work, not morbid preoccupation.

Like nightmares, painful memories are especially important to attend to because they illuminate the stepchildren of our souls, the parts of our experience that need to be reckoned with and integrated if we are to truthfully embrace our lives in full and know that they have been good enough.

Inevitably, the life review entails coming to terms with our imperfections, our sins of omission and commission, and our regrets. In his reminiscence work with elders, Marc Kaminsky has observed that guilt-ridden experiences are especially important to remember because they can lead us to necessary self-forgiveness as well as to a deeper sense of meaning and completion.[5]

The film *Evening* is a beautiful illustration of how facing painful and guilt-filled memories can lead to a more compassionate understanding of oneself and the life one has lived. The movie opens with a dying woman (played by Vanessa Redgrave) who is wrestling with the "mistakes" she has made in her life. Her memories are haunting her, and she is plagued by fear, doubt, guilt, and regret.

Then an old friend she has not seen in many years—played by Meryl Streep—comes to visit. Their tender, truthful conversation allows them to tell each other stories of the chapters they have missed in each other's life, to revisit their shared history, and to reaffirm how important they have been to each other, despite their long separation. In the process, Redgrave is able to see her life (and herself) through a wider and more compassionate lens, to lay to rest the ghosts that have been tormenting her, and to recognize that she has in fact lived "a whole life."

Befriending Bewilderment

In some Buddhist traditions, confusion and paradox are said to guard the gates of enlightenment. It's a strangely comforting thought that the more confounded we are, the closer we are to deeper understanding. In a similar way, contradiction and bewilderment can be seen as guardians of the life review. When we find ourselves in the presence of these two, we are in fertile, albeit discomforting, territory.

The life review brings us face-to-face with our immense complexity—and our contradictions. One memory illustrates our pettiness, another our generosity, and our task is to face and ultimately find a way to accept all that we are and have been. This can be bewildering work, yet as psychiatrist Carl Jung pointed out, we are not simply this or that. We are "multiplicities," composed of an enormous range of qualities, many of them apparent opposites. Strangely, it is the tension of contradiction that often brings forth some of the richest understanding of others and ourselves. As Florida Scott-Maxwell writes in her late-life memoir, "[It is] impossible to speak the truth until you have contradicted yourself."[6]

Ethnologist Barbara Myerhoff and author Deena Metzger observe that reflecting on the wide variety of memories that arises in the winter of life enables us to see ourselves and our life story more fully and more truthfully. They write,

> What is gained from this experience is the acceptance of multiple views of self, rather than a single, hard [version] . . . The self, yearning for its wholeness, considering multiplicity where before there was singleness, recognizes its fullness. . . . Only in maturity, with multiple images, is greater accuracy possible. Only then can one identify not only the false reflections of others, but the distortions one provides oneself.[7]

The Storying and Re-Storying of Life

Human beings are meaning-seeking and storytelling creatures, and these two attributes are inseparable. Stories are the way we frame and make sense of our experience and share it with others. When we come home to a loved one at the end of a day or see a friend after a long absence, we catch up, largely through the sharing of stories. We rarely just convey information, or what memoirist Maureen Murdock calls "flat facts." Usually we tell a story. We describe who was involved (the characters) and what happened (the plot), as well as the emotions we felt during and after the experience.

In telling a tale we are seeking to make sense of the events of our lives, to discover their meaning. Through sharing, we may feel less burdened by a difficult experience or be re-delighted as we recount a funny or pleasurable one. Often the listener draws from our story something of value for her own life. And the mutual sharing of stories strengthens our bonds with each another, adding texture and richness to relationships.[8]

Over time, the stories we tell ourselves about the events of our lives become the narratives by which we live, and those narratives can either enrich or impoverish us. The stories we live, sometimes called our *personal myth*, become the lens through which we perceive and interpret the events of our life. The meanings we attribute to our experiences have a powerful effect throughout our lives. The life review is an opportunity to revisit memories, including the painful and puzzling ones; to reconsider the conclusions we have drawn about our lives, the world, and ourselves; and to grow into a more life-giving narrative. As Maureen Murdock writes in her book about memoir, "We gather the jigsaw pieces of our experience and put them together in a story we tell and retell until we get it right."[9]

Here is a story from Hawaii about an old woman whose willingness to take stock of her life leads to a radical change of direction. As she acknowledges her deep unhappiness and cries out her longing for a better life, she is able to move beyond her life-as-misery narrative, into a more spacious story of courageous overcoming and contentment.

The Woman in the Moon

Long ago there lived a woman named Hina who had lived for many years. Day after day she made tapa cloths out of the bark of a tree by beating it with a mallet. Then she used the cloth to make clothing for her family. Her son and daughter had finally grown up and left home, leaving her with a husband who had become more embittered and demanding as he grew older. He offered her no help or companionship.

Each night when her cloth making was finished and the sun went down, she would fetch water with a gourd, fix the dinner, and pray for rest from her endless tasks. She would think about how she might escape from her weary existence and find peace.

One day she was pounding out the tapa cloth and cried aloud, "If only I could go away and find some rest!" The rainbow heard Hina's cry and set a rainbow in front of her. Hina decided she would follow the rainbow up to heaven and then to the sun where she would be forever at rest.

She began her long journey up the rainbow, but when she passed through the clouds the sun's rays began to burn her. She pushed herself to continue, but the rays became too hot. The sun began to singe her hair and skin, and she felt her strength ebbing away. She let her body slide back down the rainbow, grieving at her failure.

When she had returned to earth, darkness had descended. As she came to her house she saw that her husband had fetched the water. He was grumbling about this chore, and when he saw her, he reprimanded her for being gone from the house. His words strengthened her resolve to find quiet and rest.

She noticed that the sun was gone, and as she stared at the quiet coolness of the moon she realized it would be a far better place to rest than the sun. Before she left again, she entered the house and gathered up the possessions that were dear to her and placed them in an empty gourd.

As she left the house she saw that the rainbow had not deserted her, but had arched to the moon. Her husband followed her out and when he saw her with her belongings he knew she was not returning soon. "Where are you going, my wife?" he demanded brusquely.

"I am going to the moon where I can rest quietly," she answered. She began to climb the rainbow, but her husband cried out in anger, grabbed her foot, and pulled her down. Hina felt the bones in her foot break as they both fell to earth, but she pulled herself up and started up the rainbow once again. Her husband was too stunned by her determination to try to stop her again.

Hina's lameness and the pain slowed her, but her heart filled with joy as she continued to climb up the rainbow. She climbed until she came to the stars and prayed they would guide her to the moon. The stars heard her prayer and led her onward.

Finally, she came to the moon, which guided her to a place where she could keep her belongings and take her rest. Hina was overjoyed. She knew that she would never leave this place of peace and quiet.

Ever since, the people of Hawaii look up at the moon and see Hina there with her gourd of precious possessions at her side. Her foot is still lame, but her serenity and benevolence soothe all who take the time to look.[10]

Some Questions for Reflection

1. What part of this story speaks to you most, and how is that reflected in your life right now and in the past?

2. When have you experienced an unbalanced relationship like Hina and her husband's, where one person works very hard while the other contributes next to nothing? When have you been the taker? the overworked one? What did you learn from those experiences?

3. Is there a current longing in your life that you need to express? How would you finish this sentence: "If only I could . . . "?

4. When in your life have you experienced a kind of "last straw" that helped you realize you needed to make a change? What was the straw, and how did you respond to it?

5. If you were packing up for a new chapter of life and could take only five or six treasures with you, what would you choose? What value or meaning does each item have for you?

6. Who or what in your life has been like the rainbow in Hina's story—hearing your longing and helping you to go where you must?

7. When has following a dream caused you injury or pain yet also given you joy? What stood in your way? And what helped you to keep going?

8. What effect does peace and quiet—or the lack of it—have on your present life, on your emotions, thoughts, relationships, and your health?

9. When have you experienced the serenity and benevolence that come with daring to do the thing you must do?

10. If you were to take to heart the medicine of this story, what change might you make in your life?

Reflections

Hina's story demonstrates how working through suffering in the course of retrospection can free us to embrace life and find joy. Slowly, Hina allows herself to face that her life is a misery. With each recollection, she awakens further to the truth of her deep unhappiness: Her children are gone. Her husband is utterly selfish and lazy, only interested in what she can provide for him. And she is exhausted from doing the work of two and receiving nothing in return.

Hina lets herself feel her misery (rather than dismissing or minimizing it) and then begins to imagine another possibility. She cries out her longing for rest, peace, and quiet to the sky, and the rainbow hears her. In being heard, Hina hears herself more clearly and comes to know in her bones that she must leave and make a new life—or die in the attempt.

It feels important to me that Hina brings a small gourd of her treasured possessions from her old life to her new one. She does not simply run off, try to forget the past, and start from scratch. She sorts through what she has, identifies the things she most cherishes, and brings them with her. Similarly, remembrance involves sorting through memories—especially painful ones—and finding a way to carry them forward that is life-enhancing, rather than a burden.

Hina is defeated by the elements the first time she tries to leave her life of misery, and her enraged husband breaks her foot during her second attempt, but she keeps going. Allies appear, and finally she finds her way to the moon, where she is welcomed and shown the place where she belongs.

In a similar way, when we are willing to face the unresolved suffering in our own life and do the thing(s) we know we must do, we become free to embrace the present and the future. When we live in alignment with our deepest knowing, we shine and exude serenity and kindness, like Hina. A life review that brings us home to ourselves is a gift, not only to us but also to those around us.

Remembrance and Mourning

The loss of a loved one is among the most common and most difficult experiences of later life. Given that and the spiral nature of grief, it is not surprising that mourning is a common feature of the life review.

As a society, we try to hurry grief—our own and others'. We want it to be over quickly, but we do not grieve once and for all. Rather, we walk around the important losses of our lives again and again. They return in dreams and as memories; they are triggered by anniversaries and smells and particular places that bear the imprint of loss. These remembrances are painful—sometimes as excruciating as the original loss—and yet they also allow us to re-embrace whom and what we have loved, to remember them, to be grateful for them, and to let them go a little more. In her poignant book *Necessary Losses*, Judith Viorst writes:

> Perhaps the only choice we have is to choose what to do with our dead: To die when they die. To live crippled. Or to forge, out of pain and memory, new adaptations. Through mourning we acknowledge that pain, feel that pain, live past it. Through mourning we let the dead go and take them in. Through mourning we come to accept the difficult changes that loss must bring—and then we begin to come to the end of mourning.[11]

Truncated grief often morphs into grievance or despair. Grief that is allowed to flow where and how it needs to flow can carry us to new ground where we can stand in, and eventually beside, our loss.

Other sorts of losses in need of further mourning may reappear in the winter of life as well—our own unfulfilled dreams or longings, parts of ourselves that no longer exist, or abilities we once enjoyed that have faded somewhat as we've aged. In Margery Hutter Silver's study of women aged sixty-five to eighty-five, mourning was the predominant theme in her subjects' life reviews. Summarizing her own and geropsychiatrist George Pollock's observations, Silver writes:

> As people review their lives, they must mourn for parts of the self that are lost or changed, for lost others, for unfulfilled hopes and aspirations. The ability to work through grief and loss can be liberating and can result in "creative freedom, further development, joy, and the ability to embrace life."[12]

Gerontologist Marc Kaminsky elaborates on this seemingly paradoxical pairing of grief and joy: "The goal of mourning is to restore our sense of innocence and to renew our capacity to be life-glad, so that our involvement with the living takes precedence over our involvement with the dead."[13] If we are to live, life-glad, in spite of loss, we must keep finding our way through grief.

Remembrance and the Release of Resentment

Irish playwright Oscar Wilde endured mistreatment and imprisonment for being gay at a time when homosexuality was considered a criminal offense in Britain. He was sentenced to two years' hard labor and died, in exile, three years later at age forty-six. Upon his release, some friends urged him to forget what he had suffered, but he understood the necessity of coming to terms with what he had experienced:

> The important thing, the thing that lies before me, the thing that I have to do, if the brief remainder of my days is not to be maimed, marred, and incomplete, is to absorb into my nature all that has been done to me, to make it part of me, to accept it without complaint, fear, or reluctance . . . To regret one's own experiences is to arrest one's own development. To

deny one's own experiences is to put a lie into the lips of one's own life. It is no less than a denial of the soul.[14]

Like truncated grief, unresolved suffering creates emotional scar tissue that can harden the heart. The life review brings awareness of lingering resentment and the pain that lies beneath it. With that awareness comes the possibility of accepting and releasing our suffering.

Usually resentment has three elements: the experience of seemingly unjust suffering; the inability to accept what happened; and the belief that those who inflicted the harm should be punished. Memories of unresolved suffering are painful to relive; some may be truly horrific. So why would we want to go through it again? Because what happened is part of us, much as we may not want it to be. To "absorb" all that we have endured, as Wilde describes it, is to become more whole, to reclaim all we have been through, all that we are.

The first step in releasing resentment is to suffer our suffering, to allow it to be. The willingness to revisit suffering opens the door to accepting that what happened, happened. It may have been unjust or undeserved, but it is part of our lives, our inheritance. Mythologist Michael Meade has observed that our greatest gifts are usually intertwined with our deepest wounds.[15] At the time, we survive suffering, somehow. Later, when memories return and we have a broader, longer, and perhaps wiser view, we may be able to see gifts amidst the suffering. As Florida Scott-Maxwell notes in her memoir, *The Measure of My Days*, "The hardness of life I deplore creates the qualities I admire."[16]

As we relive and integrate the painful events of our life journey, we free ourselves to live beyond them. Acceptance helps dissolve resentment and the desire to punish those who have hurt us. Ultimately, the willingness to forgive another is a gift to the self because it is we who suffer most when we hold on to blame and resentment.

It is important not to confuse forgiving with forgetting, however. As Ernest Kurtz and Katherine Ketcham write, "It is through the act of facing exactly what has happened and fitting it into a whole by remembering it that the possibility of atonement (at-one-ment) occurs and forgiveness comes to fruition."[17]

Remembrance as Legacy

It is not for ourselves alone that we remember. The life review plays a vital role in bringing closure and meaning to our own lives, but it also benefits the human family. In recalling and reclaiming our life experiences, we develop wisdom, so necessary for guiding the young. And in sharing the stories of our lives and of those who have gone before, we reaffirm our interconnectedness, the continuity of life, and the endurance of the human spirit. In this hurried, virtual, rootless, and isolating postmodern world, these legacies of wisdom, belonging, and hope may be more crucial than they have ever been. As gerontologist Ron Manheimer points out, "We are mistaken . . . in thinking that people remember only for the sake of the past, when in fact old people remember for the sake of the future."[18]

The Legacy of Wisdom

The life review provides the opportunity to reexamine one's life and discover its cohesiveness and value. Everything we experience and integrate in our own life history teaches us something and endows us with understanding we might not otherwise have developed.

Traditionally, societies have looked to their elders for wisdom and entrusted them with the task of guiding the young toward meaningful lives. It is no accident that in myths and folktales around the world the wise old woman or man is the one who appears at the crucial moment in the young person's journey and points him or her toward the "Pearl of Great Price."

Storytelling has been one of the most important ways through-out history that elders transmit wisdom to the young. Gerontolo-gist Harry R. Moody writes:

The old person who has traveled on the journey before can show us, by telling a tale, where the dangers lie. The telling of the tale is *not* an amusement. It is a guidance—the best guidance, perhaps the only guidance, that one generation can give another. . . . This, in its highest form, is what reminiscence and life review can mean.[19]

The movie *The Straight Story* contains a beautiful example of the transmission of wisdom through storytelling. As part of his own life review, an older man named George sets out on a rather dangerous but necessary journey across the heartland to see his estranged brother. En route, he meets an angry, pregnant adolescent girl who has run away from home. As the two sit by George's campfire, the girl slowly lets down her defenses and tells George how she came to be alone and on the road. In response, George tells her a simple story about the strength of family ties that he used to tell his own children. In the morning, George discovers a symbolic gift the girl has left to show him she has received his wise counsel and now knows where she needs to go.

The Legacy of Belonging

In sharing the stories of our lives, we discover our kinship with one another; for as Carl Jung observed, what is most deeply personal is also most universal. At some point, we all encounter loneliness, love, loss, overcoming, shame, joy, betrayal, delight, and grief. Our life stories are about ourselves, but they are also about human experience. In telling our stories, we learn and draw strength from one another.

In her reminiscence work with groups of elders, Grace Worth was surprised to discover how much participants gained from listening to one another's stories. "Listening was as vital as talking. During the sharing time [elders] were amazed time and again at the universality of those particulars which before had seemed important only to their individual lives and persons."[20] In listening to one another's stories, we are reminded of our common humanity and of our interconnectedness. Stories dissolve isolation and reweave our sense of belonging.

The movie *Fried Green Tomatoes* (based on Fannie Flagg's book *Fried Green Tomatoes at the Whistle Stop Café*) illustrates how telling the stories of our life—even to a stranger—can create powerful bonds between people. In the movie version, a good-hearted and deeply unhappy middle-aged woman (played by Kathy Bates) befriends an old woman who tells her about the people and events of her early life in a small Alabama town. These stories of hardship and friendship are a form of life review for the old woman (played by Jessica Tandy). They also inspire the younger woman to break out of her small and confining existence and to start living with great courage and passion. Through sharing their stories, each becomes less isolated. Both find a profound sense of belonging to each other and to the larger human family.

The Legacy of Hope

In sharing our memories with the young and telling stories of what we have experienced and witnessed, we illuminate the cord of continuity that connects generations. For youth to find their way forward, they need to know from whom and whence they come. In these difficult times, stories that communicate the tenacious continuity of life and of human beings' capacity for endurance are especially important to share.

As older people, we are the guardians of the remembered past. We know a world to which the young have no access, unless we share it. Through storytelling we bring to life the people and events of the past and illuminate the bridge between generations. Our stories let the young know that generations stand behind them. They are not starting from scratch, not adrift in time. They come from people who have struggled and survived; our survival is a testament to human endurance and to the continuity of life.

Stories of how we kept going are a legacy that can lend the young strength and hope as they wrestle in their own lives. And when they are the old ones, they in turn will tell stories to their grandchildren and great-grandchildren, illuminating for them the continuous chain that links generations and connects the past, the present, and the future.

The First Grader is a powerful, almost unbearable film about a legacy of hope. An eighty-four-year-old man is determined to learn to read, and, despite daunting obstacles, he makes a place for himself in the local school, alongside fifty children from the village. As the story unfolds, horrific memories of his life emerge—excruciating losses and years of torture in British prison camps in Kenya. During the day, he lives forward (teaching children, imparting wisdom, and bearing witness to a history that must not be forgotten). At night, he remembers, and he weeps.

Somehow, he manages to redeem from the horrors that still haunt him a deep sense of purpose and a courageous commitment to a better future for the children of his country. Near the end of the film he says, "We have to learn from our past. We must not forget, but we must be better. We reap what we sow with our children."[21] Based on a true story, this is an important film to see. It is also an inspiring example of how daring to look back, to endure suffering, and to tell our stories can become a legacy of hope for future generations.

Cultivating Remembrance

Remembrance is an especially generous grace. Many of the skills and attitudes necessary for reflecting on our life's journey and finding meaning and value in it emerge in the cultivation of earlier graces. And the spontaneous return of distant memories as we age provides the raw materials for completing our life. In addition, we are aging at a time when shifting attitudes are beginning to recreate a climate that supports elders in sharing their wisdom, strength, and hope with younger generations.

Remembrance and Her Sister Graces

In cultivating Authenticity, we learn to welcome whatever arises within us, especially what disturbs us, and we acquire a deepening capacity to know what is true for us and what is genuinely meaningful.

Courage and Necessary Fierceness support us in facing the truth of what we have done and "left undone" in our lives.[22] Both of these graces lend us strength to attend to unfinished business requiring difficult action, frightening confrontation, or a profound change of heart. Courage helps us dare to share our stories in a society that often turns a deaf ear to its elders.

In cultivating Contentment, we become better able to meet distressing emotions with steadiness, equanimity, and humor. Thus, we can walk toward and work through lingering grief, guilt, resentment, and other emotional suffering that arise in the course of the life review. The Grace of Creativity enhances our capacity to be open to surprise, to entertain multiple points of view, and to meet obstacles with ingenuity and tenacity.

The Grace of Compassion helps us to bear our own suffering with tenderness and to begin to see others, especially those who have harmed us, with understanding and, ultimately, forgiveness. Simplicity teaches us to relinquish the nonessential and devote ourselves to the meaningful. The life review itself is a winnowing process in which the most important memories demand our attention, while others fade into the background.

Finally, Self-Transcending Generosity brings a sense of kinship with other human beings and with life itself. From that more-than-personal perspective, we recognize that our lives are part of a larger human story and begin to sense the importance of sharing our legacies of wisdom, belonging, and hope with younger members of the human family.

Priming the Pump

Memories usually arise of their own accord in the winter of life, but they can also be coaxed. Looking through photo albums can stimulate remembrance, as can visiting the places we have lived and the people with whom we have shared periods of our lives.

Writing in a journal or notebook on a regular basis can be an invaluable tool for inviting and working with memories and the emotions that accompany them. In "The Journal As Activity and Genre," Barbara Myerhoff and Deena Metzger describe how journaling can help connect us to ourselves and to one another:

> The materials encountered in the journal process are dealt with first in their raw, highly individual, utterly subjective state. Once examined . . . they begin to reveal familiar and even universal configurations. One's own story is thus seen to contain elements of the stories of others, common to humanity. . . . The self can now be seen as the microcosm for the macrocosm of human experience.[23]

Sharing Stories

Finding places to share our stories and our wisdom can be a challenge in an ageist society such as ours, but the value of remembrance and storytelling, especially in the winter of life, is being rediscovered. Memoir, autobiography, and other forms of life story writing are enjoying a resurgence, and these can be invaluable tools in the life review.

Life writing is not simply for the rich and famous; in fact, it seems to have particular appeal among the marginalized: elders, women, immigrants, prisoners, and survivors of all sorts. In *Death in Life: Survivors of Hiroshima*, psychiatrist Robert Jay Lifton observes that people who survive large-scale disasters like Hiroshima, as well as those who have endured devastating personal loss, often find their way back from the edge through telling their stories.

Senior centers, lifelong learning institutes, and other organizations frequently offer courses and workshops in memoir, autobiography, life story, and life history writing. Many programs are composed of elders and young adults, which appears to have particular advantages. In their life history work with elders and college students, for example, Barbara Myerhoff and Virginia Tufte observed "the natural affinity between people of alternate generations, so often observed by anthropologists." They describe the benefits of pairing life-reviewing older adults with young interviewer/listeners:

> It offers to the elderly . . . the chance to be heard, be seen and recorded as having existed, and . . . to integrate their historical experiences and thus to construct and manifest a valuable identity, a personal mythology. . . . It gives an opportunity, too, for the younger people to see and know a model for the future, thus complete themselves, and to recognize the full scope of the human life cycle with all its limits and possibilities. Finally, it provides intergenerational continuity, integrating the teller and listener into a web of common meaning.[24]

Many books offer instructions and some rich examples of various approaches to life story writing, including Maureen Murdock's *Unreliable Truth*, Marc Kaminsky's *The Uses of Reminiscence*, Barbara Myerhoff's *Remembered Lives*, and William Randall and Gary Kenyon's *Ordinary Wisdom*.

Poetry as Life Story

Poetry can be an especially potent way to tell our stories because of its brevity and emotionally evocative language. Here are two simple suggestions for writing life story poems; neither requires rhyming:

1. Distill a memory into a Haiku (just three lines, consisting of five, seven, and five syllables, respectively)—see what happens.

2. Turn a memory into an un-poem[25]—arrange the lines as you wish, but limit yourself to nine to thirteen syllables for the whole poem.

If this practice appeals to you, consider creating a series of poems as a form of life review and a possible legacy. My friend Linda, a retired teacher and therapist, recently created a book (*Memory of Rain*) from the poems she had written over the past fifty years. Although it wasn't her intent, Linda's book-making became a kind of a life review as she sorted through what she had written at various points in her life, revisited the events and the emotions they stirred, decided which poems to include and which not, and in time found a way of organizing and sequencing her poems that felt right. She later said the experience helped her connect to something bigger than herself and brought to light a thread of continuity running through her life. And it was such a gift to her children and grandchildren—and to her friends.

John Fox's *Finding What You Didn't Lose* is a good resource for poem making. See also Janet Bloom's "Minerva's Doll" and George Getzel's "Old People, Poetry, and Groups," both in Marc Kaminsky's *The Uses of Reminiscence*.

Stories Without Words

Life stories can also be shared without words, for example through creating collages, assembling photographs, or working with other art media. My friend and colleague Geri has been making jewelry and dolls for years, and as we've aged, more and more of her work seems to incorporate old photographs and family memorabilia. In addition to honoring her ancestors and their gifts, her pieces reflect and deepen her connection to parts of herself and her life story that words alone might not convey.

Another friend, Judy, creates assemblages from treasured and found objects. She recently assembled small items that had belonged to her father into a powerful piece to honor his life and commemorate his death. The process helped her to better understand her dad's experience as a young fighter pilot in World War II and its impact on his life and his family.

And a third friend, Marti, has recently begun creating cards for her children and other family members that each include an old photograph along with a few words about the event captured in the photo. Each card is a gift to someone in her family, a form of life review for Marti, and has stimulated rich conversations across generations.

Consider assembling photographs and memorabilia of your own life (and, if possible, of your ancestors' lives) as a form of life review. Or explore other wordless ways you might re-experience and express the important events and people of your life, for yourself and as a possible legacy for others.

Learning from Film

The movies described earlier in this chapter illustrate the push toward remembrance in the winter of life: *Evening*, *The First Grader*, *The Straight Story*, and *Fried Green Tomatoes*. All are gems in their own right and also beautiful examples of the healing grace of remembering and sharing life stories with one another. Also highly recommended: *The Woman in Gold*, *The Best Exotic Marigold Hotel*, *Water for Elephants*, and *Enchanted April*.

Reading Others' Stories

The memoirs, autobiographies, and journals of long-lived people can provide a powerful experience of the life-review process and may inspire reflection on our own journey. See, for example, *The*

Book of Elders (edited by Sandy Johnson), *Grandmothers Counsel the World* (edited by Carol Schaefer), *The Measure of My Days* (Florida Scott-Maxwell), *Loving and Leaving the Good Life* (Helen Nearing), and the late-life diaries of May Sarton (for example, *After the Stroke*, *At Seventy*, and *Endgame*.)

Celebrating Lives

Celebrations of milestone birthdays (eighty, ninety, one hundred, or . . .) can provide a wonderful opportunity to see, hear, and feel the richness of our lives in the presence of loved ones. Invariably, people tell stories and share memories of the honoree, and a display of photographs from various chapters in the person's life, assembled by friends or family, adds another dimension to the celebration. Rather than— or in addition to—honoring someone at her memorial service, how much richer for everyone involved to do so while she is alive!

For more introverted souls or for those with loved ones who live far away, one-on-one visits or small gatherings may be more appealing. A friend, who has friends and family living in various places, celebrated her seventieth birthday by taking each of the significant people in her history out to dinner over the course of a year.

Rituals of Remembrance

In the last few years I have participated in a community-wide celebration of the Days of the Dead. All over town people create altars of remembrance and decorate them with candles, marigolds, photographs, and other cherished items that are reminiscent of departed loved ones. There are candle-lit processions, silent vigils, and the sharing of grief and celebration.

The Celts and other indigenous peoples around the world have held ceremonies in late fall for millennia, to mark the dying of the old year and to remember the departed. Traditionally, rituals happen in community, but private rituals of remembrance can also help us to honor the dead and to let them go. The anniversary of a spouse's or a dear friend's death can be celebrated alone or with others who knew the one for whom we still grieve.

Rituals of remembrance can also mark other meaningful milestones in one's life. For example, it is not uncommon for a person in recovery to receive a tattoo at some point in the process that symbolizes his or her coming back to life. It is an ever-present reminder of the choices and the journey that have been made, and perhaps it also serves as a talisman against forgetting.

If you're inclined, celebrate the Days of the Dead (October 31–November 2) alone, with a few close friends, with a large community—or all of the above. Anniversaries of a loved one's death are also ripe times for pausing to remember, to celebrate, to grieve, to honor, and to let go. See Kay Turner's *Beautiful Necessity* for examples of altars created by women for remembrance, healing, protection, and other purposes.

Looking Way Back

One of my cousins, Cliff, is engaged in researching the Avery branch of our family. His primary focus is the distant past—our ancestors who came to the colonies from Wales, Scotland, and Ireland. I'm appreciating the similarities across generations that we're discovering as Cliff supplies us with family history—a love of farming, rivers, writing, and singing; humor that is at once serious and irreverent; and recurring names that some of us gave our children, without knowing that they also belonged to our ancestors. Seeing our own life in the context of an extended family across generations adds richness to the life review and can deepen our sense of belonging and continuity.

10: The Grace of Agelessness

"There is an unspeakable dawn in happy old age."
—Victor Hugo, *Les Misérables*

Agelessness is the capacity to be old and young and in between. It means wearing our years lightly—having access to all ages, but not being confined or defined by any of them. The Grace of Agelessness emerges as we recognize that old and young are not mutually exclusive and that our years are a gift yet need not determine how we feel and act.

One of the most liberating of Winter's Graces, Agelessness frees us from the negative stereotypes of old age. Two daunting yet enlivening tasks stand between us and that freedom, however: releasing the attachment to youth and claiming our years. The willingness to wrestle with these two challenges releases us from the grip of the past and from a dread of the future. No longer fearing old age nor measuring the present against the yardstick of youth, we are free to discover for ourselves the unexpected dimensions of late-life agelessness: physical and cognitive vitality, enduring beauty, and lifelong passion.

Prologue: Kissing the Hag

In many of the world's folktales, a young person in some kind of trouble encounters an ugly hag who is sitting by the side of a river or a path. The crone asks the young one to wash the sores on her back, to give her a kiss, or to help her in some way. The youth's willing-ness to care for the old woman in spite of her hideous appearance is the catalyst that transforms the crone into an ally who helps the young person grow into her or his destiny.[1] Often these tales contain another character as well, who is repulsed by the old hag and mis-treats her. His or her arrogance and mean-spiritedness usually lead to an unhappy outcome.

One way to understand folktales is to imagine that each char-acter is an aspect of ourselves. We all carry within us a wounded old one who needs our kindness and care. Rare is the woman in postmodern America who has not been scarred to some degree by demeaning attitudes toward older women. We are also the one who treats the old woman with disdain. Living in an environment that denigrates old age, we learn to look harshly on our own and others' aging.

And we all have within us a heroine who does not turn away from the old one and willingly washes her sores. As we face and care for the wounded old woman within us, she becomes a wise and nurturing ally who has a great deal to teach us, including this ageless secret: *owning old does not mean losing young.*

Young and old appear to be opposites, which leads to the fear that if we admit to age we somehow lose access to youth. However, as a woman comes to accept the reality of her age, she finds—per-haps to her astonishment—that old and young are not mutually exclusive. They coexist. As the author Madeleine L'Engle notes, "The great thing about getting older is that you don't lose all the other ages you've been."[2] Women's spirituality scholar Patricia Monaghan concurs, "Women in their prime are maids and crones at once. Every aged woman knows still the wild spring winds."[3] In claiming the winter of life we do not lose access to our younger selves. We become women of all seasons, at home in each, impris-oned by none.

Scientists are confirming that we are many ages at once, and that chronological age is relatively unimportant. Walter Bortz, a professor at the Stanford School of Medicine, observes, "[Chronological] age is becoming increasingly irrelevant to how we live, what we experience, and who we are becoming."[4] Rather than a singular number measured in years, age is increasingly regarded as multi-dimensional, with chronological, biological, cognitive, social, and psychological dimensions. At any one time, we might be chronologically one age, while our other ages could span decades.

At the moment, I'm chronologically seventy-two but biologically closer to fifty-five (with the exception of my sun-damaged skin). Cognitively I'm about fifty most days but eighty when short on sleep or under stress. Emotionally I move between twenty and eighty, and socially I'm seventy-something (I'm retired and a grandmother, both of which have traditionally been associated with later life). In the company of young children, I often feel thirty and sometimes catch a glimpse of my four-year-old self. We are multi-aged, and our years are a gift.

The Changing Face of Aging

Early research on late life was conducted with hospitalized elders, which led to a mistaken view of aging as an inevitable decline into disability and illness. Social gerontologist Peter Öberg explains that problems usually ascribed to old age—such as loneliness, unhappiness, and debilitating illness—"do not correspond to old people's own experiences . . . The [gerontology] field has been dominated by a 'misery perspective' focusing on 'problems of aging.' However, we know that it is often only a minority of older people who experience these difficulties."[5] More recent studies have established that emotional well-being often improves with age (see the Grace of Contentment) and that physical health, cognitive vitality, and other areas believed to atrophy with age in fact remain accessible in later life.

Physical and Cognitive Vitality

A growing body of late-life research suggests that most of the physical changes once assumed to be part of the aging process are related to how we live, rather than how long ago we were born. Dr. Mike Evans, for example, writes, "The really exciting thing is that we used to think that problems such as reduced cardiovascular and respiratory function, muscle wasting, and bone loss were just a natural part of aging, but it's clear now that most are actually the result of inactivity."[6]

Most so-called "problems of age" are the consequence of behaviors and attitudes, not chronological age, and can be prevented, delayed, or offset by regular exercise and other health-friendly practices. And the catastrophic conditions mistakenly equated with age, such as severe dementia and debilitating frailty, are the exception, not the rule. The vast majority of older adults do not experience them.[7]

Dr. John Rowe and Robert Kahn's extensive MacArthur study, for example, revealed that health and well-being in later life are, in fact, the norm.

> Older people . . . are much more likely to age well than to become decrepit and dependent. . . . Research provides very strong evidence that we are, in large part, responsible for our own old age. . . . People often blame aging for losses that are in fact caused by lifestyle—overeating and poor nutrition, smoking, excessive use of alcohol, lack of regular exercise, and insufficient mental exertion.[8]

Dr. Christiane Northrup concurs that there is much we can do (and refrain from doing) to maintain health and well-being as we age. She writes,

> As a physician and health educator, I know you can minimize the possibility of degenerative disease and premature aging if you make good lifestyle choices. . . . Cognitive

decline is not a normal part of getting older. . . . Mental habits play a huge role in our health and longevity . . . [and] belief in the positive aspects of aging strongly affects your biology and thus your survival.[9]

As Dr. Northrup points out, debilitating cognitive decline is not a normal part of aging. The late-life brain has a far greater capacity for continuing development, resilience, and rewiring than early studies suggested. In fact, as Dr. Gene Cohen observes, some changes in the aging brain actually enhance the quality of later life (see the Grace of Contentment, *Reflection and the Maturing of Vision* and *Emotional Climate of Later Life*). For more on maintaining cognitive vitality, I recommend Gene Cohen's *The Mature Mind*, Ellen Langer's *Mindfulness*, and Hansen and Mendius's *Buddha's Brain*.

Enduring Beauty

Like cognitive and physical vitality, beauty is also mistakenly assumed to decline with age—especially for women—at least in our culture, which equates beauty with youth and women's appearance with their worth. Research confirms that a double standard of aging exists. Men and women alike judge visible signs of age such as graying hair and wrinkles more harshly in women than in men and describe the same characteristics as "old" in a woman but "distinguished" in a man.[10]

In contrast, the Japanese actually have a word (*shibui*) that describes the beauty of age. Unlike flawless or flashy beauty that draws attention to itself, shibui is characterized by beautiful imperfection, effortlessness, elegant simplicity, and understatement. Shibui is apparent in weathered wood and stones, simple handmade pottery, the bark and bend of ancient trees, and in the faces of many elders. William Shakespeare observed that "beauty is in the eye of the beholder," and we can learn to recognize and appreciate the beauty of age.

The British film *Calendar Girls* presents a refreshingly affirming view of older women's beauty, inspired by the statement of one of the characters, a man in midlife: "The flowers of Yorkshire are like the women of Yorkshire—the last stage of their growth is the most glorious."[11] Rather than worrying about "losing our looks," we can broaden our definition of beauty and perhaps even celebrate some of the changes, like Maggie Kuhn, founder of the Gray Panthers: "I wish all my peers could enjoy their wrinkles as much as I enjoy mine. I regard them as badges of distinction that I have worked hard for."[12] The fresh beauty of youth is a delight and is easy to appreciate. But the fine lines at the corners of older eyes and those that reflect decades of laughter (and even distress) reveal a person's character and life story, adding texture and richness that I find equally beautiful.

The kind of beauty that comes with age shines from the inside out, and the winter of life offers some of the most potent beauty secrets available: self-acceptance (Authenticity), connectedness and generosity (Self-Transcending Generosity), humor and gratitude (Contentment), playful engagement (Creativity), kindness (Compassion), savoring small pleasures and living our genuine priorities (Simplicity), and making peace with our lives (Remembrance). These qualities may not preserve prettiness, but they do radiate beauty.

Lifelong Passion

Stereotypes aside, research reveals that regular sexual enjoyment is the norm for healthy elders with partners, and that physical intimacy often becomes more satisfying with age.[13] For an enjoyable, and perhaps surprising, experience, check out Connie Goldman's *Late-Life Love*, a collection of stories of older couples. One of her subjects confided, "For me, physical intimacy is better [at eighty] than it has ever been in my whole life." Another woman mused, "I wonder if young people have as much fun and pleasure in bed as we do!" (She is eighty-five; her husband is ninety.)[14]

In the majority of tribal and village cultures, sexual activity among elders is expected and tends to occur regularly until very late in life. According to Winn and Newton who studied elders' sexual behavior in 106 indigenous cultures, women in very late life typically have greater interest in sex than very old men and often choose younger men as partners.[15] Elaborating on Winn and Newton's findings, Davis and Leonard write, "In seventy percent of these [indigenous] societies [postmenopausal women] serve as sexual initiators of young men. Apparently the prevailing wisdom is that older women have the perspective and expertise to cultivate healthy sexuality in the next generation."[16]

In industrialized countries, longitudinal evidence indicates that most healthy, older married couples report continued, regular sexual enjoyment. In their extensive study of sexuality in later life, Starr and Weiner note, "As a 72-year-old woman explained, speaking for many of our respondents, 'Sex is so much more relaxed . . . I know my body better and we know each other better. Sex is unhurried and the best in our lives.'"[17] The primary reasons for a lack of sexual activity among celibate elders are the lack of a partner (especially for women) and poor health, rather than chronological age or a lack of interest in sex.[18]

Myth and folklore have long revealed the older woman's continuing enjoyment of sexuality. In fact, in some cases the goddess of sexuality herself is an old woman, for example the frightening yet alluring Aztec goddess Tlazolteotl and Huitaca, the Columbian goddess of joy, intoxication, and sexual abandon who encourages the enjoyment of all forms of pleasure, despite the disapproval of her straight-laced husband.

Several older and multi-aged goddesses of sexuality were honored in the Middle East—Anat and Ishatar, for example—and the complex, shape-shifting Samdzimari was worshipped in the Caucasus mountains. Celtic folklore is replete with sexually active older goddesses, like Achtland; the smiling, vulva-splaying Sheila na Gig; and the over-eager Mal, who died pursuing a much younger man along the Irish coast.[19]

Despite recent research and historical and cross-cultural evidence to the contrary, ageist stereotypes in the United States portray older people as asexual. Younger people typically find the idea of sexual activity in elders disturbing and somehow unnatural, as reflected in such pejorative phrases as "dirty old man" and "foolish old woman." And many senior care facilities prohibit sexual "fraternizing" between elders. As Marilyn Elias points out, "Retirement and nursing homes can make it especially tough for older folks to get together. These institutions often have rules that restrict contact between the sexes and bar overnight visits."20

May Sarton writes passionately on the desexualizing of older people: "How unnatural the imposed view . . . that passionate love belongs only to the young, that people are dead from the neck down by the time they are forty, and that any deep feeling, any passion after that age, is either ludicrous or revolting!"21

Late-life passion can, of course, take many forms, and sexual activity is only one of them. Many artists and scientists are engaged in some of their most passionate work in the last decades of life or begin new creative endeavors. (For more about this trend, see the Grace of Creativity.) Jungian analyst Jean Bolen describes passion or "juice" as the defining characteristic of an ageless older woman. "A crone is a juicy older woman with zest, passions, and soul. . . . The juice that truly vitalizes us is unconditional love, which is the one source of energy that is never depleted."22

Ageless heroines have appeared in several stories throughout this book. Some of these older women demonstrate remarkable physical stamina ("The Hedley Kow" and "The Woman in the Moon"), and many walk great distances with apparent ease ("The Little Old Woman Who Went to the North Wind," "The Midwife of Dakar," and "The Haunted House"). Their cognitive vitality is revealed in their creative and wise responses to important problems ("The Wise Woman" and "The Running Stick," for example), and their passionate engagement with life is often apparent (as in "Ubong and the Headhunters" and "Poppet Caught a Thief"). And the following folktale from Syria reveals the importance of sexuality in late life, despite stereotypes to the contrary:

The Cure

An old widow had only one son. When he grew to be a man she found him a bride, but she was jealous of her daughter-in-law and began to complain of imaginary sicknesses. Every day she would nag her son and say, "Bring me the doctor, my boy. Let the doctor come!"

The son did nothing for a while, but eventually he gave in and went to fetch the doctor. While he was out, the widow washed herself and lined her eyes with *kohl* [cosmetic powder]. She put on her best gown and wound a sash of silk about her waist. She donned a velvet vest and her daughter-in-law's wedding headdress and placed an embroidered kerchief over it. Then she sat and waited.

When the doctor arrived and asked for his patient, the son showed him in and said, "There she is. It is my mother. From the moment I married she has been grumbling like a hen, and not one day has brought her joy or pleasure."

"This lady needs a husband," said the doctor.

"But she is my mother!"

"Yes," said the doctor, "and she needs a groom."

"She's over ninety years old. Surely she can't be thinking of marriage again!"

"You are wrong, my son," said the doctor. "As often as her skirts are lifted by the wind, the thought of a bridegroom enters her mind."

"Sir," said the son. "If she had wanted a husband she could have married long ago. Why don't you examine her and see what is the matter with her?"

"I have already told you what is wrong."

At this the old woman sprang up from her corner and said to her son, "My boy, may you find favor in the sight of God, do you fancy yourself a greater expert than the wise doctor?"[23]

Some Questions for Reflection

1. What part of this story stands out for you, and how is that relevant to your life right now?

2. In what ways are you like the old woman at the start of the story, complaining about imaginary illnesses, "grumbling like a hen," and unable to find joy or pleasure in life?

3. Where in your life do you act like the son, sure that you know what others need better than they do?

4. To what degree have you, like the old woman's son, internalized the idea that older people are no longer sexual beings?

5. How would you describe your current sexual life? What do you wish it were like? If there is a gap between reality and wish, how might you begin to close it?

6. If you were to take to heart the medicine of this story, what shift might you make in your life?

Reflections

This very short story illustrates the all-too-common disconnect between an old woman's desire for sexual intimacy and the tenacious belief of a younger person that such a thing is impossible.

Despite the wise doctor's insistence that the root of the old woman's unhappiness is her unfulfilled longing for a husband, her son is incredulous. "But she's my mother," he exclaims. "She's over ninety years old!" As children, most of us have trouble imagining our parents as sexual beings; when they are in their nineties it can be even more difficult. However, the longing for physical affection and intimacy does not fade with youth.

Initially we are told that this old woman is jealous of her son's wife. (Perhaps living with newlyweds makes her aware of her own longing for a partner?) Yet her complaining of imaginary illnesses is more than the nagging litany of a bitter woman who refuses to find joy or pleasure in anything. It is a creative strategy to convince her son to bring the doctor for a visit.

The old woman goes to elaborate lengths to bathe, dress, and decorate herself before the doctor arrives, including the donning of her daughter-in-law's wedding headdress. What I appreciate about this part of the story is the audacious passion with which the old woman expresses what matters to her, even though she is living with people who do not understand. Rather than denying her longing to herself, or concealing it for fear of being ridiculed as "foolish," she goes all out—then sits and waits.

The doctor is an important ally. He sees and speaks the truth: "This lady needs a husband." Free from limiting ideas about old age, the doctor calmly repeats his prescription three times; each time the son insists he must be wrong.

Finally, the old woman springs from her seat in the corner and challenges her son's arrogance with a simple question: "Do you fancy yourself a greater expert than the wise doctor?" We are left to imagine what happens next. Does the son finally recognize the truth? Does he find his mother a suitable husband?

Whatever the outcome, the doctor's visit is a gift. He validates our heroine as a "lady" and a sexual being, thus providing a powerful antidote to her son's insistence that she should be long past such concerns. Even if the visit does not alter the circumstances of her life, it may have a lasting effect on its quality. The doctor's visit and validation have helped the old woman to communicate more directly, to stand up for herself, and to honor her own needs. I think it's unlikely that things in their home will be exactly the way they were before.

⫸ *Cultivating Agelessness* ⫷

Robert Frost once said: "The best way out is always through."[24] He further advised, "Fall in with what you're asked to accept, you know; fall in with it—and turn it your way. . . . Hold [your] own *with* whatever's going—not *against*, but *with*."[25] For me, Frost's wise counsel and the hag-kissing stories referred to at the beginning of this chapter provide some essential guidelines for growing into the Grace of Agelessness. In these folktales, a crucial moment occurs when the young heroine moves toward the old woman and agrees to wash her sores. Much as we might wish it didn't, the path to agelessness passes by the wounded old woman who resides in most, if not all, of us. To wash her sores means becoming aware of the ways in which we are injured by ageist attitudes and treating those sore places in ourselves with kind attention and care. "The best way out is always through. . . . not *against*, but *with*."

Claiming Our Years

Frost suggests that we "fall in" with what is given, but accepting our age is the last thing that most women in our culture want to do. One of the great paradoxes of the human psyche, however, is that the willingness to accept something invariably creates a shift, while resistance to it usually leads to its persistence. As we entertain a more heartening (and accurate) narrative of age and begin to treat our aging selves with tenderness rather than scorn, we may discover that it is possible to keep hold of the baby (our years) and throw out the bathwater (ageist ideas about what our years are supposed to mean).

There are a number of reasons for claiming our age; the first is gratitude. Long years are a gift. To affirm and be grateful for our age (our life!) is important, as is gratitude for health, loved ones, and all our blessings—including life's challenges. My father died at fifty-six, and my friends Elizabeth and Robin, at fifty-seven and sixty. I'm grateful to be seventy-two.

Claiming our age also allows us to be attentive students in the wisdom school of later life, which is a very exciting and essential classroom. It is difficult to address the tasks of winter and embrace its gifts and graces if we are still preoccupied with the concerns of youth: appearance, acquisition, and achievement. Focusing on the values of youth in the second half of life keeps us looking for fulfillment in the wrong places.

The agendas of the two halves of life are complementary in sequence, but they pull in very different directions. Youth looks outward and moves upward; age looks inward and moves downward. Youth is concerned with personal identity, achievement, and success, while in later life we are pulled beyond the little self and become more concerned with meaning, integrity, and being of service. As Jung observed, "We cannot live the afternoon of life according to the program of life's morning; for what was great in the morning will be little at evening, and what in the morning was true will at evening have become a lie."[26]

Claiming our age also helps overturn lingering ageist stereotypes. The world needs elders, older men and women who are willing to "come out," if future generations are to have more accurate, hopeful, and healthy views of old age. We are potentially teachers and role models of what is possible in the winter of life—let us be courageous and authentic about aging! If we refuse to claim our years, what message are we sending to younger generations about growing old? And if we conceal our years in an effort to pass for forty, how will our youth know where to turn for seasoned guidance that has been tested and strengthened by decades of living?

Releasing the Attachment to Youth

The attachment to youth and the aversion to age are two expressions of the same ageist fallacies: that youth is good and age is bad; that the first half of life is valuable, and the second half is a mistake, a disaster, or a failure. Growing older is not the problem; our attachment to youth and the aversion to age that lies beneath it are the problem.

In the face of demeaning ageist stereotypes, many women invest enormous amounts of time, money, and energy in attempting to pass for young. But pretending to be younger than we are makes us vulnerable to being found out, like a fugitive in our own life. The attachment to youth keeps the focus on appearance, which often goes hand in hand with competing with other women for attention and position. Snow White's stepmother, who began each day by asking her mirror, "Who's the fairest of us all?" is a chilling example of what can happen when an older woman's assurance that she's "still got it" remains her most pressing concern. Focusing on looking young can also distract us from the tasks of later life and easily undermines Authenticity, Self-Transcending Generosity, Courage, and other graces.

Just as it's possible to hold on to the baby of our years and throw out the bathwater of ageism, it is possible to release the fear-based attachment to youth and still retain access to qualities often associated with the spring of life, like passion, beauty, and vitality. Helen Mirren, a wonderfully multi-aged woman, points out, "You only have two options in life: Die young or get old. There is nothing else . . . You just have to find a way of negotiating getting old psychologically and physically."[27]

Enlivening Attitudes

Our attitudes and beliefs have a powerful effect on our experience of aging and on our health and well-being, and three are essential to late-life thriving: healthy defiance, optimism, and an openness to change.

Healthy Defiance

In his cross-national study of centenarians, psychologist Mario Martinez found that the single greatest determinant of vibrant old age is "healthy defiance" of limiting cultural messages about aging. He observes, "While Western cultures tend to conclude that value, potency, and activity decrease with age, centenarians do not buy into this proposition; they view their journey through life . . . [as increasing] their worthiness, complexity, and passion."[28] Martinez's *The MindBody Code* includes powerful exercises, drawn from neuroscience and contemplative traditions, which help replace limiting ideas about aging with those that support "healthy defiance" and thus healthy aging.

An essential first step toward healthy defiance is staying alert to ageist comments and questioning them, whether they come through others or from within ourselves. Offhand remarks about how awful getting older is are all around us: "That's age for you," "I hate getting old," and "It's only going to get worse." A simple heartfelt statement, such as, "In some ways I like being seventy more than being twenty," can move the conversation in a more age-friendly direction. Over time, gently challenging mistaken assumptions about age can help wear down negative attitudes and stereotypes.

Being aware of our own age-unfriendly attitudes is especially important. For example, many of us terrorize ourselves with the fear of dementia whenever we (temporarily) forget a name, a word, or the reason we walked into a particular room. Statistically, it is far more likely that we are under stress, not really paying attention, or getting insufficient sleep—and we can do something about each of these.

Doing what we can to take care of ourselves as we grow older—rather than blaming age for our troubles—is essential for health and well-being in later life. I've noticed myself periodically wanting to make age the villain, for example when my knees hurt. While decades of use likely did contribute to the wearing away of my meniscus, my attitude and behavior also play a part. When I'm honest with myself, I know there are things I can do to lessen knee pain. Through trial and error, it's become apparent that when I walk every day and choose fruits and vegetables over inflammatory foods, my joints hurt far less.

Moving beyond the mistaken linking of old age and pathology is vital because our beliefs and expectations have an enormous impact on our behavior and experience. A loss-focused view of aging typically goes hand in hand with unhealthy practices like smoking and a lack of exercise. If we believe that it is all downhill anyway, it is easy to slip into a defeated, why-bother attitude and to stop taking care of ourselves. But it *is not* all downhill!

Optimism

An optimistic outlook—about aging in particular and about life in general—is essential for agelessness. Negative attitudes toward growing old are easily and often unconsciously absorbed, and they restrict our sense of what is possible. On the other hand, the combination of affirming our age, realistically facing limits, and remaining focused on possibilities rather than problems engenders agelessness. Connie Goldman and Richard Mahler observe:

> The sensation of being fully alive, spirited, and aware in later life is not a function of being young in the chronological sense. . . . The secret of remaining truly youthful means tapping into . . . the winning combination of a fresh, optimistic outlook with the kind of wisdom and self-knowledge that comes with each passing day.[29]

Anthropologist Sula Benet's extensive study of the long-living Abkhasian people of the Caucasus Mountains revealed a number of reasons for their longevity; chief among these is their optimistic engagement with life. Dr. Benet observes, "Abkhasians are a life-loving, optimistic people . . . [They] expect a long and useful life and look forward to old age." Quoting an optimistic and ageless ninety-nine-year-old man from the village of Achandara, she writes, "It isn't time to die yet. I am needed by my children and grandchildren, and it isn't bad in this world—except that . . . it has become difficult to climb trees."[30]

Probably the most significant finding about optimism is that it is a learnable skill, rather than a characteristic that we either have or lack. Cognitive psychologists and neuroscientists have demonstrated that self-defeating attitudes and ways of thinking can be changed through awareness and practice. (See Mario Martinez's *The Mind-Body Code*, Martin Seligman's *Learned Optimism*, and *Buddha's Brain* by Rick Hansen and Richard Mendius.)

Openness to Change

Researchers have identified openness to change as an essential attitude for healthy aging. Erika Landau and Benjamin Maoz, for example, found that elders who are open to change continue to grow psychologically and experience a sense of meaning and purpose in their lives. In contrast, those who cling to former ways and rigid patterns of behavior tend to be "emotionally-bound" and are more frightened of death.[31]

In their study of "late bloomers"—people who are thriving in their later years—Connie Goldman and Richard Mahler found that "an attitude that accepts change and encourages growth can be a guiding force in remaining healthy, upbeat, and invigorated, whatever the date on your birth certificate."[32] On the other hand, resisting change or remaining focused on what we have lost, rather than on what is now possible, is a prescription for misery.

My friend Joanne, a retired nurse, is an inspiring example of the enlivening effects of openness and optimism. At eighty-six, she is a woman of all seasons and apparently immune to limiting ageist stereotypes. She and the almost ninety-year-old "love of [her] life" regularly drive long distances in order to spend time together (they live four states apart). Recently, she came over to give me some advice on pruning an out-of-control plum tree. I was expecting a conversation, with both of us on the ground, but after a few minutes of looking at the tree, Joanne asked me for a ladder. Compact pruning saw in hand (she had brought her own), she climbed the ladder without a second thought and began removing some of the smaller rogue branches.

Her ageless attitude inspires me. She is not reckless (she made sure I was holding the ladder and didn't try to climb the entangled tree), but she is a wonderful model of the active, open, optimistic style that is associated with healthy aging. When I asked Joanne if she had any advice for aging well, she demurred at first and then mused, "So much of it is attitude, really—staying interested and doing what you can to help out." (She is active in local affordable-housing efforts and is a first responder at ICE raids, sometimes in the middle of the night, lending support to families and making sure that no laws are broken during the process.) She added, "In your eighties, maintenance takes a lot more time, and you just have to do it." Joanne walks every day, is an avid gardener, and does aquatic exercise two or three times a week. She also makes sure to get as much rest as she needs, which is sometimes nine or ten hours a night.

Tools for Cultivating Agelessness

Some of the tools below address the task of claiming and celebrating our years; others focus on releasing the attachment to youth or healing the aversion to age. Some may be useful in maintaining late-life health and vitality, and others support ageless attitudes. Many of the practices that nurture other graces also contribute to agelessness, and references to those are included here as well.

Stay Physically Active. The evidence is irrefutable: the greatest gift we can give ourselves and the single most important contributor to agelessness in body and mind is regular physical exercise—and it's never too late to start. Regardless of age or physical condition, find activities you enjoy and do one of them for at least thirty minutes daily: walk, bike, swim, dance, do tai chi or yoga, or play golf.

Exercise alone, enlist a buddy, or join a class (there are many online and on television). Do whatever it takes to stay active.

Tune In to Age-Friendly Messages. The air is thick with limiting ageist notions, but evidence of agelessness is all around us too, if we're willing to look and listen for it. Spend time with ageless older people who are thriving in their later decades, and watch movies with ageless older heroines like *Calendar Girls, Enchanted April*, and *The Best Exotic Marigold Hotel* (and the sequel, *The Second Best Exotic Marigold Hotel*). *The Age of Adaline* is a must-see for any woman who has ever longed to remain forever young (which is not the same as being ageless).

Nurture Your "Little Gray Cells." A growing body of research has revealed that cognitive vitality is much more common in late life than previously thought and that it is enhanced by mental and physical exercise. Brains thrive on activity and variety, and they deteriorate when we spend too much time on autopilot. Here are a few simple suggestions for keeping your brain healthy:

Vary routines—take a different route when you walk, change the order in which you brush your teeth, eat breakfast at dinnertime, rearrange your furniture, try a new recipe, mix up your wardrobe by combining items of clothing you've never worn together before, and occasionally write with your "wrong" hand. See *Consult Your Nondominant Hand* (p. 107 in Creativity).

Engage all your senses during the day—take time to smell the roses or a scented candle; listen to music, the sounds of nature, or the squeals of children in the park; chew your food slowly and savor its tastes and textures; spend time really looking at something of beauty, as if for the first or last time; give yourself a head rub, pamper your cat or dog with some extended petting time, or treat yourself to a bubble bath and some loving touch. The capacity for savoring deepens in late life; enjoy! See *Savoring and Delight* (p. 189 in Simplicity).

Keep learning—let your interests lead you into new territory. Explore lifelong learning opportunities through local colleges, senior centers, and other venues; start playing your viola or recorder again, or take up a new instrument; learn a new language; enjoy crossword and other puzzles, and play games (such as scrabble, chess, and bridge).

Pay attention to what is going on around and within you. Keep the television, computer, and other potentially mind-numbing devices off when you are not purposefully using them. Avoid multitasking; practice mindfulness. See *Monotasking* (p. 45 in Authenticity) and *Stay Awake* (p. 84 in Courage).

Stay open to the unexpected—see what adventures arise when things fail to go according to plan. Take appealing and semi-sensible risks; surprise yourself or a friend with something out of the ordinary. Befriending change is not only an ally of cognitive vitality; it also enhances emotional well-being in late life. See *Venture Beyond the Familiar* (p. 103 in Creativity) and *Befriending the Wild Woman* (p. 173 in Necessary Fierceness).

Stay Connected. Research suggests that feeling part of a meaningful social network—regardless of size—is critical for staying healthy, for recovering from illness when it does occur, and for maintaining life satisfaction.[33] For your own and others' sake, stay in touch with people you value—through visits, phone calls, and/ or email—no matter what.

Volunteering can be a mutually nourishing experience and is related to satisfaction in late life. If you are in transition and are not sure where meaning lies for you at this point, explore options for volunteering. Jimmy Carter's *The Virtues of Age* and Ram Dass and Mirabi Bush's *Compassion in Action* are good places to start. See *Serve in Winter* (p. 152 in Compassion) and *Express Kinship* (p. 63 in Self-Transcending Generosity).

Don't let confinement—temporary or otherwise—stop you. If you have telephone and/or computer access, you can send emails and make phone calls in support of causes that matter to you. Share yourself and your gifts—the world needs all of us.

Practice Gratitude and Optimism. Optimism is essential to ageless-ness, and the best method I know for cultivating it is to practice gratitude on a daily basis until it becomes a way of being. Every evening before sleep, write down six blessings of that day—see if you can come up with six different gifts every day for at least a month.

Granted, some days are far harder than others; these are the days when gratitude is most important. Gratitude trains the eye and the heart to notice the innumerable ways we are blessed each day, regard-less of circumstances. It teaches us to look at the half-full glass and see what is there, rather than what is missing, lost, or no longer pos-sible. See *Savoring the Good* (p. 126), *Expressing Gratitude* (p. 127), and *Taming the Wolves of Discontent* (p. 128) in Contentment—and *Slowing Down* (p. 194) and *Being in Nature* (p. 199) in Simplicity.

Savor the Blessings of Your Years. The life review described in the Grace of Remembrance brings greater awareness of the gifts our years have brought, including the experiences that have entailed suffering. Reminiscence also enhances psychological well-being, deepens our store of wisdom, enriches the legacies we have to share with younger members of the human family, and brings a sense of meaning and cohesiveness to our own life. See *The Storying and Re-Storying of Life* (p. 206), *Sharing Stories* (p. 220), and *Stories Without Words* (p. 222) in the Grace of Remembrance.

Celebrate Birthdays. Consider marking (rather than ignoring or denying) your birthdays by reviewing the year you've just lived and honoring or expressing it in some way—making a collage, writing a poem, or . . . And/or make a birthday feast for the people who have been important to you during the year and toast them and their gifts. If getting them all together isn't feasible, how else might you say thank you, for your friends and for this year of your life?

Also see *Celebrating Lives* (p. 224 in Remembrance) and *Celebrate Your Birth Date with a Stretch* (p. 85 in Courage).

Enjoy Your Age in Your Own Way. As Robert Frost advised, "Fall in with what you're asked to accept . . . and turn it your way." Dust off your eccentricity license (p. 30 in Authenticity) and follow your heart. Pursue a new career at sixty if you're inclined, get married at eighty-six if you want to, go somewhere you've always wanted to go at any age. You're only old once—enjoy!

Remember to Laugh and Play. Young children laugh and play as easily and naturally as they breathe, and both of these engender agelessness. Every day presents us with myriad opportunities to laugh—at ourselves, at life events, at human foibles—if we train our eyes to see them, and the capacity for laughter often increases in later life. See *Laughing with Ourselves and Each Other* (p. 127 in Contentment).

Play—like laughter—engenders agelessness, and the lack of it can make us old at any age. It has been said that we do not quit playing because we get old, but rather that we grow old because we stop playing.[34] If it's been a while since you let yourself play, check out Diane Ackerman's *Deep Play* for inspiration. As she notes, play is for adults as well as children, and it's pleasurable, satisfying, absorbing, challenging, restoring, and rejuvenating. See *Remember to Play* (p. 103), *Play with Art Media* (p. 107), and *Enjoy Art* (p. 108) in the Grace of Creativity.

Train Your Shibui Eye. It may take practice to learn to appreciate the beauty of age. Start with nature. Notice the stark beauty of the landscape in winter—the hush of snow, the grace of bare tree limbs, the glistening of raindrops on spider webs, the soft light of the low-hung sun, the endless shifting of exquisite cloud formations, the passion of a winter storm. Take time to see and touch old furniture and well-worn quilts and to notice the radiance of joyful old people's faces and the stories those faces tell.

Then spend some time training your eye to see the beauty in your own face and body. Do not compare what you see to what used to be, but look for the beauty in what is now. What can you find to appreciate? to love?

When I did this last exercise and really looked at myself, I realized that my gray-silver-golden-white hair is much more interesting than it was in its younger, simply auburn years. And I could see beauty in the wrinkles (laugh lines) around my eyes and mouth.

Lingering doubts about the capacity for late-life beauty will likely be softened by gazing at the photographs in these books: Joyce Tenneson's *Wise Women*, Charlotte Painter and Pamela Valois's *Gifts of Age*, and Chester Higgins's *Elder Grace* (portraits of older African American men and women). *The Art of Frank Howell* (with text by Michael French) also contains exquisite paintings, primarily of older Native American women and men.

Grieve Together. A few years ago, three friends and I got together one morning to talk about aging. At the time, all of us were professional (or retired) women in our late sixties with fulfilling lives. None of us is especially focused on appearance, yet the first topic that emerged was our aging bodies and the shame and grief we were feeling about being visibly older women.

We each talked about the things we were finding the hardest to accept: crepey skin, sunspots, thinning hair, and loss of muscle tone. Speaking vulnerably and listening to each other was strangely healing—a sort of group confessional. As each woman described her "imperfections," her beauty, intelligence, and courage were also very apparent to those of us listening. By extension, we were able to see our aging selves in a kinder, more balanced, and loving light.

Consider doing something similar with a few trustworthy companions.

Pursue Meaningful Activities and Non-Activities. Zest and vitality are natural by-products of a meaningful life, and winter is an optimal time to pursue what most matters to us. Engaging in what calls to us most deeply is not the same as "keeping busy"; in fact, it may be antithetical. Living our priorities requires saying no to things that no longer matter in order to free time, energy, and focus for what does. See *Clarifying Genuine Priorities* and *Saying NO to Distractions and Nonessentials* (pp. 196, 197) in Simplicity.

In a culture like ours that emphasizes activity, speed, and extroversion, quieter ways of being—for example, contemplation, meditation, reflection, and prayer—tend to be underappreciated. However, in late life especially, these "non-activities" become more appealing, even essential, for many of us. And research suggests that they have a beneficial impact on those around us too.[35]

Several sources on meditative practices are noted throughout this book (see especially Authenticity, Simplicity, and Contentment). A few of my current favorites are *The Way of the Small* (by Michael Gellert); *Real Happiness: The Power of Meditation* (by Sharon Salzberg); *Listening Below the Noise* (by Anne LeClaire); and *Meditations from the Mat* (by Rolf Gates).

Keep Learning. Information on wellness in the winter of life is readily available through books, newsletters, TED talks and other videos, and on numerous websites. Many universities provide a wealth of cutting-edge material about late-life health and well-being. See, for example, publications by the Stanford Center on Longevity (longevity.stanford.edu/scl-publications), The Harvard Health Letter (www.health.harvard.edu/newsletters/harvard_health_letter), and the University of California, Berkeley Wellness Letter (www.berkeleywellness.com).

Recommended Readings on Agelessness

Bortz, Walter: *We Live Too Short and Die Too Long*

Carstensen, Laura: *A Long Bright Future*

Goldman, Connie: *Late-Life Love*

Goldman, Connie, and Richard Mahler: *Secrets of Becoming a Late Bloomer*

Higgins, Chester, Jr.: *Elder Grace*

Hill, Robert D.: *Seven Strategies for Positive Aging*

Jamison, Kay Redfield: *Exuberance*

Martinez, Mario: *The MindBody Code*

Nuland, Sherwin: *The Art of Aging*

Painter, Charlotte, and Pamela Valois: *Gifts of Age*

Rowe, John W., and Robert L. Kahn: *Successful Aging*

Sadler, William: *The Third Age*

Tenneson, Joyce: *Wise Women*

11: The Grace of Wisdom

*"To understand wisdom fully and correctly probably
requires more wisdom than any of us have . . . [and]
it is almost certainly not something we can ever achieve. . . .
The recognition that total understanding will always
elude us is itself a sign of wisdom."*
—Robert Sternberg, *Wisdom: Its Nature,
Origins, and Development*

Experience is an excellent teacher, provided we are willing students in the school of wisdom that is human life. Long years bring a rich store of experiences from which we can garner insight and understanding—provided our eyes, ears, and minds stay open, and our hearts remain teachable.

Witnessing the unfolding of our own and others' lives over decades, we become better able to see situations as they are and to sense how best to respond. At the same time, we learn that the vast, complex, and unpredictable mystery of life is beyond our comprehension and control. Thus, the Grace of Wisdom is a paradoxical mix of active engagement and detached reflection, clear seeing and healthy uncertainty, and effective action and holy inaction.

Wisdom and Folly

Wisdom, from the root *weid,* which means "to see," is difficult to put into words, let alone to reduce to a single definition. And wisdom

252 ❄ Winter's Graces

can take widely varying forms, as gerontologists William Randall and Gary Kenyon point out: "Wisdom might express itself . . . in the late-life political activism of a Bertrand Russell, or in the eccentric behavior of a Zen [master] . . . [or] in words . . . or in a touch, in a look, or even in silence and simply *being there*."[1] Despite its disparate forms and its resistance to being pinned down by words, we usually recognize wisdom when we encounter it.

As a starting place, wisdom can be viewed as a breadth and depth of understanding, coupled with the capacity to apply it sensitively and effectively in specific situations, especially important, complex, and uncertain ones. Wisdom begins with experience and is illuminated by some sort of reflection. It is refined by the perennial willingness to ask questions and entertain doubt. The latter is especially important, as this well-known folktale demonstrates:

Several blind men are trying to discover what an elephant is by touching it. Each man feels a different part—leg, tail, trunk, ear, tusk, or belly—and concludes that the elephant is like a pillar, a rope, a tree branch, a fan, a pipe, or a wall.

When the men compare notes, of course, they are in complete disagreement. Each argues that his impression of the elephant is the truth and that others are mistaken. In some versions of the story, the men come to blows. In others, they stop arguing and start listening to each other, and thus begin to understand the elephant more fully.[2]

Like a blind man who is unwilling to question what he thinks he knows, a foolish woman mistakes her own point of view for the truth. A wise woman, on the other hand, recognizes that her knowledge is limited. She listens to others' experience and continually seeks to understand more fully.

Gerontologist James Meacham observes that without the capacity for doubt we fall into "the error of believing that [we] can see all that can be seen . . . [and know] all that can be known."[3] William Randall and Gary Kenyon agree: "The instant we congratulate ourselves on how sage we have become, we taint any insight we have managed to attain."[4]

Wisdom in Winter

The link between old age and wisdom is intuitive, universal, and long-standing. In village and tribal cultures especially, wise elders are honored and consulted on important matters. In folktales, it is often an old man or woman who appears as a wisdom figure to assist the young hero at a crucial moment in the story. And in ancient myths from around the world, the goddess of wisdom is often personified as an older woman—Sophia, for example, and Oshun, Sapientia, Metis, Egeria, Anahita (disambiguation), Danu, Chokmah, Sigurdrifta, Voluspa, Tara, Hecate, and others.

Age does not guarantee wisdom, of course, nor youth preclude it, yet long years provide a wealth of experiences that are the beginning of wisdom. As psychologist Deirdre Kramer points out, "The endless source of stress and opportunities for growth in one's life will provide the person with ongoing possibilities for maintenance and development of wisdom-related capacities."[5]

In addition, a number of late-life developments discussed in earlier chapters provide a rich harvest of attitudes and aptitudes that contribute to wisdom, especially the taste for reflection, the broadening and deepening of perspective, tolerance for uncomfortable emotions, the befriending of adversity, and a growing appreciation for paradox and for letting be. Each of Winter's Graces fosters capacities that support the flowering of wisdom in late life.

The Grace of Authenticity, for example, brings a taste for reflection, deeper awareness and appreciation of who we really are (our gifts and wounds), and the ability to stand with what we know (even in the face of opposition or criticism). The Grace of Self-Transcending Generosity enables us to see beyond our personal agenda and engenders humility, which helps us question our current understanding. The foundation of wisdom is the effective use of the authentic self, coupled with the recognition that we are instruments of something greater than ourselves.

The Grace of Courage fosters the willingness to risk our personal comfort and safety on behalf of something important. Psychological courage is particularly important in helping us to face the truth about ourselves and the world and to keep learning from experience. The Grace of Creativity brings freedom, flexibility, and the capacity to learn from our mistakes. Courage and Creativity both give us important training in living on the edge and leaping in the dark. They help us to remain flexible as we encounter important, complex, and uncertain situations.

The Grace of Contentment broadens and deepens our vision so that we can see situations from multiple perspectives, learn from adversity, tolerate paradox, and let go and let be, when appropriate. The Grace of Compassion begins with loving kindness toward ourselves and helps us to view others' distress with tolerance and understanding. This pair of graces helps us work free of our emotional limitations so that we are able to see situations clearly and respond to others effectively and with kindness.

Necessary Fierceness enables us to be ferocious when gentler means are insufficient and to set important limits, as needed. The Grace of Simplicity teaches us to honor what is most meaningful and to relinquish distractions and nonessentials. Both of these graces encourage the development of discernment and detachment, which are integral to wisdom.

The Grace of Remembrance entails the privilege of reviewing the whole of our life and garnering its wisdom. It helps us to recognize the deeper human story of which we are a part and to clarify the legacies we have to offer the human family. The Grace of Agelessness reconnects us to all the ages we have been and the varied blessings of each of life's seasons. These two graces entail looking back as well as living forward, bringing greater awareness of our gifts and vulnerabilities and the wisdom and hope we have to share with others.

The heroines in the stories throughout this book illustrate the ways in which each grace contributes to the crowning grace of Wisdom, in its various dimensions. For example, these wise women exhibit deep understanding of the human heart ("The Running Stick"), yet listen to others' input and adapt to unexpected developments ("The Little Old Woman Who Went to the North Wind"). They are motivated by concern for the greater good ("Ubong and the Headhunters"), and at the same time honor their own important needs ("The Woman in the Moon"). Some step forward to help in an important and uncertain situation ("The Wise Woman" and "Poppet Caught a Thief"), while others watch and wait for the ripeness of time ("The Rope of Ash" and "The Son of a Goblin").

Here is one last folktale, from Haiti, about an old woman who embodies many facets of the Grace of Wisdom: knowing and continuing to learn; giving and setting limits; and acting on behalf of something important, or letting it be, as needed. The four characters in the story—two old women and two young ones—provide some instructive contrasts between a life of wisdom (based on openness and generosity) and a life of foolishness (rooted in arrogance and selfishness).

Mother of the Waters

There was once a young girl whose mother and father were both dead. As she had no way to get anything to eat, she had to hire herself out as a servant. She worked for a woman who lived by the river. But even though the woman had a daughter the same age as the servant girl, she showed no kindness to her. She beat her and spoke roughly to her and gave her only scraps to eat.

One day, the woman sent the servant girl to the river to wash the silverware. As the girl was washing the silver, a tiny silver teaspoon slipped through her fingers and was carried away by the water. The servant girl reached for the teaspoon, but the current was moving too swiftly. She went back to the house and told her mistress what had happened.

"Find my teaspoon," the woman screamed, "or never return to my house!"

The servant girl returned to the river and followed the stream. She walked all day without finding the teaspoon, and as the sun began to set in the sky, she started crying. An old woman sitting on a stone near the river's edge asked her why she was crying.

"I have dropped my mistress's silver teaspoon in the river. She says if I do not find it, I may not return. I will have no work. How will I eat?"

The old woman did not answer. Instead, she asked, "Will you wash my back?"

"Of course," the girl answered.

She soaped and scrubbed the old woman's back, but it was rough and hard and covered with sores and thistles, and the girl's hands were soon bleeding.

"What is it?" the woman asked.

"It is nothing," the girl answered.

"Let me see your hands," the old woman said.

The girl held them out. The old woman spit on them. The cuts closed up, and the girl's hands were as they were before.

"Come home with me," the old woman said, "and I will give you dinner."

She led the girl to her home in the mountains and gave her banana pudding. Then they went to sleep. The next day, after the girl had swept the yard, the woman gave her a bone, a grain of rice, and one bean and told her to make dinner.

"Grandmother," the girl said respectfully, "please forgive me, but I do not know how to make dinner with these."

"It is simple," the old woman said. "Place them in a pot of boiling water and dinner will soon be ready."

The girl followed the woman's directions, and by noon a delicious-smelling casserole of rice, beans, and meat was steaming inside the pot.

As they ate the old woman told the girl: "I will be going out.

In a few hours, a wild cat will come and beg for food. Do not give it any food. Beat it with my stick."

A few hours after the woman had left, the girl heard a mewing outside the door. *Me-ow. Me-ow. Me-ow.* The cat was so thin and hungry the girl did not have the heart to hit it. She brought it a saucer of milk and watched it eat. After a while the cat went away.

A short time later the old woman returned. She was pleased with the girl, so the servant girl stayed on with her. The girl helped the old woman, who always gave her enough to eat. Then, after several months, the old woman told her it was time for her to return to her mistress.

"Yes," said the girl, "but how can I go back without the silver teaspoon?"

"Walk down the road," the old woman said. "When you come to the first crossroads you will see a pile of eggs lying on some straw. The larger ones will call out: *Take me, take me!* Take one of the smaller eggs and break it open at the next crossroads."

The servant girl thanked the old woman and set out. At the first crossroads, she saw the pile of eggs. The larger ones cried: *Take me, take me!*

The girl chose the smallest egg, and when she cracked it open at the next crossroads, out came a tiny box, which grew and grew until it filled her arms. The girl opened it and inside were forks and knives and spoons—all made of silver.

The woman and her daughter were so jealous when they saw the servant girl's box of silverware that they made her tell the story of how she had gotten it, three times.

Then, the very next morning, the mother sent her own daughter down to the river to wash the silverware. The girl didn't even bother to wash the silverware. She simply threw the small coffee teaspoon into the river and went home.

"I have lost the coffee spoon," the girl declared.

"Then go and find it," the mother said knowingly, "and do not come home until you do."

The daughter walked alongside the river all day. Then, toward evening, she saw the old woman sitting on a stone. Immediately, she began to cry.

"Why are you crying?" the woman asked.

"Oh-oh. I have lost my mother's silver spoon. She says I may not go home unless I find it. What shall I do?"

"Will you wash my back?" the woman asked.

The girl took the soap and began to wash the woman's back, when the thistles on the woman's back cut her hands.

"Oh-oh!" she cried.

"What is it?" asked the woman.

"It's your filthy rotting back. It cut my hands, and they are bleeding!"

The old woman took the girl's hands and spit on them, and they were healed. Then she brought her to the mountain and fed her supper.

The next morning, the woman gave the girl a bone, a grain of rice, and one bean and told her to make dinner.

"With this garbage?" said the girl.

"What a sorry tongue you have," the woman answered. "I only hope you are not as nasty as your words. Place what I have given you in a pot of boiling water, and dinner will soon be ready."

At noon, the pot was filled with rice and beans and meat. They ate their meal, then the old woman said, "I am going out. In a few hours, a wild cat will come and beg for food. Do not give it any food. Beat it with my stick."

Some time after the old woman left, the girl heard a mewing outside. *Me-ow. Me-ow. Me-ow.*

She grabbed the old woman's stick and rushed for the cat. She hit it and hit it and hit it and hit it until she broke one of its legs. Much later that evening, the old woman returned. She was leaning on a cane and limping, for one of her legs was broken.

The next morning, she told the girl: "You must leave my house today. You will not learn, and I cannot help you anymore."

"But I will not go home without my silverware," the girl insisted.

"Then I shall give you one last bit of advice. At the next cross-roads, you will find a pile of eggs lying on some straw. The larger ones will call out: *Take me, take me!* Choose one of the smaller eggs and break it open at the next crossroads."

The girl ran out of the house and down the road. When she came to the first crossroads the larger eggs called out, *Take me, take me!*

"I am not foolish," said the girl. "If an egg speaks to me, I will listen. If it is a large one, all the better."

She chose the largest egg and broke it open at the next cross-roads. Out came all kinds of lizards, goblins, demons, and devils and ate the girl up.[6]

Some Questions for Reflection

1. What part of this story speaks to you most strongly, and how is that related to your life?

2. When have you felt like a mistreated servant, and how did you respond?

3. Who are the people whom you have treated unkindly, in thought, word, or deed?

4. How willing are you to allow yourself to cry when you are sad? To say, "I don't know" when you don't?

5. What are the sore places within you that need care, and how do those wounds inadvertently injure others?

6. How willing are you to trust in life when it seems you have limited resources (like a bone, a grain of rice, and one bean with which to make a meal)?

7. How able are you to take instruction but also to follow the dictates of your own heart when the two conflict?

8. Where do you see evidence of the stingy mistress and of the generous old woman within yourself?

9. How might your life benefit from the old woman's advice to choose the small and simple, even though the big things "call" to you?

10. Where and how do jealousy and greed poison your life, as they did the mistress and her daughter's?

11. Where in your life are you cutting corners and going through motions like the daughter? What does that cost you and others?

12. What parts of you interfere with your ability to learn?

13. What/who are the situations or people in your life that you would be wise to send on their way, as the old woman does with the second girl?

14. If you were to take to heart the medicine of this story, what shift—large or small—would you make in your life?

Reflections

This is a fine teaching tale about wisdom and the qualities that nurture it (openness, genuineness, generosity, compassion, humility, and courage). In contrast, the cruel woman and her daughter demonstrate the dead end toward which greed, pretense, selfishness, laziness, impatience, cruelty, and arrogance lead.

The old woman sitting by the river embodies the blend of detachment and engagement with the world that Erik Erikson describes as the essence of wisdom.[7] Her interactions with the young women—framed as questions, requests, and suggestions—leave them free to find their own way. She does not coerce, interfere, or manipulate; she allows each to make her own choices and, hopefully, to learn from them. Her detached concern is also apparent in her taking the girls under her wing for a time, serving them as best she can, and, when the time is right, releasing each to her fate.

Three Questions. The old woman enters the story at an important juncture, responding to the cries of a girl in distress. She begins by asking three simple yet masterful questions that quickly get to the crux of the matter and reveal a great deal about the girl's character: "Why are you crying?" "Will you wash my back?" and "What's the matter?"

The servant girl is vulnerable, truthful, and kind in her responses. Her tears are a genuine expression of her emotions; she is willing to help the old woman, though she is in distress herself; and she demonstrates discretion and graciousness in not mentioning the cuts she receives in washing the old woman's back. The girl is frightened, hungry, and kindhearted.

In contrast, the same three questions reveal the second girl's pretense, selfishness, and cruelty. She is playing a game, going through motions in order to receive her own chest of silver, and her tears are a manipulation. She agrees to the old woman's request for help but shames her for her "filthy rotting back" and blames her angrily for cutting her hands.

Though this girl's character and ulterior motives are obvious, the old woman heals her cuts and offers to take her home and feed her. Rather than write her off as an unpleasant and hopeless case, she extends the same healing, hospitality, and opportunities that she gives the first girl and then waits to see what will happen.

Three Tasks. The old woman gives each girl a series of tasks. Like the three questions, these scenarios are tests of the girls' character and capacity for learning. The first—making dinner from a single grain of rice, one bean, and a bone—reveals the servant girl's willingness to admit her lack of knowledge, to follow direction, and to trust that something good can come from meager resources. In contrast, the second girl complains that the old woman has not given her enough to work with and dismisses the simple ingredients as "garbage." Her arrogance and unkindness are becoming more apparent, and the old woman gives her a warning: "I only hope you are not as nasty as your words."

The second task—not to feed a hungry wild cat and to beat it with a stick—is a test of discernment, an essential dimension of wisdom. The first girl does not "have the heart" to hit the cat and instead gives it a saucer of milk. In this instance, she does not follow the old woman's instructions because they go against her own sense of what is good and right. She responds with compassion and generosity, rather than doing what she is told.

For the second girl, there is no conflict and thus no opportunity to learn discernment; the old woman's directions are entirely compatible with her own cruel inclinations. She immediately grabs the stick and beats the cat so badly that she breaks its leg. And she fails to make the connection between the cat's and the old woman's broken legs and her own behavior. It's worth noting that the woman does not instantly toss the girl out at this point. Instead, she waits until morning and in three short statements communicates a great deal:

"You must leave my house today" sets a clear boundary and time frame. (*A wise woman takes care of herself and sets necessary limits, without apology.*)

"You will not learn" is a gift, the truth expressed in a nonjudgmental way. Rather than berating the girl for her cruelty, stubbornness, and other flaws, the old woman states a fact, which is potentially a useful piece of information that could serve the girl if she would heed it. Sadly, but not surprisingly, she doesn't. (*A wise woman speaks the truth with as much kindness as possible.*)

And in saying, "I cannot help you anymore," the old woman is acknowledging the truth of the situation and her own limits. She has done all she can, and it was not enough to turn the girl's heart. (*A wise woman recognizes her limitations and senses when it is time to let go and let be.*)

The third task comes into play when it is time for each girl to leave the old woman's home and find her own way. The girls are departing under very different circumstances, but again they are given the same opportunity and instructions: at the first crossroads, choose one of the smaller eggs—not the big ones that call out—and break it open at the second crossroads.

The servant girl thanks the old woman and follows her sage advice, picking the smallest egg at the first crossroads and cracking it open at the second. She has been a good student. She has learned to listen to herself and to the old woman's wise counsel, to respond to others' suffering with kindness and compassion (even when told to do otherwise), to see beneath appearances, and to make thoughtful choices.

When the second girl is told to leave, she refuses to go without her silver. Instead of gratitude, she expresses defiance and entitlement. The old woman gives her the same instructions about the eggs, but once again the girl is led astray by her arrogance ("I am not foolish") and her refusal to learn.

The Crossroads. The girls must make a choice at the first crossroads, though they cannot yet see what lies inside the eggs. This important yet uncertain moment is a test of the girls' capacity for wisdom, for seeing in the dark. The girl-who-would-not-learn makes a choice based on arrogance, greed, and external advice. (Take me!) The young heroine's decision reflects her ability to see beneath appearances and to listen to the voice of wisdom, her own and the old woman's.

It is not until the second crossroads, however, that the eggs are broken open and the fruits of these choices become apparent. As Randall and Kenyon observe, "Wisdom requires that, in the end, we jump or leap, and whether an action is deemed to be wise or not is often not known until after the fact."[8] It is so often the case that we must make the best decision we can at a given time and then wait to see how it unfolds. Part of wisdom is reflecting on decisions we have made after the fact and learning from them, regardless of the outcome.

⟫⟫ *Cultivating Wisdom* ⟪⟪

The crowning grace of winter, Wisdom emerges naturally from the interplay and cultivation of the rest of Winter's Graces. Five practices—most of them mentioned earlier—encourage the flowering of this grace: continuing to learn, spending time in nature, staying connected, moving toward challenges, and continuing to play and celebrate.

Continuing to Learn

Remaining open-minded and openhearted encourages the flowering of wisdom; becoming enamored with what we think we know undermines it. Psychologist Robert Sternberg has identified four common fallacies that lead toward folly rather than wisdom:

- *The Egocentrism Fallacy:* thinking that the world revolves around you, and acting in ways that benefit yourself, regardless of the effect on others
- *The Omniscience Fallacy:* believing that you know all there is to know and therefore do not need to listen to others' counsel
- *The Omnipotence Fallacy:* believing that your intelligence and/or education somehow make you all-powerful
- *The Invulnerability Fallacy:* believing that you can do whatever you want and that others will not be able to expose, harm, or hold you accountable[9]

The glaring and seemingly growing presence of this gruesome quartet on the world stage (and in our daily interactions) is painfully obvious. Watch for these fallacies and other attitudes in yourself that cause suffering for others and stunt the growth of wisdom.

A wise woman understands that the gathering of wisdom is a lifelong endeavor and remains open to doubt and new learning. She watches and listens to others; reflects on her own experience; observes her thoughts, emotions, speech, and actions (and their effects); and makes adjustments as needed.

Spending Time in Nature

Nature is a remarkable teacher. Spending time in her presence can inspire, restore, and heal us. It can also teach us a great deal about the cycles of life, broaden and deepen our perspective, and remind us of our true place in the world. Wise men and women in the East and West have long prescribed time in Mother Nature's abundantly beautiful (and sometimes fierce) schoolhouse.

In *The Second Half of Life*, Angeles Arrien points out that being in nature slows us down so that we can do the kind of reflecting that wisdom requires. "Nature's rhythm is medium to slow. . . . [and] there are two things we can never do in the fast lane: we can neither deepen our experience nor integrate it, both essential tasks in the second half of life."[10]

A wise woman visits Mother Nature often and keeps learning from her.

Staying Connected

A nourishing social network is widely regarded as one of the essential components of healthy aging (p. 245 in Agelessness). In addition to their positive effects on physical health and emotional well-being, mutually beneficial relationships support the development of wisdom. Psychologist Ruthellen Josselson observes that for women in the second half of life in particular, relationships are an important path to wisdom.

> The capacity to embrace differences in relationship enlarges the self. . . . This is a soulful knowing, in which one feels a deeper and more meaningful connection to others who are experienced in their contradictory—and often frustrating—wholeness. . . . Understanding more about others . . . may transform a woman's view of the world and her place in it. Through reflection on their experiences in relationships, women come to find new significance in old truths, knowing what they always in some sense knew, but knowing it in a new, deeper sense.[11]

Randall and Kenyon suggest that most of us can benefit from what they call "wisdom environments," where we can tell and listen to one another's stories in a nonjudgmental way. Friendship can serve as a wisdom environment, as can marriage, psychotherapy, a life-review group, or even a soulful conversation with someone we meet in passing. Reading James Meacham's phrase "supportive and sharing relationships within a wisdom atmosphere,"[12] I thought of my women's group:

When we were in our twenties and thirties, the group spontaneously developed a process we called Name That Gift. We invoked it when one of us was describing a difficult experience and was struggling to make sense of it. Sometimes it took all of our efforts to identify a potential gift or opportunity for learning inside the trouble. In our youth, Name That Gift was a way of helping each other through hard times, but now I see it as a group effort at distilling wisdom too—listening to one another, looking deeply into an experience, and seeking to learn from it. I think that these decades of sharing our stories and searching for meaning in our own and each other's life experience has helped us grow into wiser versions of ourselves than we might have otherwise.

A wise woman invests herself in a few genuinely nourishing relationships, sharing and listening in ways that help bring out the best in herself and in others.

Moving Toward Life

It has been said that fools rush in where wise ones fear to tread, but it is also the case that wise ones are enriched by moving toward challenges that the foolish might avoid out of fear. Situations that are important, complex, and uncertain test our mettle and our courage; they are also potentially our greatest wisdom teachers. I love this statement by author and naturalist Diane Ackerman about risk, passion, and lived experience, from which wisdom flows:

> The great affair, the love affair with life, is to live as variously as possible, to groom one's curiosity like a high-spirited thoroughbred, climb aboard, and gallop over the thick, sunstruck hills every day.
>
> Where there is no risk, the emotional terrain is flat and unyielding, and, despite all its dimensions, valleys, pinnacles, and detours, life will seem to have none of its magnificent geography, only a length.
>
> It began in mystery, and it will end in mystery, but what a savage and beautiful country lies in between.[13]

A wise woman keeps exploring. She moves toward important experiences (even frightening ones) and garners wisdom from discomfort and adversity, as well as from joy and delight.

Celebrating

A wise man once taught me something of great value: the importance of celebrating. We worked together in a market research firm, where we were often engaged in three or more projects at once—completing one, starting another, and exploring possibilities of others. Before there was a word for multitasking, and the business world was hurried but not yet moving at warp speed, he taught me to take time to pause at the end of a project and review it—to appreciate what went well, to identify what I might do differently next time, and above all to celebrate the ending before moving on to something else.

Rabbi Abraham Joshua Heschel points out that such celebrating is not frivolous and, in fact, is vitally important for psychological and spiritual development:

> [People] of our time [are] losing the power of celebration. Instead of celebrating, [we seek] to be amused or entertained. Celebration is an active state, an act of expressing reverence or appreciation. To be entertained is a passive state—it is to receive pleasure afforded by an amusing act or a spectacle. . . . Celebration is a confrontation, giving attention to the transcendent meaning of one's [life].[14]

Consider doing some kind of ritual, writing, or art project to celebrate the crowning grace of Wisdom before ten more of "the 10,000 things" pull your attention elsewhere. Pausing to celebrate is a gift to the nervous system and helps integrate and enrich experience. And it can be fun. Write a few haiku, make a collage or a wisdom doll, weave a crown of wisdom for yourself from willow or grapevine cuttings, or create a feast for a few people who have supported you in becoming your best and wisest self.

A wise woman makes the time to play and express herself and to celebrate important moments and milestones in her life, alone and with those she loves.

Suggested Readings on Wisdom

Arrien, Angeles: *The Second Half of Life*

Bianchi, Eugene: *Aging as a Spiritual Journey*

Bolen, Jean Shinoda: *Goddesses in Older Women*

Bourgeault, Cynthia: *The Wisdom Jesus*

Chittister, Joan: *The Gift of Years*

Dass, Ram: *Still Here*

Estés, Clarissa Pinkola: *The Dangerous Old Woman* (audio series)

Friedman, Jerry: *Earth's Elders*

Moore, Thomas: *Care of the Soul*

Randall, William, and Gary Kenyon: *Ordinary Wisdom*

Rohr, Richard: *Falling Upward*

Schachter-Shalomi, Zalman, and Ronald S. Miller: *From Age-ing to Sage-ing*

Schaefer, Carol: *Grandmothers Counsel the World*

Somé, Malidoma Patrice: *The Healing Wisdom of Africa*

Sternberg, Robert: *Wisdom*

Woodman, Marion: *The Crown of Age* (audiobook)

Young-Eisendrath, Polly, and Melvin E. Miller: *The Psychology of Mature Spirituality*

Blessing

In his poem "Vacillation," William Butler Yeats describes a joyful epiphany he experienced in the late autumn of his life:

> My body of a sudden blazed;
> And twenty minutes more or less
> It seemed, so great my happiness,
> That I was blessed and could bless.

To reflect on our years and recognize that we are indeed blessed is one of the sweetest gifts of age. And it is intertwined with a second: to know that we are capable of blessing others. As winter's women, we have decades of experience from which to draw. We each have memories, stories, and hopefully wisdom gathered from it all. We have survived heartbreak and known joy and delight in small if not in large things. And as grandmothers, we have the privilege of blessing the world—especially the young—guiding them as best we can, while remembering that they must find their own way—as we must.

The word *old* derives from the root *al-*, which means "to grow" and "to nourish." As older adults, these are our tasks: to continue growing and to nurture others in becoming their deepest and best selves. These are not easy tasks, but they are vital, meaningful, and often joyful ones. And, like the heroines and heroes in myths and folktales, we have allies.

Nature is our ally. Developmental trends in the winter of life support us in becoming more authentic, compassionate, humble, generous, and wise. We can resist these nudges, just as we can rail against difficult situations in which we find ourselves, or we can bless them, work with them, and learn and grow from them.

In his beautiful book *Falling Upward*, Franciscan brother Richard Rohr describes the ebb and flow of necessary suffering and spacious grace that characterize later life:

> There is still darkness in the second half of life—in fact maybe even more. But there is now a changed capacity to hold it creatively and with less anxiety. . . . Life is much more spacious now, the boundaries of the container having been enlarged by the constant addition of new experiences and relationships. You are like an expandable suitcase, and you became so almost without your noticing.[1]

Folklore is our ally. Myths and folk stories from around the world illustrate that a vital, creative, meaningful, and generous late adulthood is a real possibility. In addition, the International Council of Thirteen Indigenous Grandmothers, Malidoma Somé, and other tribal peoples have begun sharing some of their traditions and wisdom with the broader human family, helping us to remember the vital role that elders play in guiding the young and in protecting the beauty and balance of the natural world.[2]

Trustworthy visionaries are our allies. Meredith Little, Michael Meade, Richard Rohr, and others offer workshops rooted in traditional wisdom, some of which are specifically designed for emerging elders.[3] An increasing number of courses and seminars around the country address the challenges and blessings of the second half of life, and the books and audiotapes of Clarissa Pinkola Estés, Marion Woodman, Jean Bolen, Harry Moody and David Carroll, Eugene Bianchi, and others offer guidance on growing into elderhood. Also see the wisdom-filled poetry of Rumi, Mary Oliver, Wendell Berry, John O'Donohue, David Whyte, and others.[4]

We are one another's allies. Women seem to have a natural affinity for gathering in circles and sharing their experiences with one another, especially their struggles. In lifelong learning classes and in workshops, I've witnessed the healing that can occur when women (and men) talk with trustworthy others about their fears of growing old and about the challenges of aging as well as its blessings. If you aren't already part of such a group, I encourage you to seek one or create one, and see what happens.

Life itself is an ally. There is a delightful bit of dialogue in the film *Shakespeare in Love* between an older man and young Will. They are talking about the nature of the theater business in sixteenth-century London, but they could easily be referring to the challenges of aging:

In a moment of discouragement, the older man says: "The natural condition is one of insurmountable obstacles on the road to imminent disaster."

"What do we do?" asks young Will anxiously.

"Nothing. Strangely enough, it all turns out well."

"How?"

"I don't know," the older man responds. "It's a mystery."[5]

Despite seemingly insurmountable obstacles and rumors of disasters on the road ahead, things do turn out well. Not necessarily how or when we expect, but they do turn out. And the wheel of life keeps turning.

Disasters happen, but so do enormous acts of courage, generosity, and kindness—every day. And while there may be little we can do to change "the natural condition," there is a lot that we can do—and refrain from doing—that will make the world a far better place than it would otherwise be.

For the sake of the world and its children, it matters that we be the kindest and wisest human beings we can possibly be. That entails continually facing the truth of who we are with firm gentleness and ceasing to do those things that create suffering for others and ourselves. It means mustering our courage, humor, and trust in this beautiful Mystery in order to keep sharing whatever we have been given until the moment of our death. It means stepping into our elder shoes.

According to some, the Buddha's last words to his disciples were, "Be a light." May we each be a light in the world, a "shining person," as Richard Rohr would say.[6] May we be old in the truest sense, continuing to grow and nurturing those around us, especially the young ones. May we all—regardless of age—recognize that we are blessed and keep discerning each day how best to bless one another.

Credits

Permission to reprint their copyrighted material is gratefully acknowledged to the following:

Leslau, Charlotte and Wolf, eds. "The Midwife of Dakar," from *African Folk Tales*. Mount Vernon, NY: Peter Pauper Press, 1963. Reprinted with the permission of the authors' daughter, Sylvia Grotz.

Ramanujan, A. K. "Tell It to the Walls," from *Folktales from India*, copyright © 1991 by A. K. Ramanujan. Used by permission of Pantheon Books, an imprint of the Knopf Doubleday Publishing Group, a division of Penguin Random House LLC. All rights reserved.

Randolph, Vance. "Poppet Caught a Thief," from *Who Blowed Up the Church House? and Other Ozark Folk Tales*. New York: Columbia University Press, 1952. Reprinted with the permission of the University of Arkansas, Special Collections.

Wolkstein, Diane. "Mother of the Waters," from *The Magic Orange Tree and Other Haitian Folktales*. New York: Alfred A. Knopf, 1978. Reprinted with the permission of the author's daughter, Rachel Zucker.

Notes

Introduction

1. Initial studies in gerontology were conducted with elders in hospitals, which led to a negatively skewed view of aging. Psychologists Mary and Kenneth Gergen describe this misunderstanding of late life as an artifact of these early "Dark Ages of aging." (Gergen, "Positive Aging," 3.) Despite a steady stream of research since the 1970s that refutes the loss-focused view of late life, the fear of aging persists, most notably in the United States.

2. Two of the earliest books offering a more balanced and positive view of aging are Dr. Robert Butler's *Why Survive? Being Old in America* and Henri Nouwen's *Aging: The Fulfillment of Life*. More recent titles on the topic are noted throughout the book.

3. Practices for maintaining health and well-being in old age have been well documented by gerontologists, physicians, and others. See, for example, Dr. Christiane Northrup's *Goddesses Never Age*; Mario Martinez's *The MindBody Code: How to Change the Beliefs That Limit Your Health, Longevity, and Success*; Dr. Sherwin B. Nuland's *The Art of Aging: A Doctor's Prescription for Well-Being*; and Dr. Gene Cohen's *The Mature Mind: The Positive Power of the Aging Brain*.

4. Not only is the percentage of adults who suffer from dementia relatively low; it continues to decline. In "Dementia Rates Are Falling in the U.S.," Howard Gleckman relates the results of a 2016 study:

In 2000, about 11.6 percent of all those 65 and older had dementia. By 2012, that had fallen to about 8.6 percent, a decline of almost one-quarter. . . . Even among the very old, the decline in dementia risk was noticeable—falling from 34 percent in 2000 to a bit below 30 percent in 2012.

And in terms of physical disability, only about 5 percent of adults over sixty-five are so frail that they require full-time care in nursing homes. According to Rowe and Kahn, "Older people . . . are much more likely to age well than to become decrepit and dependent. . . . Relatively few elderly people live in nursing homes . . . only 5.2 percent" (Rowe and Kahn, *Successful Aging*, 16). Furthermore, very few older people who do not live in nursing homes are debilitatingly frail. According to the CDC, only 6.4 percent of noninstitutionalized adults over sixty-five need help with personal care from others ("Older Persons' Health," National Center for Health Statistics, Centers for Disease Control and Prevention, updated May 3, 2017, www.cdc.gov/nchs/fastats/older-american-health.htm).

5. Gerontologists have observed the "chronological non-conformity" of older adults, and many now question the predictive value of chronological age. As Dr. Walter Bortz observes, "[Chronological] age is becoming increasingly irrelevant to how we live, what we experience, and who we are becoming" (Bortz, *We Live*, 199).

6. McCoy, *Celtic Women's Spirituality*, 69.

7. The term *winter's graces* came to me upon waking one winter's morning when I had been struggling for some time with the challenge of how to talk about old age without scaring people. Later on, a woman in my Gifts of Age class told me that Carl Jung had alluded to "the graces of winter" decades earlier. I've since looked and haven't been able to find that phrase in his *Collected Works*. I may have seen it somewhere at some point and forgotten, or it may simply have bubbled up from the unconscious. I'm glad it came, by whatever means.

8. Bolen, *Crones Don't Whine*.

9. Woodman, *Crown of Age*, and Gardner, *Celebratin*

10. According to the Population Reference Bureau's 2016 report, there are over 46 million Americans over sixty-five; that number is expected to reach 98 million by 2060.

11. I am especially grateful to the inspiring elder students in my classes at the Osher Lifelong Learning Institute at Sonoma State University, who taught me a great deal about later life.

12. When he was six, my son Logan came up with the phrase "a full grown-up" in the midst of a conversation with my sister, who had just told him she was returning to school (at about age forty). He paused for a moment—clearly puzzled—and then said, "Oh, then you're not a full grown-up?"

Presumably, he had always considered Helen a grown-up, but in his pre-operational mind, children go to school and adults do not. So an adult going to school was bewildering. I loved his turn of phrase, and "full grown-up" seems an apt description of what the graces of winter support us in becoming.

13. Yolen, *Gray Heroes*, xxix, xxxiv.

14. Estés, *Women Who Run*, 15–16.

1: *The Grace of Authenticity*

1. The phrase about "[wearing] other people's faces" in the youthful pursuit of acceptance and approval comes from May Sarton's "Now I Become Myself" (*Collected Poems*, 156).

2. In her pioneering work, *Feminine Psychology*, Karen Horney (1885–1952) challenged Freud's view of women as masochistic and asserted that we are trained to place primary value on relationships and others' needs, to the detriment of our autonomy and self worth. Psychologist Carol Gilligan elaborates on this theme in her book, *In a Different Voice*.

3. Lamott, *Plan B*, 171–72.

4. Allen, "Indian Summer," in Pearsall, *The Other Within*, 236–38.

5. Barbara Walker's *The Crone* and Demetra George's *Mysteries of the Dark Moon* present two excellent and quite different accounts of the rise of patriarchy and the fear of women's power, which culminated in the European (and, later, North American) witch hunts between the fifteenth and eighteenth centuries.

I also highly recommend *The Goddess Trilogy* (directed by Donna Read [National Film Board of Canada, 1989]), a beautifully crafted documentary on the history of the sacred feminine and its impact on the lives of women. Part Two specifically addresses the "Burning Times," but all three parts are well worth seeing.

6. "The Little Old Woman Who Went to the North Wind" is reprinted with permission from ABC-CLIO. Barchers, *Wise Women*, 305–7.

7. "Medicine," in this context, refers to the intrinsic capacity of a time-tested story to touch each person who hears it in a unique and powerfully healing way. As Clarissa Pinkola Estes explains, "Stories are medicine . . . . They have such power; they do not require that we do, be, act anything – we need only listen. The remedies for the repair or reclamation of any lost psychic drive are contained in stories. Stories engender the excitement, sadness, questions, longings, and understandings that spontaneously

bring [whatever is needed] . . . back to the surface." Estes, *Women Who Run*, 15-16.

8. Jungian analyst Allan Chinen uses the phrase *emancipated innocence* to refer to this freedom from social convention enjoyed by elders in many cultures. Chinen, *In the Ever*, 80–82.

9. "The Wise Woman" is reprinted with permission from ABC-CLIO. Barchers, *Wise Women*, 323–24.

10. Griffith, *In Her Own Right*, 216.

11. Rohr, *Falling Upward*, 127–36. Also see Johnson and Ruhl, *Living Your Unlived Life*.

12. Maslow, *Toward a Psychology*, 211–33, and *Farther Reaches*, 40–51; Kirschenbaum and Henderson, *Carl Rogers Reader*, 399–429; and Meade, *The Genius Myth*.

13. Oliver, *New and Selected*, 114–15.

14. Paul and Margret Baltes first described the importance of selectivity, compensation, and maximization in their book *Successful Aging*. Laura Carstensen's observations of "socioemotional selectivity" in later life confirm and expand on the increasing importance of selectivity as we age (Carstensen, "Older People").

15. Gilligan, *In a Different*.

16. I am deeply grateful to Anita Eliot, MFT, for bringing my awareness to the role that the fear of selfishness plays in undermining authenticity.

17. I love this gentle phrase, "slowly by slowly," which a friend learned while visiting South Africa. Like "baby steps," it underscores the years of learning and unlearning that becoming "a full grown-up" entails.

18. Palmer, *Let Your Life*, 7.

19. Le Guin, *Dancing*, 4.

20. Winerman, "The Mind's Mirror," 48–51.

21. Psychiatrist Fritz Perls (1893–1970) was a passionate early advocate of trusting the human organism and recognizing the intrinsic pleasure that accompanies meeting its genuine needs. *Gestalt Therapy* (by Frederick Perls, Ralph Hefferline, and Paul Goodman) contains a number of engaging exercises for enhancing awareness of one's experience, one's body, and the world.

2: The Grace of Self-Transcending Generosity

1. Midlarsky and Kahana, *Altruism*, 82.

2. Rohr, *Falling Upward*, 120.

3. See Carl Jung's *The Structure and Dynamics of the Psyche*.

4. Woodman, *The Crown of Age*.

5. Tornstam, "Maturing into Gerotranscendence," 171–72. Also see Tornstam's book *Gerotranscendence*.

6. Erikson, Erikson, and Kivnick, *Vital Involvement*, 45, 50–53.

7. Peck, "Psychological Developments," in Neugarten, *Middle Age*, 90–91.

8. Bolen, *Crones Don't Whine*, 18.

9. Galvin, "Ubong and the Headhunters," 67–71.

10. Muir, *My First Summer*, 211. For fascinating accounts of the vital role that trees play in the deep interconnectedness of life, see *The Songs of Trees: Stories of Nature's Great Connectors* by David George Haskell and *The Hidden Life of Trees: What They Feel, How They Communicate* by Peter Wohlleben.

11. See Huxley, *The Perennial Philosophy*.

12. Mitchell, *Tao Te Ching*, 16.

13. McGaa, *Mother Earth*, 203–9.

14. Gallese, quoted in Winerman, "The Mind's Mirror," 51.

15. Einstein, quoted in Walter Sullivan, "The Einstein Papers: A Man of Many Parts," *New York Times*, March 29, 1972.
    In her 2005 *The New Quotable Einstein*, Alice Calaprice verifies the first two sentences of this quotation, but she did not find the rest of it in Einstein's papers.

16. Waxman, *Astronomical Tidbits*, xiii–xiv.

17. Episcopal Church, *Book of Common Prayer*, 594–95.

18. Dass and Bush, *Compassion*, 170.

3: The Grace of Courage

1. Monroe, *The Heart of Altruism*, 63–90.

2. Ibid., 67.

3. Elizabeth Bugental, conversation with author, May 2005.

4. Putman, "Psychological Courage." Also see Putman's book *Psychological Courage*.

5. De Mille, "The Grand Dame of Dance," 94.

6. Cohen, *The Creative Age*.

7. Leslau, *African Folk Tales*, 58–60. Reprinted with permission of the authors' daughter, Sylvia Grotz.

8. Le Guin, *Lathe of Heaven*, 159.

9. White et al., "Young Adults."

10. For further information, see abuelas.org.ar.

11. Hasan, *Folktales of Uttar Pradesh*, 28–29. Reprinted with the permission of the author, Seemin Hasan.

12. For other stories of the creative and collaborative courage of later life, see "The Wise Woman" (Authenticity), "Ubong and the Headhunters" (Self-Transcending Generosity), "The Running Stick" (Compassion), and "The Son of a Goblin" (Necessary Fierceness).

13. The late-life capacity to wait and to cooperate with life's unfolding is developed in the Graces of Contentment and Wisdom.

14. Roosevelt, *You Learn by Living*, 29–30.

15. Eliot, "East Coker," 31–32.

16. Arrien, *The Second Half*, 37.

17. Winerman, "The Mind's Mirror," and Keltner, Marsh, and Smith, *The Compassionate Instinct*, 6.

4: The Grace of Creativity

1. Richards, *Everyday Creativity*.

2. Maslow, *Farther Reaches*, 55–97. Maslow observed that human beings are endowed with what he called "primary creativeness," which makes us improvisational by nature. He recognized the ways in which enculturation often stifles creativity, yet he found that many adults maintain their creativity or regain access to it in their later years. Maslow's decades-long study of self-actualizing (healthy) adults led him to view creativity as a defining characteristic of essential humanness, related to qualities such as openness, boldness, courage, freedom, spontaneity, integration, and self-acceptance.

3. Amabile, quoted in Goleman, Kaufman, and Ray, *Creative Spirit*, 57.

4. Kastenbaum, "Serious Play," 5-6.

5. Simonton, "Creative Productivity," 16. Also see Simonton, "Age and Outstanding Achievement: What Do We Know after a Century of Research?"

6. Baltes, "The Aging Mind."

7. Cohen, *The Mature Mind*, 38–39, 98–101.

8. "Poppet Caught a Thief" is reprinted with permission from the Unversity of Arkansas, Special Collections. Randolph, *Who Blowed Up the Church*, 99–101.

9. Matisse, "Looking at Life," 3.

10. Kanter, "What Makes a Good Leader," www.alumni.hbs.edu/stories/Pages/story-bulletin.aspx?num=3059.

11. Ma, "In Pursuit of Neuroscience."

12. Csikszentmihalyi, *Creativity*, 75.

13. Nakamura and Csikszentmihalyi, "Creativity in Later Life," in Sawyer et al., *Creativity and Development*, 186–216.

14. Cohen, *Creative Age*, 17, 183.

15. Kastenbaum, "Serious Play," 5.

16. Nakamura and Csikszentmihalyi, "Creativity in Later Life," in Sawyer et al., *Creativity and Development*, 203.

17. Heimel, "Lower Manhattan Survival," 26.

18. Touhy and Jett, *Ebersole and Hess' Toward Healthy*, 467.

19. McCartney, quoted in MacDonald, *Revolution in the Head*, 157.

20. Davies, *Happy Alchemy*, 142.

21. Vaillant, *The Wisdom of the Ego*, 284.

22. Werner and Smith, *Vulnerable but Invincible*.

23. Chinen, "The Return of Wonder," 45, 48. Also see Chinen's *In the Ever After*, 1–7, 95–103, 129–37.

24. Landau and Maoz, "Creativity and Self-Actualization," 117–27.

25. Cohen, *Creative Age*, 11.

26. Ibid., 11, 12.

27. Jung, *Collected Works*, 6:123.

28. Joyce, *Ulysses*, 190.

29. Estés, *The Creative Fire*.

30. Pauling, as quoted by Francis Crick during a talk at the Pauling Symposium, Oregon State University, "The Impact of Linus Pauling on Molecular Biology," February 28, 1995. http://oregonstate.edu/dept/Special_Collections/subpages/ahp/1995symposium/crick.html.

31. There is significant evidence that participating in various forms of creativity—dance, expressive writing, and music making, for example—has positive impacts on physical and cognitive health and on emotional and social well-being in later life. For good summaries of a number of studies, see Tony Noice, Helga Noice, and Arthur F. Kramer, "Participatory Arts for Older Adults: A Review of Benefits and Challenges," *Gerontologist* 54, no. 5 (October 2014): 741–53. Also see Barbara Bagan, "Aging: What's Art Got To Do With It?" *Today's Geriatric Medicine*, www.todaysgeriatricmedicine.com/news/ex_082809_03.shtml.

Julia Cameron's *It's Never Too Late to Begin Again*, Cathy Malchiodi's *The Soul's Palette*, and Jan Phillips's *Marry Your Muse* are excellent resources for exploring art making.

32. Cameron, *The Artist's Way*, 42–44.

33. James Aw, "Art for Life's Sake: The Health Benefits of Culture," *National Post*, August 23, 2011, http://nationalpost.com/health/art-for-lifes-sake-the-health-benefits-of-culture.

Also see Koenraad Cuypers, Steinar Krokstad, Turid Lingaas Holmen, Marguun Skjel Knudtsen, Lars Olov Bygren, and Jostein Holmen, "Patterns of Receptive and Creative Cultural Activities and Their Association With Perceived Health, Anxiety, Depression, and Satisfaction With Life Among Adults; the HUNT Study, Norway," *Journal of Epidemiology and Community Health* 66, no. 8 (2012): 698–703.

5: The Grace of Contentment

1. Graham and Pozuelo, "Happiness, Stress, and Age," 1, 12–13. Also see Carstensen, "Older People."

2. Lyubomirsky, *How of Happiness*, 41.

3. King and Hicks, "Whatever Happened," 631–34.

4. Haidt, *Happiness Hypothesis*, 141.

5. Remen, *Kitchen Table Wisdom*, 75.

6. Kahneman and Deaton, "High Income," 89, 92.

7. Lyubomirsky, *How of Happiness*, 43–44.

8. O'Connor, *Happy at Last*, 20, 13.

9. Hanson, *Buddha's Brain*, 5, 6.

10. Cohen, *Mature Mind*, 36–39, 96–98.

11. Carstensen, Fung, and Charles, "Socioemotional Selectivity," 113–15, 118–19.

12. Mather et al., "Amygdala Responses," 259, 262. Also see Cohen, *Mature Mind*, 17–18.

13. Keltner, *Born to Be Good*, 45. Also see Scheibe and Carstensen, "Emotional Aging."

14. Goleman, *Emotional Intelligence*, 57.

15. Ramanujan, *Folktales from India*, 3. Reprinted with permission, Penguin Random House.

16. Niebuhr, *Justice and Mercy*, v.

17. King and Hicks, "Whatever Happened," 634.

18. Jacobs, *More English*, 55–59.

19. Fredrickson, "The Broaden-and-Build Theory," in Csikszentmihalyi and Csikszentmihalyi, *A Life Worth Living*, 90–97. Also see Ong et al., "Psychological Resilience."

20. Hanson, *Buddha's Brain*, 69.

21. Keltner, *Born to Be Good*, 97–145.

22. Heschel, *Insecurity of Freedom*, 78.

23. Chödrön, *When Things Fall*, 14, 17, 23.

6: The Grace of Compassion

1. Eckhardt, *Compassion*, 2. Also see Armstrong, *Twelve Steps*, 3–64, and Keltner, *Born to Be Good*, 225–49, for excellent overviews of the virtue and the science of compassion.

2. Armstrong, *The Spiral Staircase*, 293.

3. Dalai Lama, *The Art of Happiness*, 69, 56.

4. Keltner, Marsh, and Smith, *The Compassionate Instinct*, 6.

5. Moore et al., "From Suffering to Caring," 185. In studies of over one thousand adults over fifty years old, Raeanne Moore and her associates found that late-life compassion was especially strong in older women. The desire to help others in distress seemed to be related to high levels of psychological resilience and a history of challenging life events.

6. Chödrön, *When Things Fall Apart*, 104, 110.

7. Dass and Bush, *Compassion in Action*, 227–28.

8. According to the University of Alaska's Native Language Center, the name *Eskimo* is commonly used in Alaska to refer to all Inuit and Yupik people, even though others consider it a derogatory term given by non-indigenous people and believed to mean "eater of raw meat." Linguists now believe that *Eskimo* derived from an Ojibwa word meaning "to net snowshoes." The term *Inuit*, although preferred in parts of Canada and the United States, is more specific and does not include all language groups in Alaska. Hence, the use of *Eskimo* here. (See "Inuit or Eskimo: Which name to use?" www.uaf.edu/anlc/resources/inuit-eskimo.)

9. Riggs, *Animal Tales*, 61–67.

10. Underwood, "Compassionate Love," in Fehr, Sprecher, and Underwood, *Science of Compassionate Love*, 6–8.

11. Campbell, *The Hero*, 23.

12. Meade, *The Water of Life*, 295.

13. Biedermann, *Dictionary of Symbolism*, 39–40.

14. Kornfield, *The Art of Forgiveness*, 100.

15. For good summaries of a number of studies describing the effects of meditation on compassion (and related benefits), see these three articles:

"18 Science-Based Reasons to Try Loving-Kindness Meditation" by Emma Seppala, science director of Stanford University's Center for Compassion and Altruism Research and Education (https://emmaseppala.com/18-science-based-reasons-try-loving-kindness-meditation-today)

Northeastern University psychology professor David DeSteno's "The Kindness Cure" (www.theatlantic.com/health/archive/2015/07/mindfulness-meditation-empathy-compassion/398867/)

Stacey Colino's "The Surprising Benefits of Compassion Meditation" (https://health.usnews.com/wellness/articles/2016-03-23/the-surprising-benefits-of-compassion-meditation)

16. Salzberg, *Real Happiness*, 21. (This is also available as an audio-book, read by the author, HighBridge, 2011.)

17. Edelman, *Families in Peril*, 107.

18. Johnson and Ruhl, *Contentment*, 113.

7: The Grace of Necessary Fierceness

1. For an exploration of how traditional gender training has led women to silence their unique voice and disown their power, see Carol Gilligan's *In a Different Voice* and Karen Horney's *Feminine Psychology*. Also see Reiser, *Reflections on Anger*, 9–19, for a discussion of the differences between women's and men's conditioning regarding anger.

2. Suzanne Barchers's *Wise Women: Folk and Fairy Tales from Around the World* and Kathleen Ragan's *Fearless Girls, Wise Women, and Beloved Sisters* both contain inspiring little-known folktales about spirited women of all ages.

3. For a more complete version of the myth of Durga, see Galland, *The Bond Between Women*, xvi–xx.

4. See Bolen, *Goddesses in Older Women*, 85–88, for a longer telling of Sechmet's story, with commentary.

5. *The Goddess Trilogy* from the National Film Board of Canada illustrates the connection between women's struggle in owning their power and fierceness, the demonizing of the fierce old woman in myth and later in folklore, and the killing of between thirty and one hundred thousand wise and powerful old women during the witch hunts in Europe and later in North America. The three DVDs are available through many libraries and can be purchased online: *Goddess Remembered*, *The Burning Times*, and *Full Circle*.

6. Underwood, "Clan Mothers," 158.

7. Pearson, *Awakening the Heroes*, 104. For further discussion of the wise warrior archetype also see 94–117.

8. Carstensen, "Older People."

9. Bolen, *Crones Don't Whine*, 44; also see *Goddesses in Older Women*, 78–79.

10. Arnansan, "The Son of the Goblin," 177-81.

11. Temperance (*sophrosyne* in Greek) is one of four cardinal virtues in the West and one of five foundational restraints in the yoga tradition (*brahmacharya*). And it is among the six character strengths identified by positive psychologists. Temperance is generally defined as moderation or control over excess and has many forms, including prudence, self-regulation, humility, forgiveness, and mercy.

12. Tavris, *Anger*, 253.

13. Fischer, *Transforming Fire*, 151.

14. Reiser, *Reflections on Anger*, 28. Also see Reiser, *Reflections on Anger*, 21–28; Tavris, *Anger*, 15–25; and Thomas, *Women and Anger*, 1–39.

15. For discussions of the effects of culture (including gender and race) on anger, see Fischer, *Transforming Fire*, 11; Thomas, *Women and Anger*, 31; Tavris, *Anger*, 46–65; and Reiser, *Reflections on Anger*, 9–19.

16. Lorde, *Sister Outsider*, 129.

17. Tavris, *Anger*, 23.

18. Campbell, *Men, Women, and Aggression*, 8.

19. Williams, *Refuge*, 12.

20. Deming, *We Cannot Live*, 51.

21. Ibid., *Revolution and Equilibrium*, 207.

22. See the writings of Barbara Deming on nonviolence and Dennis Sullivan and Larry Tifft's *Handbook of Restorative Justice*.

8: *The Grace of Simplicity*

1. "Your one wild and precious life" is from Mary Oliver's "The Summer Day," *New and Selected Poems*, 94.

2. See Paul and Margret Baltes's *Successful Aging* and Laura Carstensen on "socioemotional selectivity."

3. Erikson, Erikson, and Kivnick, *Vital Involvement*, 333.

4. Woodman, *Crown of Age*; Bolen, *Crones Don't Whine*, 56–59.

5. Bolen, *Crones Don't Whine*, 56.

6. De Leeuw, "The Haunted House," 81–88.

7. Nearing, *Loving and Leaving*, 191.

8. Marion told this story at a workshop in London, Ontario, in March 2008. Used with permission of the Marion Woodman Foundation.

9. Scott-Maxwell, *The Measure*, 90–91, 112.

10. Peck, "Psychological Developments," in Neugarten, *Middle Age*, 91.

11. Elgin, *Voluntary Simplicity*, 142–43.

12. Slavitt, *Seneca*, xv.

13. Elgin, *Voluntary Simplicity*, 33, 32. Also see Michael Gellert's *The Way of the Small: Why Less Is Truly More*.

14. Segal, *Graceful Simplicity*, 209, 160.

15. Pfeiffer, *Frank Lloyd Wright*, 34.

16. Arrien, *The Second Half*, 150–51.

17. Moore, *The Re-Enchantment*, 293.

18. Elgin, *Voluntary Simplicity*, 163–64.

9: *The Grace of Remembrance*

1. Butler, "The Life Review," in Neugarten, *Middle Age*, 489–90.

2. Erikson, Erikson, and Kivnick, *Vital Involvement*, 288.

3. Kaminsky, "Transfiguring Life," in Kaminsky, *The Uses of Reminiscence*, 13.

4. McMahon and Rhudick, "Reminiscing," in Levin and Kahana, *Psychodynamic Studies*, 73. McMahon and Rhudick also noted that some older adults did not appear to engage in reminiscence to any significant degree.

5. Kaminsky, "Transfiguring Life," in Kaminsky, *The Uses of Reminiscence*, 3–25.

6. Scott-Maxwell, *The Measure*, 34.

7. Myerhoff and Metzger, "The Journal As Activity," in Myerhoff, *Remembered Lives*, 358, 344.

8. Another benefit of sharing stories is that we shelter one another's memories. In the almost fifty years that our women's group has been meeting, it has become increasingly the case that one woman will retell a relevant anecdote or a memorable statement that another woman shared years ago but no longer remembers. When shared again, these treasures, stored in another's memory, are a gift to the one who forgot, and they enrich our shared history.

9. Murdock, *Unreliable Truth*, 16.

10. "The Woman in the Moon" is reprinted with permission from ABC-CLIO. Barchers, *Wise Women*, 313–14.

11. Viorst, *Necessary Losses*, 264.

12. Silver, "The Significance," in Levkoff, Chee, and Noguchi, *Aging in Good Health*, 31. (Margery Silver credits George Pollock for the last eleven words of this quotation.)

13. Kaminsky, "Transfiguring Life," in Kaminsky, *The Uses of Reminiscence*, 12.

14. Wilde, *De Profundis*, 36, 38.

15. I first heard mythologist Michael Meade speak about the intertwining of wounds and gifts at one his workshops years ago. (See mosaicvoices.org for workshops, community-building projects [including some for elders and youth], books, CDs, and downloads.)

16. Scott-Maxwell, *The Measure*, 47.

17. Kurtz and Ketcham, *Spirituality of Imperfection*, 224.

18. Manheimer, "Remember to Remember," in Kaminsky, *All That Our Eyes*, 98.

19. Moody, "Reminiscence and the Recovery," in Kaminsky, *The Uses of Reminiscence*, 158, 162.

20. Worth, "At the Center," in Kaminsky, *The Uses of Reminiscence*, 59.

21. Justin Chadwick, dir., *The First Grader.* United Kingdom: BBC Films, 2010. DVD.

22. The phrasing *what we have done and left undone* is based on the "Confession" in *The Book of Common Prayer*, 23. ("We have left undone those things which we ought to have done, and we have done those things which we ought not to have done.")

23. Myerhoff and Metzger, "The Journal As Activity," in Myerhoff, *Remembered Lives*, 358.

24. Myerhoff and Tufte, "Life History As Integration," in Myerhoff, *Remembered Lives*, 254–55.

25. I learned this process from the late Lars Peterson, a creative writing teacher. The un-poem format, for me, combines the best of Haiku (brevity and non-rhyming) with greater flexibility in terms of poem length and line placement.

10: The Grace of Agelessness

1. One of these hag-embracing stories, "Mother of the Waters," appears in the next chapter, the Grace of Wisdom.

2. L'Engle, quoted in Susan Heller Anderson and David W. Dunlap, "New York Day by Day: Authors to Readers," *New York Times*, April 25, 1985. Quotation was a response to a fourth grader's question, "How old are you?"

3. Monaghan, *Seasons*, 3–4.

4. Bortz, *We Live Too Short*, 199.

5. Öberg, "Images Versus Experience," in Faircloth, *Aging Bodies*, 129.

6. Evans, quoted in Allison, "Improving the Odds," 6.

7. See note 4 in the Introduction.

8. Rowe and Kahn, *Successful Aging*, 16, 30, 44.

9. Northrup, *Goddesses Never Age*, 2, 7, 8. Chapters 1 (pp. 1–21) and 4 (pp. 78–113) contain a wealth of information about maintaining health and well-being in later life.

10. Sontag, "The Double Standard of Aging." Subsequent studies have confirmed the double standard of aging. One revealed that older subjects discriminated less on the basis of gender and evaluated women more positively than younger subjects did. See Francine M. Deutsch, Carla M. Zalenski, and Mary E. Clark, "Is There a Double Standard of Aging?" *Journal of Applied Social Psychology* 16, no. 9 (December 1986): 771.

11. Nigel Cole, dir., *Calendar Girls*. United Kingdom: Touchstone Pictures, 2003. DVD.

12. Kuhn, "Insights on Aging," 18. This article is well worth reading and can be accessed at http://hearth.library.cornell.edu/cgi/t/text/pageviewer-idx?c=hearth;cc=hearth;q1=kuhn;rgn=full%20text;idno=4732504_70_004;didno=4732504_70_004;view=image;seq=20;node=4732504_70_004%3A6.6;page=root;size=s;-frm=frameset.

13. Elias, "Late-Life Love," 1–3. Also see Starr and Weiner, *Sex and Sexuality*, 41–46.

14. Goldman, *Late-Life Love*, 24, 30.

15. Winn and Newton, "Sexuality in Aging," 289–94.

16. Davis and Leonard, *The Circle of Life*, 175.

17. Starr and Weiner, *Sex and Sexuality*, 11.

18. Starr and Weiner, *Sex and Sexuality*, 13–14, 47–50, and Chapter 9, "Older Women Alone," 161–83; Elias, "Late-Life Love," 1–3.

19. For a good introduction to these sensuous crones and other goddesses, see Patricia Monaghan's *The New Book of Goddesses and Heroines*.

20. Elias, "Late-Life Love," 3.

21. Sarton, *Journal of a Solitude*, 90.

22. Bolen, *Crones Don't Whine*, 19, 22.

23. "The Cure," from Inea Bushnaq's *Arab Folktales*, 331–32, is reprinted with the permission of Penguin Random House.

24. Frost, "A Servant to Servants," 66.

25. Frost, "The Commencement Address," 14–15.

26. Jung, *Structure and Dynamics*, 399.

27. Helen Mirren, "Helen Mirren in Light and Shadow," interview by Robert Love, *AARP Magazine* (December 2016–January 2017), 32.

28. Martinez, *The Mind/Body Code*, 98. Also see Ashton Applewhite's *This Chair Rocks: A Manifesto Against Ageism*.

29. Goldman and Mahler, *Secrets of Becoming*, 20.

30. Sula Benet, "Why They Live to Be 100, Or Even Older, in Abkhasia," *New York Times*, December 26, 1971, www.nytimes.com/1971/12/26/archives/why-they-live-to-be-100-or-even-older-in-abkhasia-faces-in-an.html.

31. Landau and Maoz, "Creativity and Self-Actualization," 117–27. Also see Ryff, "In the Eye," 195–210.

32. Goldman and Mahler, *Secrets of Becoming*, 20.

33. Rowe and Kahn, "Successful Aging," 45–47, 152–66. Ryff, "In the Eye," 195–210.

34. Hall, *Adolescence*, 235. The idea that a lack of play is a cause, rather than the result, of aging is attributed to many. The following paragraph from G. Stanley Hall's *Adolescence* establishes him—and Karl Groos, whom he quotes—as early proponents of this concept:

"Gross (sic) well says that children are young because they play, and not vice versa; and he might have added, men grow old because they stop playing, and not conversely, for play is, at bottom, growth, and at the top of the intellectual scale it is the eternal type of research from sheer love of truth."

Hall is referencing page 68 of Karl Groos's 1896 edition of *Die Spiele der Thiere* (*The Play of Animals*), in which he writes, "*die Thiere spielen nicht, weil sie jung sind, sondern sie haben eine Jugend, weil sie spielen müssen*" ("the animals do not play because they are young, rather, they have youth because they must play").

35. Research suggests that meditation stimulates areas of the brain associated with kindness, empathy, and concern for others (see *Practice Lovingkindness*, p. 145 in Compassion and note 15, p. 291). According to psychologist Clay Routledge, prayer has been shown to enhance self-control, reduce aggressive reactivity, increase trust and the capacity for forgiveness, and offset the negative effects of stress (see www.psychologytoday.com/blog/more-mortal/201406/5-scientifically-supported-benefits-prayer).

11: The Grace of Wisdom

1. Randall and Kenyon, *Ordinary Wisdom*, 28.

2. The story of the blind men and the elephant originated in India and has spread throughout Asia, the Middle East, and Europe. Versions appear in several spiritual traditions, including Jainism, Hinduism, Buddhism, Sufism, and Baha'i.

3. Meacham, "The Loss of Wisdom," in Sternberg, *Wisdom*, 183, 187.

4. Randall and Kenyon, *Ordinary Wisdom*, 2.

5. Kramer, "Conceptualizing Wisdom," in Sternberg, *Wisdom*, 281.

6. "Mother of the Waters" from Diane Wolkstein's *The Magic Orange Tree and Other Haitian Folktales*, 152–56, is reprinted with the permission of the author's daughter, Rachel Zucker.

7. Erikson, *The Life Cycle*, 61.

8. Randall and Kenyon, *Ordinary Wisdom*, 22.

9. Robert Sternberg, "It's Not What You Know, but How You Use It: Teaching for Wisdom," *Chronicle of Higher Education*, June 28, 2002.

10. Arrien, *The Second Half*, 157.

11. Josselson, "Relationship," in Young-Eisendrath and Miller, *The Psychology*, 96, 100.

12. Meacham, "The Loss of Wisdom," in Sternberg, *Wisdom*, 209.

13. Ackerman, *A Natural History of the Senses*, 309.

14. Heschel, *The Wisdom*, 152.

Blessing

1. Rohr, *Falling Upward*, 117, 119.

2. See *Grandmothers Counsel the World* (Carol Schaefer); *The Healing Wisdom of Africa* (Malidoma Somé); *The Book of Elders* (Sandy Johnson); *Medicine Cards* (Jamie Sams and David Carson); and *Sacred Path Cards* (Jamie Sams).

3. See Michael Meade (mosaicvoices.org); Meredith Little (http://schooloflostborders.org); and Richard Rohr, Cynthia Bourgeault,

and James Finley's Living School at the Center for Action and Contemplation (https://cac.org/living-school/living-school).

4. For more on becoming a "shining" elder, see Angeles Arrien's *The Second Half of Life*; Jean Bolen's *Crones Don't Whine*; Eugene Bianchi's *Aging as a Spiritual Journey*; Clarissa Pinkola Estés's *The Dangerous Old Woman* (audio series); Steven Foster and Meredith Little's *The Roaring of the Sacred River*; Richard Leider and David Shapiro's *Claiming your Place at the Fire*; Harry Moody and David Carroll's *The Five Stages of the Soul*; William Randall and Gary Kenyon's *Ordinary Wisdom*; Richard Rohr's *Falling Upward*; Zalman Schachter-Shalomi and Ronald Miller's *From Age-ing to Sage-ing*; Carol Schaefer's *Grandmothers Counsel the World*; and Marion Woodman's *Crown of Age* (audiobook).

For further inspiration, see Wendell Berry's *Collected Poems: 1957–1982*; John O'Donohue's *To Bless the Space Between Us*; Mary Oliver's *New and Selected Poems*; David Whyte's *River Flow*; and *The Essential Rumi* (Coleman Barks, translator).

5. John Madden, dir., *Shakespeare in Love*. United Kingdom: Universal Pictures, 1999. DVD.

6. The phrase "shining person" comes from Richard Rohr: "Just watch true elders sitting in any circle of conversation . . . This is human life in its crowning . . . All you have to do is meet one such shining person and you know that he or she is surely the goal of humanity." (Rohr, *Falling Upward*, 119, 123, 126.)

Bibliography

Ackerman, Diane. *A Natural History of the Senses*. New York: Vintage, 1995.

———. *Deep Play*. New York: First Vintage Books, 1999.

Allen, Paula Gunn. "Indian Summer." In *The Other Within Us: Feminist Explorations of Women and Aging*, edited by Marilyn Pearsall, 233–38. Boulder, CO: Westview Press, 1997.

Allison, Malorye. "Improving the Odds." *Harvard Health Letter* 16, no. 4 (February 1991): 3–6.

Amabile, Teresa. Growing Up Creative: Nurturing a Lifetime of Creativity. Amherst, MA: Creative Education Foundation Press, 1989.

Andrews, Cecile. *The Circle of Simplicity: Return to the Good Life*. New York: Harper Perennial, 1997.

Applewhite, Ashton. *This Chair Rocks: A Manifesto Against Ageism*. New York: Networked Books, 2016.

Armstrong, Karen. *The Spiral Staircase: My Climb Out of Darkness*. New York: Anchor Books, 2005.

———. *Twelve Steps to a Compassionate Life*. New York: Alfred A. Knopf, 2011.

Arnasan, Jón. "The Son of the Goblin." In *Legends of Iceland*, translated by George E. J. Powell and Eirikur Magnússon, 177-81. London: Richard Bentley, 1864.

Arrien, Angeles. *The Second Half of Life: Opening the Eight Gates of Wisdom*. Boulder, CO: Sounds True, 2005.

Baltes, Paul. "The Aging Mind: Potential and Limits." *The Gerontologist* 33, no. 5 (October 1993): 580–94.

Baltes, Paul, and Margret Baltes. *Successful Aging: Perspectives from the Behavioral Sciences.* Cambridge: Cambridge University Press, 1990.

Barchers, Suzanne I. *Wise Women: Folk and Fairy Tales from Around the World.* Englewood, CO: Libraries Unlimited, 1990.

Berry, Wendell. *Collected Poems: 1957–1982.* New York: North Point, 1994.

Biedermann, Hans. *Dictionary of Symbolism: Cultural Icons and the Meanings Behind Them.* Translated by James Hulbert. New York: Meridian Books, 1989.

Blair, Nancy. *Amulets of the Goddess: Oracle of Ancient Wisdom.* Oakland, CA: Wingbow Press, 1993.

Bloom, Janet. "Minerva's Doll." In Kaminsky, *The Uses of Reminiscence,* 115–33.

Bolen, Jean Shinoda. *Crones Don't Whine: Concentrated Wisdom for Juicy Women.* Boston: Conari Press, 2003.

———. *Goddesses in Older Women: Archetypes in Women Over Fifty.* New York: HarperCollins, 2001.

Boorstein, Sylvia. *Happiness is an Inside Job: Practicing for a Joyful Life.* New York: Ballantine Books, 2008.

Bortz, Walter, II. *We Live Too Short and Die Too Long: How to Achieve and Enjoy Your Natural 100-Year-Plus Life Span.* New York: Select Books, 2007.

Bourgeault, Cynthia. *The Wisdom Jesus: Transforming Heart and Mind—A New Perspective on Christ and His Message.* Boston: Shambhala, 2008.

Breathnach, Sarah Ban. *Simple Abundance: A Daybook of Comfort and Joy.* New York: Warner Books, 1995.

Bugental, Elizabeth. *Love Fills in the Blanks: Paradoxes of Our Final Years.* Oakland, CA: Elders Academy Press, 2008.

Bushnaq, Inea. *Arab Folktales.* New York: Pantheon Books, 1986.

Butler, Robert. *Why Survive? Being Old in America.* New York: Harper & Row, 1975.

―――. "The Life Review: An Interpretation of Reminiscence in the Aged." In Neugarten, *Middle Age*, 486–96.

Calaprice, Alice. *The New Quotable Einstein*. Princeton, NJ: Princeton University Press, 2005.

Cameron, Julia. *The Artist's Way: A Spiritual Path to Higher Creativity*, 10th anniversary ed. New York: Jeremy P. Tarcher/Putnam, 2002.

―――. *It's Never Too Late to Begin Again: Discovering Creativity and Meaning at Midlife and Beyond*. New York: TarcherPerigree, 2016.

Campbell, Anne. *Men, Women, and Aggression*. New York: Basic Books, 1993.

Campbell, Joseph. *The Hero with a Thousand Faces*. Novato, CA: New World Library, 2008.

Carstensen, Laura. *A Long and Bright Future: Happiness, Health, and Financial Security in an Age of Increased Longevity*. New York: Broadway Books, 2011.

―――. "Older People Are Happier" (TED Talk, New York, NY, November 2011). www.ted.com/talks/laura_carstensen_older_people_are_happier#t-8505.

Carstensen, Laura, Helene Fung, and Susan Charles. "Socioemotional Selectivity Theory and the Regulation of Emotion in the Second Half of Life." *Motivation and Emotion* 27, no. 2 (June 2003): 103–23.

Carstensen, Laura, Bulent Turan, Susanne Scheibe, Nilam Ram, Hal Ernesner-Hershfield, Gregory Samanez-Larkin, Kathryn Brooks, and John Nesselroade. "Emotional Experience Improves with Age: Evidence Based on Over Ten Years of Experience Sampling." *Psychology and Aging* 26, no. 1 (March 2011): 21–33.

Carter, Jimmy. *The Virtues of Aging*. New York: Ballantine, 1998.

Chinen, Allan. *In the Ever After: Fairy Tales and the Second Half of Life*. Wilmette, IL: Chiron Publications, 1989.

―――. "The Return of Wonder in Old Age." *Generations* 15, no. 2 (Spring 1991): 45–48.

Chittister, Joan. *The Gift of Years: Growing Older Gracefully.* New York: BlueBridge, 2008.

Chödrön, Pema. *When Things Fall Apart: Heart Advice for Difficult Times.* Boston: Shambhala, 2000.

Cohen, Gene. *The Creative Age: Awakening Human Potential in the Second Half of Life.* New York: HarperCollins, 2000.

———. *The Mature Mind: The Positive Power of the Aging Brain.* New York: Basic Books, 2005.

Crick, Francis. "The Impact of Linus Pauling on Molecular Biology." Talk delivered at the Pauling Symposium, Oregon State University, Corvallis, OR, February 28, 1995. http://oregonstate.edu/dept/Special_Collections/subpages/ahp/1995symposium/crick.html.

Csikszentmihalyi, Mihaly. *Creativity: Flow and the Psychology of Discovery and Invention.* New York: HarperCollins, 2013.

Dass, Ram, and Mirabai Bush. *Compassion in Action: Setting Out on the Path of Service.* New York: Bell Tower, 1992.

Davies, Robertson. *Happy Alchemy: On the Pleasures of Music and the Theater.* Toronto: McClelland and Stewart, 1997.

Davis, Elizabeth, and Carol Leonard. *The Circle of Life: Thirteen Archetypes for Every Woman.* Berkeley, CA: Celestial Arts, 2002.

De Leeuw, Adele. "The Haunted House." In *Legends and Folk Tales of Holland*, 81–88. New York: Thomas Nelson and Sons, 1963.

De Mille, Agnes. "The Grand Dame of Dance." By John Leongard and Gordon Tenney. *Life Magazine* 55, no. 20 (November 15, 1963): 89–90, 92, 94.

Deming, Barbara. *Revolution and Equilibrium.* New York: Grossman Publishers, 1971.

———. *We Cannot Live Without Our Lives.* New York: Grossman Publishers, 1974.

Deren, Jane, Ronald Manheimer, and Sylvia Riggs Liroff, eds. *Portraits and Pathways: Exploring Stories of Aging.* Washington, DC: National Council on Aging, 1988.

Deutsch, Francine M., Carla M. Zalenski, and Mary E. Clark. "Is There a Double Standard of Aging?" *Journal of Applied Social Psychology* 16, no. 9 (December 1986): 771–85.

Eckhardt, William. *Compassion: Toward a Science of Value.* Oakville, Ontario: CPRI Press, 1972.

Edelman, Marian Wright. *Families in Peril: An Agenda for Social Change.* Cambridge, MA: Harvard University Press, 1987.

Edens, Cooper. *If You're Afraid of the Dark, Remember the Night Rainbow.* La Jolla, CA: Green Tiger Press, 1978.

Elgin, Duane. *Voluntary Simplicity: Toward a Way of Life That Is Outwardly Simple, Inwardly Rich.* New York: William Morrow, 1981.

Eliot, T. S. "East Coker." Chap. 2 in *The Four Quartets.* New York: Houghton Mifflin Harcourt, 2014.

Elias, Marilyn. "Late-Life Love." *Harvard Health Letter* 18, no. 1 (November 1992): 1–3.

Episcopal Church. *The Book of Common Prayer.* New York: The Church Pension Fund, 1945.

Erikson, Erik. *The Life Cycle Completed: A Review.* New York: Norton, 1982.

Erikson, Erik, Joan Erikson, and Helen Kivnick. *Vital Involvement in Old Age.* New York: W. W. Norton, 1986.

Estés, Clarissa Pinkola. *The Creative Fire: Myths and Stories on the Cycles of Creativity.* Boulder, CO: Sounds True, 1991.

———. *The Dangerous Old Woman.* Audiobook series. 6 CDs. Boulder, CO: Sounds True, 2010.

———. *Women Who Run with the Wolves: Myths and Stories of the Wild Woman Archetype.* New York: Random House, 1997.

Fischer, Kathleen. *Transforming Fire: Women Using Anger Creatively.* New York: Paulist Press, 1999.

Foster, Steven, and Meredith Little. *The Roaring of the Sacred River: The Wilderness Quest for Vision and Self-Healing.* New York: Prentice Hall, 1989.

Fox, John. *Finding What You Didn't Lose: Expressing Your Truth and Creativity Through Poem-Making.* New York: Jeremy P. Tarcher/ Putnam, 1995.

Fredrickson, Barbara. "The Broaden-and-Build Theory of Positive Emotions." In *A Life Worth Living: Contributions to Positive Psychology,* edited by Mihaly Csikszentmihalyi and Isabella Selega Csikszentmihalyi, 85–103. New York: Oxford University Press, 2006.

Frost, Robert. "A Servant to Servants." In *North of Boston,* 64–72. New York: Henry Holt, 1917.

———. "The Commencement Address." *Dartmouth Alumni Magazine,* July 1955, 14–15.

Galland, China. *The Bond Between Women: A Journey to Fierce Compassion.* New York: Riverhead Books, 1998.

Galvin, A. D. "Ubong and the Headhunters." In *On the Banks of the Barum,* 67–71. Privately published, Malaysia, n.d.

Gardner, Ruth. *Celebrating the Crone: Rituals & Stories.* St. Paul, MN: Llewellyn Publications, 1999.

Gates, Rolf. *Meditations from the Mat: Daily Reflections on the Path of Yoga.* New York: Anchor Books, 2002.

Gellert, Michael. *The Way of the Small: Why Less Is Truly More.* Lake Worth, FL: Nicolas-Hays, 2008.

George, Demetra. *Mysteries of the Dark Moon: The Healing Power of the Dark Goddess.* San Francisco: Harper San Francisco, 1992.

Gergen, M. M. and K. J. Gergen. "Positive Aging: New Images for a New Age." *Ageing International* 27, no. 1 (2001): 3–23.

Getzel, George. "Old People, Poetry, and Groups." In Kaminsky, *The Uses of Reminiscence,* 193–99.

Gilligan, Carol. *In a Different Voice: Psychological Theory and Women's Development.* Cambridge, MA: Harvard University Press, 1982.

Gimbutas, Marija. *The Language of the Goddess.* Harper San Francisco, 1989.

Gleckman, Howard. "Dementia Rates Are Falling in the U.S." *Forbes*, November 21, 2016. www.forbes.com/sites/howard-gleckman/2016/11/21/dementia-rates-are-falling-in-the-us/#a7ad43a10338.

Goldman, Connie, ed. *Late-Life Love: Romance and New Relationships in Later Years.* Minneapolis: Fairview Press, 2006.

Goldman, Connie, and Richard Mahler. *Secrets of Becoming a Late Bloomer: Extraordinary Ordinary People on the Art of Staying Creative, Alive, and Aware in Midlife and Beyond.* Center City, MN: Hazelden, 1995.

Goleman, Daniel. *Emotional Intelligence: Why It Can Matter More Than IQ.* New York: Bantam Books, 1995.

Goleman, Daniel, and Paul Kaufman. "The Art of Creativity." *Psychology Today* 25 no. 2 (March 1992): 40–45. Also online: www.psychologytoday.com/articles/199203/the-art-creativity.

Goleman, Daniel, Paul Kaufman, and Michael Ray. *The Creative Spirit.* New York: Pume/Penguin Group, 1992.

Graham, Carol, and Julia Ruiz Pozuelo. "Happiness, Stress, and Age: How the U Curve Varies across People and Places." *Journal of Population Economics* 30, no. 1 (January 2017): 225–64.

Griffith, Elisabeth. *In Her Own Right: The Life of Elizabeth Cady Stanton.* New York: Oxford University Press, 1985.

Haidt, Jonathan. *The Happiness Hypothesis: Finding Modern Truth in Ancient Wisdom.* New York: Basic Books, 2006.

Hall, G. Stanley. *Adolescence: Its Psychology and Its Relations to Physiology, Anthropology, Sociology, Sex, Crime, Religion and Education.* New York: D. Appleton and Company, 1904.

Hanson, Rick, and Richard Mendius. *Buddha's Brain: The Practical Neuroscience of Happiness, Love, and Wisdom.* Oakland, CA: New Harbinger Publications, 2009.

Hasan, Amir, and Seemin Hasan. *Folktales of Uttar Pradesh Tribes.* Gurgaon, India: Academic Press, 1982.

Haskell, David George. *The Songs of Trees: Stories From Nature's Great Connectors.* New York: Viking/Random House, 2017.

Heimel, Cynthia. "Lower Manhattan Survival Tactics." *Village Voice* 13 (1983): 26.

Heschel, Abraham Joshua. *The Insecurity of Freedom: Essays on Human Existence*. Basingstoke, UK: Macmillan, 1963.

Heschel, Abraham Joshua, trans. by Ruth M. Goodhill. *The Wisdom of Heschel*. New York: Farrar, Straus and Giroux, 1975.

Higgins, Chester, Jr. *Elder Grace: The Nobility of Aging*. Boston: Bullfinch Press, 2000.

Hill, Robert D. *Seven Strategies for Positive Aging*. New York: W. W. Norton, 2008.

His Holiness the Dalai Lama and Desmond Tutu, with Douglas Abrams. *The Book of Joy: Lasting Happiness in a Changing World*. New York: Avery (Penguin Random House), 2016.

His Holiness the Dalai Lama and Howard Cutler. *The Art of Happiness: A Handbook for Living*, 10th anniversary ed. New York: Riverhead Books, 2009.

Hollis, James. *Finding Meaning in the Second Half of Life: How to Finally, Really Grow Up*. New York: Gotham Books, 2005.

Honoré, Carl. *In Praise of Slowness: Challenging the Cult of Speed*. San Francisco: Harper San Francisco, 2005.

Horney, Karen. *Feminine Psychology*. New York: W. W. Norton, 1967.

Huxley, Aldous. *The Perennial Philosophy*. New York: Harper & Brothers, 1945.

Jacobs, Joseph. *More English Fairy Tales*. New York: Putnam, n.d.

Jalāl al-Dīn Rūmī, Maulana. *The Essential Rumi*. Translated by Coleman Barks. New York: HarperCollins, 1995.

Jamison, Kay Redfield: *Exuberance: The Passion for Life*. New York: Vintage Books, 2004.

Johnson, Robert. *Inner Work: Using Dreams and Active Imagination for Personal Growth*. San Francisco: Harper & Row, 1986.

Johnson, Robert, and Jerry Ruhl. *Contentment: A Way to True Happiness*. New York: HarperCollins, 1999.

————. *Living Your Unlived Life: Coping With Unrealized Dreams and Fulfilling Your Purpose in the Second Half of Life.* Jeremy P. Tarcher/Penguin, 2007.

Johnson, Sandy, ed. *The Book of Elders: The Life Stories and Wisdom of Great American Indians.* Harper San Francisco, 1994.

Josselson, Ruthellen. "Relationship as a Path to Integrity, Wisdom, and Meaning." In Young-Eisendrath and Miller, *The Psychology of Mature Spirituality,* 2000, 87–102.

Joyce, James. *Ulysses.* New York: Modern Library, 1992.

Jung, Carl. *The Collected Works of C. G. Jung.* Vol. 6, *Psychological Types.* Princeton, NJ: Princeton University Press, 2014.

————. *The Structure and Dynamics of the Psyche.* Princeton, NJ: Princeton University Press, 1960.

Kahn, Michael. *The Tao of Conversation: How to Talk About Things That Really Matter, in Ways That Encourage New Ideas, Deepen Intimacy, and Build Effective and Creative Working Relationships.* Oakland, CA: New Harbinger Publications, 1995.

Kahneman, Daniel, and Angus Deaton. "High Income Improves Evaluation of Life but Not Emotional Well-Being." *Proceedings of the National Academy of Sciences of the United States of America* 107, no. 38 (September 21, 2010): 16,489–93.

Kaminsky, Marc. "Transfiguring Life: Images of Continuity Hidden Among the Fragments." In Kaminsky, *The Uses of Reminiscence,* 3–25.

————, ed. *The Uses of Reminiscence: New Ways of Working With Older Adults.* New York: Haworth Press, 1984.

Kanter, Rosabeth Moss. "What Makes a Good Leader." By Deborah Blagg and Susan Young. *Harvard Business School Bulletin,* February 1, 2001.

Kastenbaum, Robert. "Serious Play and Infinite Limits." *Generations* 15, no. 2 (Spring 1991): 5–6.

Keltner, Dacher. *Born to Be Good: The Science of a Meaningful Life.* New York: W. W. Norton, 2009.

Keltner, Dacher, Jason Marsh, and Jeremy Adam Smith, eds. *The Compassionate Instinct: The Science of Human Goodness*. New York: W. W. Norton, 2010.

King, Laura A., and Joshua A. Hicks. "Whatever Happened to 'What Might Have Been'? Regrets, Happiness, and Maturity." *American Psychologist* 62, no. 7 (October 2007): 625–36.

Kirschenbaum, Howard, and Valerie Land Henderson, eds. *The Carl Rogers Reader*. Boston: Houghton Mifflin, 1989.

Kondo, Marie. *The Life-Changing Magic of Tidying Up: The Japanese Art of Decluttering and Organizing*. Berkeley, CA: Ten Speed Press, 2014.

Kornfield, Jack. *The Art of Forgiveness, Lovingkindness, and Peace*. New York: Bantam Books, 2002.

Kramer, Deirdre. "Conceptualizing Wisdom: The Primacy of Affect-Cognition Relations." In Sternberg, *Wisdom*, 279–316.

Kuhn, Maggie. "Insights on Aging." *Journal of Home Economics* 70, no. 4 (Fall 1978): 18–20.

Kurtz, Ernest, and Katherine Ketcham. *The Spirituality of Imperfection: Storytelling and the Search for Meaning*. New York: Bantam Books, 1992.

Lamott, Anne. *Plan B: Further Thoughts on Faith*. New York: Penguin, 2006.

Landau, Erika, and Benjamin Maoz. "Creativity and Self-Actualization in the Aging Personality." *American Journal of Psychotherapy* 32, no. 1 (January 1978): 117–27.

Langer, Ellen J. *Mindfulness*. Reading, MA: Perseus Books, 1989.

LeClaire, Anne. *Listening Below the Noise: The Transformative Power of Silence*. New York: Harper Perennial, 2009.

Leder, Drew. *Spiritual Passages: Embracing Life's Sacred Journey*. New York: Jeremy P. Tarcher/Putnam, 1997.

Le Guin, Ursula. *Dancing at the Edge of the World: Thoughts on Words, Women, Places*. New York: Grove Press, 1989.

———. *The Lathe of Heaven*. New York: Simon and Schuster, 2008.

Leider, Richard, and David Shapiro. *Claiming Your Place at the Fire: Living the Second Half of Your Life on Purpose*. San Francisco: Berrett-Koehler Publishers, 2004.

Lerner, Harriet. *The Dance of Anger: A Woman's Guide to Changing the Patterns of Intimate Relationships*. New York: Harper Perennial, 1987.

Leslau, Charlotte, and Wolf Leslau, eds. *African Folk Tales*. Mount Vernon, NY: Peter Pauper Press, 1963.

Lifton, Robert Jay. *Death in Life: Survivors of Hiroshima*. New York: Simon and Schuster, 1967.

Lindbergh, Anne Morrow. *Gift from the Sea*. New York: Pantheon Books, 1975.

Lorde, Audre. *Sister Outsider: Essays and Speeches*. Freedom, CA: Crossing Press, 1984.

Lyubomirsky, Sonja. *The How of Happiness: A Scientific Approach to Getting the Life You Want*. New York: Penguin Books, 2007.

Ma, Yo-Yo. "In Pursuit of Neuroscience: Yo-Yo Ma." By Philip Ball. *Financial Times*, September 16, 2011.

MacDonald, Ian. *Revolution in the Head: The Beatles' Records and the Sixties*. 3rd ed. Chicago: Chicago Review Press, 2007.

Malchiodi, Cathy. *The Soul's Palette: Drawing on Art's Transformative Powers for Health and Well-Being*. Boston: Shambhala, 2002.

Manheimer, Ron. "Remember to Remember." In *All That Our Eyes Have Witnessed: Aging, Reminiscence, Caring*, edited by Marc Kaminsky. New York: Horizon Press, 1982.

Martinez, Mario. *The MindBody Code: How to Change the Beliefs That Limit Your Health, Longevity, and Success*. Boulder, CO: Sounds True, 2014.

Maslow, Abraham. *The Farther Reaches of Human Nature*. New York: Penguin, 1976.

———. *Toward a Psychology of Being*. 3rd ed. New York: John Wiley & Sons, 1999.

Mather, Mara, Turhan Canli, Tammy English, Sue Whitfield, Peter Wais, Kevin Ochsner, John D.E. Gabrieli, and Laura L.

Carstensen. "Amygdala Responses to Emotionally Valenced Stimuli in Older and Younger Adults." *Psychological Science* 15, no. 4 (April 2004): 259–63.

Matisse, Henri. "Looking at Life with the Eyes of a Child." *Art News and Review*, February 6, 1954.

McCoy, Edain. *Celtic Women's Spirituality: Accessing the Cauldron of Life*. St. Paul, MN: Llewellyn Publications, 1998.

McGaa, Ed. *Mother Earth Spirituality: Native American Paths to Healing Ourselves and Our World*. San Francisco: Harper & Row Publishers, 1990.

McMahon, Arthur, and Paul Rhudick. "Reminiscing in the Aged: An Adaptational Response." In *Psychodynamic Studies on Aging: Creativity, Reminiscing, and Dying*, edited by Sidney Levin and Ralph Kahana, 64–78. New York: International Universities Press, 1967.

Meacham, James. "Wisdom and the Context of Knowledge: Knowing That One Does Not Know." *Contributions to Human Development* 8 (1983): 111–134.

———. "The Loss of Wisdom." In Sternberg, *Wisdom*, 181–211.

Meade, Michael. *The Genius Myth*. Seattle, WA: Greenfire Press. 2016.

———. *The Water of Life: Initiation and the Tempering of the Soul*. Seattle, WA: Greenfire Press, 2006.

Mellick, Jill. *The Natural Artistry of Dreams: Tools for Creative Dream Work*. Berkeley, CA: Conari Press, 1996.

Mitchell, Stephen, trans. *Tao Te Ching*. New York: Harper & Row, 1988.

Monaghan, Patricia. *The New Book of Goddesses and Heroines*. St. Paul, MN: Llewellyn Publications, 2000.

———. *Seasons of the Witch*, 2nd ed. St. Paul, MN: Llewellyn Publications, 2002.

Monroe, Kristen Renwick. *The Heart of Altruism: Perceptions of a Common Humanity*. Princeton, NJ: Princeton University Press, 1996.

Moody, Harry R. "Reminiscence and the Recovery of the Public World." In Kaminsky, *The Uses of Reminiscence*, 157–66.

Moody, Harry R., and David Carroll. *Five Stages of the Soul: Charting the Spiritual Passages That Shape Our Lives*. New York: Anchor Books, 1997.

Moore, Raeanne C., A'verria Sirkin Martin, Allison R. Kaup, Wesley K. Thompson, Matthew E. Peters, Dilip V. Jeste, Shahrokh Golshan, and Lisa T. Eyler. "From Suffering to Caring: A Model of Differences Among Older Adults in Levels of Compassion." *International Journal of Geriatric Psychiatry* 30, no. 2 (February 2015): 185–91.

Moore, Thomas. *Care of the Soul: A Guide for Cultivating Depth and Sacredness in Everyday Life*. New York: HarperCollins, 1992.

———. *The Re-Enchantment of Everyday Life*. New York: Harper Collins, 1996.

Muir, John. *My First Summer in the Sierra*. New York: Houghton Mifflin, 1911.

Murdock, Maureen. *Unreliable Truth: On Memoir and Memory*. New York: Seal Press, 2003.

Myerhoff, Barbara, ed. *Remembered Lives: The Work of Ritual, Storytelling, and Growing Older*. Ann Arbor, MI: University of Michigan Press, 1992.

Myerhoff, Barbara, and Deena Metzger. "The Journal As Activity and Genre." In Myerhoff, *Remembered Lives*, 341–59.

Myerhoff, Barbara, and Virginia Tufte. "Life History As Integration." In Myerhoff, *Remembered Lives*, 249–55.

Nakamura, Jeanne, and Mihaly Csikszentmihalyi. "Creativity in Later Life." In *Creativity and Development*, by R. Keith Sawyer, Vera John-Steiner, Seana Moran, Robert J. Sternberg, David Henry Feldman, Jeanne Nakamura, and Mihaly Csikszentmihalyi, 186–216. New York: Oxford University Press, 2003.

Nearing, Helen. *Loving and Leaving the Good Life*. Post Falls, VT: Chelsea Green, 1992.

Neugarten, Bernice L., ed. *Middle Age and Aging: A Reader in Social Psychology.* Chicago: University of Chicago Press, 1973.

Niebuhr, Reinhold. *Justice and Mercy.* Edited by Ursula Niebuhr. New York: Harper & Row, 1974.

Nin, Anaïs. *The Diary of Anaïs Nin.* Vol 3. New York: Mariner Books, 1971.

Northrup, Christiane. *Goddesses Never Age: The Secret Prescription for Radiance, Vitality, and Well-Being.* Carlsbad, CA: Hay House, 2015.

Nouwen, Henri. *Aging: The Fulfillment of Life.* Garden City, NY: Doubleday, 1976.

Nuland, Sherwin. *The Art of Aging: A Doctor's Prescription for Well-Being.* New York: Random House, 2007.

Öberg, Peter. "Images Versus Experience of the Aging Body." In *Aging Bodies: Images and Everyday Experience,* edited by Christopher A. Faircloth, 103–39. Walnut Creek, CA: AltaMira Press, 2003.

O'Connor, Richard. *Happy at Last: The Thinking Person's Guide to Finding Joy.* New York: St. Martin's, 2008.

O'Donohue, John. *To Bless the Space Between Us: A Book of Blessings.* New York: Doubleday, 2008.

Oliver, Mary. *New and Selected Poems.* Boston: Beacon Press, 1992.

Ong, Anthony, C. S. Bergeman, Toni Bisconti, and Kimberly Wallace. "Psychological Resilience, Positive Emotions, and Successful Adaptation to Stress in Later Life." *Journal of Personality and Social Psychology* 91, no. 4 (October 2006): 730–49.

Palmer, Parker. *Let Your Life Speak: Listening for the Voice of Vocation.* San Francisco: Jossey-Bass and Sons, 2000.

Pearson, Carol S. *Awakening the Heroes Within: Twelve Archetypes to Help Us Find Ourselves and Transform the World.* Harper San Francisco, 1991.

Peck, Robert C. "Psychological Developments in the Second Half of Life." In Neugarten, *Middle Age,* 88–92.

Perls, Frederick. *Ego, Hunger, and Aggression.* New York: Vintage Books, 1969.

Perls, Frederick, Ralph Hefferline, and Paul Goodman. *Gestalt Therapy: Excitement and Growth in the Human Personality.* Gouldsboro, ME: The Gestalt Journal Press, 1994.

Pfeiffer, Bruce Brooks, ed. *Frank Lloyd Wright Collected Writings.* Vol. 1, *1894–1930.* New York: Rizzoli Publishing, 1992.

Phillips, Jan. *Marry Your Muse: Making a Lasting Commitment to Your Creativity.* Wheaton, IL: Quest Books, 1997.

Putman, Daniel. "Psychological Courage." *Philosophy, Psychiatry, and Psychology* 4, no. 1 (March 1997): 1–11.

———. *Psychological Courage.* Lanham, MD: University Press of America, 2004.

Ragan, Kathleen. *Fearless Girls, Wise Women, and Beloved Sisters: Heroines in Folktales from Around the World.* New York: W. W. Norton, 1998.

Ramanujan, A. K. *Folktales from India: A Selection of Oral Tales from Twenty-Two Languages.* New York: Pantheon Books, 1991.

Randall, William L., and Gary M. Kenyon. *Ordinary Wisdom: Biographical Aging and the Journey of Life.* Westport, CT: Praeger Publishers, 2001.

Randolph, Vance. *Who Blowed Up the Church House? And Other Ozark Folk Tales.* New York: Columbia University Press, 1952.

Reiser, Christa. *Reflections on Anger: Women and Men in a Changing Society.* Westport, CT: Praeger, 1999.

Remen, Rachel Naomi. *Kitchen Table Wisdom: Stories That Heal.* New York: Riverhead Books, 2006.

Richards, Ruth, ed. *Everyday Creativity and New Views of Human Nature: Psychological, Social, and Spiritual Perspectives.* Washington, DC: American Psychological Association, 2007.

Riggs, Renée C. *Animal Stories from Eskimo Land.* New York: Frederick A. Stokes, 1923.

Rohr, Richard. *Falling Upward: A Spirituality for the Two Halves of Life.* San Francisco: Jossey-Bass, 2011.

Roosevelt, Eleanor. *You Learn by Living: Eleven Keys for a More Fulfilling Life*. Louisville, KY: Westminster John Knox Press, 1960.

Rowe, John W., and Robert L. Kahn. *Successful Aging*. New York: Dell Publishing, 1998.

Ryff, Carol. "In the Eye of the Beholder: Views of Psychological Well-Being Among Middle-Aged and Older Adults." *Psychology and Aging* 4, no. 2 (1989): 195–210.

Sadler, William. *The Third Age: Six Principles for Growth and Renewal after Forty*. New York: Quill/HarperCollins, 2000.

Salzberg, Sharon. *Lovingkindness: The Revolutionary Art of Happiness*. Boston: Shambhala, 1995.

———. *Real Happiness: The Power of Meditation*. New York: Workman Publishing, 2010.

Sams, Jamie. *Sacred Path Cards: The Discovery of Self Through Native Teachings*. San Francisco: Harper San Francisco, 1990.

Sams, Jamie, and David Carson. *Medicine Cards: The Discovery of Power Through the Ways of Animals*. Santa Fe, NM: Bear and Company, 1988.

Sarton, May. *Collected Poems (1930–1973)*. New York: W. W. Norton, 1974.

———. *Journal of a Solitude*. New York: W. W. Norton, 1992.

Schachter-Shalomi, Zalman, and Ronald S. Miller. *From Age-ing to Sage-ing: A Profound New Vision of Growing Older*. New York: Grand Central Publishing, 2014.

Schaefer, Carol. *Grandmothers Counsel the World: Women Elders Offer Their Vision of Our Planet*. Boston: Trumpeter Books, 2006.

Scheibe, Susanne, and Laura Carstensen. "Emotional Aging: Recent Findings and Future Trends." *Journal of Gerontology Series B: Psychological Sciences and Social Sciences* 65B, no. 2 (March 2010): 135–44.

Scott-Maxwell, Florida. *The Measure of My Days: One Woman's Vivid, Enduring Celebration of Life and Aging*. New York: Penguin Books, 1968.

Segal, Jerome M. *Graceful Simplicity: Toward a Philosophy and Politics of Simple Living.* New York: Henry Holt, 1999.

Seligman, Martin. *Learned Optimism: How to Change Your Mind and Your Life.* New York: Pocket Books, 1998.

Silver, Margery Hutter. "The Significance of Life Review in Old Age." In *Aging in Good Health: Multidisciplinary Perspectives,* edited by Sue Levkoff, Yeon Kyung Chee, and Shohei Noguchi, 29–40. New York: Springer Publishing, 2001.

Simonton, Dean. "Age and Outstanding Achievement: What Do We Know after a Century of Research?" *Psychological Bulletin* 104, no. 2 (1988): 251–67.

———. "Creative Productivity Through the Adult Years." *Generations* 15, no. 2 (Spring 1991): 13–16.

Slavitt, David R., ed. *Seneca: The Tragedies*, Vol. 2. Baltimore, MD: Johns Hopkins University Press, 1995.

Somé, Malidoma Patrice. *The Healing Wisdom of Africa: Finding Life Purpose Through Nature, Ritual, and Community.* New York: Jeremy P. Tarcher/Putnam, 1998.

Sontag, Susan. "The Double Standard of Aging." *Saturday Review,* September 23, 1972.

Starr, Bernard, and Marcella Bakur Weiner. *The Starr-Weiner Report on Sex and Sexuality in the Mature Years.* New York: Stein and Day Publishers, 1981.

Sternberg, Robert J. *Wisdom: Its Nature, Origins, and Development.* New York: Cambridge University Press, 1990.

Stewart, Susan. "Collage." *Winters Graces* (blog). http://winters-graces.com/collage.

St. James, Elaine. *Simplify Your Life: 100 Ways to Slow Down and Enjoy the Things That Really Matter.* New York: Hyperion, 1994.

Sullivan, Dennis, and Larry Tifft. *Handbook of Restorative Justice.* New York: Routledge, 2007.

Tavris, Carol. *Anger: The Misunderstood Emotion.* New York: Simon and Schuster, 1989.

Thomas, Sandra P., ed. *Women and Anger.* New York: Springer Publishing, 1993.

Tornstam, Lars. *Gerotranscendence: A Developmental Theory of Positive Aging.* New York: Springer Publishing, 2005.

———. "Maturing into Gerotranscendence." *The Journal of Transpersonal Psychology* 43, no. 2 (2011): 166–180.

Touhy, Theris, and Kathleen Jett, eds. *Ebersole and Hess' Toward Healthy Aging: Human Needs and Nursing Response*, 8th ed. St Louis, MO: Elsevier, 2012.

Turner, Kay. *Beautiful Necessity: The Art and Meaning of Women's Altars.* New York: Thames and Hudson, 1999.

Tutu, Desmond. *No Future Without Forgiveness.* New York: Doubleday Books, 1999.

Underwood, Lynn G. "Compassionate Love: A Framework for Research." In *The Science of Compassionate Love: Theory, Research, and Applications*, edited by Beverley Fehr, Susan Sprecher, and Lynn G. Underwood. 3–25. Chichester, West Sussex, UK: John Wiley & Sons, 2009.

Underwood, Paula. "Clan Mothers and the Twenty-First Century." In *The Fabric of the Future: Women Visionaries Illuminate the Path to the Future*, edited by M. J. Ryan. 150–62. Berkeley, CA: Conari Press, 1998.

Vaillant, George. *The Wisdom of the Ego.* Cambridge, MA: Harvard University Press, 1993.

Viorst, Judith. *Necessary Losses: The Loves, Illusions, Dependencies, and Impossible Expectations That All of Us Have to Give Up in Order to Grow.* New York: Simon and Schuster, 1986.

Walker, Barbara. *The Crone: Woman of Age, Wisdom, and Power.* San Francisco: Harper San Francisco, 1988.

Ward, Linda. *Memory of Rain.* Self-published, Blurb Book (blurb.com), 2014.

Waxman, Gerald. *Astronomical Tidbits: A Layperson's Guide to Astronomy.* Bloomington, IN: AuthorHouse, 2010.

Werner, Emmy, and Ruth Smith. *Vulnerable but Invincible: A Longitudinal Study of Resilient Children and Youth*. New York: McGraw-Hill, 1982.

White, Kathleen M., J. C. Speisman, and D. Costos. "Young Adults and Their Parents: From Individuation to Mutuality." *New Directions for Child and Adolescent Development*, no. 22 (1983): 61–76.

Whyte, David. *River Flow: New and Selected Poems*. Langley, WA: Many Rivers, 2007.

Wilde, Oscar. *De Profundis and the Ballad of Reading Gaol*. Leipzig, Germany: Tauchnitz, 1908.

Williams, Terry Tempest. *Refuge: An Unnatural History of Family and Place*. New York: Pantheon Books, 1991.

Winerman, Lea. "The Mind's Mirror." *Monitor on Psychology* 36, no. 9 (2005): 48–51.

Winn, Rhonda, and Niles Newton. "Sexuality in Aging: A Study of 106 Cultures." *Archives of Sexual Behavior* 11, no. 4 (August 1982): 283–98.

Wohlleben, Peter. *The Hidden Life of Trees: What They Feel, How They Communicate*. Translated by Jane Billinghurst. Vancouver, BC: Greystone Books, 2016.

Wolkstein, Diane. *The Magic Orange Tree and Other Haitian Folktales*. New York: Alfred A. Knopf, 1978.

Woodman, Marion, *The Crown of Age*. Audiobook. 2 CDs. Boulder, CO: Sounds True, 2002.

Worth, Grace. "At the Center of the Story." In Kaminsky, *The Uses of Reminiscence*, 53–66.

Yolen, Jane. *Gray Heroes: Elder Tales from Around the World*. New York: Penguin Books, 1999.

Young-Eisendrath, Polly, and Melvin E. Miller, eds. *The Psychology of Mature Spirituality: Integrity, Wisdom, Transcendence*. London: Routledge, 2000.

Acknowledgments

This project has spanned more than a decade, and many people have helped bring *Winter's Graces* to completion—family, friends, and circles of friends; students, colleagues, and other professionals; and assorted angels who have helped me keep going in various ways when doubt and discouragement were calling for a strike.

I am grateful to Barrett Briske for her support and skill as editor, technical consultant, and information sleuth; to book midwife Caroline Pincus, therapist Anita Eliot, and dear friend Ellen Katzman for their steadfast encouragement; to Linda Lee Boyd and Abbey Levine for their generosity and many forms of support; and to all those who provided helpful feedback on early versions of the work: David Sowerby, Mary Ann Clark, Sami Lange, Jackie Cato, Jim Wiley, Noelle Oxenhandler, Frances Frazier, Margaret Potts, Marti Shortridge, Victoria Temple, Nancy Bertelsen, Sue Thollaug, Jeannette Myers, Geri Olson, Suzanne Gray, Patricia Tuttle-Brown, Pam Mercer, Dee Bell, Kathleen Kraemer, Dinah Bachrach, "Mike" Michaels, and Doris Ober.

Thank you to the inspiring elder students in my "Gifts of Age" classes at Sonoma State University and to Marion Woodman, Elizabeth Bugental, Joanne Woodland, Sharon Rivkin, Dena Bliss, Judy Foley, and others whose life stories illustrate the graces of later life throughout the book.

Three circles of friends have lent their support as readers and sounding boards: Bruce and Jeanne Feldman and David Van Nuys; the community of St. John's Episcopal Church in Petaluma; and our women's group of forty-eight years—Linda Ward, Sandra Rucker, Judy White, Chris Evans, and Annie and Jann Kalbaugh.

Last and not least, I am grateful for these assorted angels: Jack Ritchie and his colleagues at Sonoma State University's library; Maria Ruiz and friends at Della Fattoria for their early morning kindness and cappuccinos; Jean Wasp, retired Media Relations Coordinator, and Elaine Leder, retired Dean of the School of Social Sciences at Sonoma State University, for their backing and encouragement; and my family—ancestral, extended, and nuclear: my sister Helen Nichols and brother-in-law Ron Sidell; Logan and Kanjana Stewart and their wonder-filled children, Lona and Lukas; Avery Stewart and his wonderful daughters Madison and Natalie, whose research and other skills helped bring *Winter's Graces* to fruition. And a final thank you for their invaluable assistance to publicists Julia and Jared Drake at Wildbound PR, to web designer Stephanie Raccine at Off the Page Creations, and to Brooke Warner, Lauren Wise, and the talented staff at She Writes Press.

About the Author

photo © Madison Stewart

Susan Stewart, PhD, is an emerita professor of psychology, a retired psychotherapist, and a workshop facilitator. A baby boomer who turned seventy-two just before publishing this book, she belongs to a women's group that has been meeting for forty-eight years. She is blessed with two grown sons, Avery and Logan, and four grand-children—Lukas, Lona Louisa, Madison, and Natalie, ages four, six, nineteen, and twenty-two, respectively, at the time of this book's publication. Susan is a singer and cellist and loves to dance.

Selected Titles From She Writes Press

She Writes Press is an independent publishing company founded to serve women writers everywhere. Visit us at www.shewritespress.com.

Flip-Flops After Fifty: And Other Thoughts on Aging I Remembered to Write Down by Cindy Eastman. $16.95, 978-1-938314-68-1. A collection of frank and funny essays about turning fifty—and all the emotional ups and downs that come with it.

The Shelf Life of Ashes: A Memoir by Hollis Giammatteo. $16.95, 978-1-63152-047-1. Confronted by an importuning mother 3,000 miles away who thinks her end is nigh—and feeling ambushed by her impending middle age—Giammatteo determines to find The Map of Aging Well, a decision that leads her on an often-comic journey.

Where Have I Been All My Life? A Journey Toward Love and Wholeness by Cheryl Rice. $16.95, 978-1-63152-917-7. Rice's universally relatable story of how her mother's sudden death launched her on a journey into the deepest parts of grief—and, ultimately, toward love and wholeness.

Green Nails and Other Acts of Rebellion: Life After Loss by Elaine Soloway. $16.95, 978-1-63152-919-1. An honest, often humorous account of the joys and pains of caregiving for a loved one with a debilitating illness.

Role Reversal: How to Take Care of Yourself and Your Aging Parents by Iris Waichler. $16.95, 978-1-63152-091-4. A comprehensive guide for the 45 million people currently taking care of family members who need assistance because of health-related problems.

The Space Between: A Memoir of Mother-Daughter Love at the End of Life by Virginia A. Simpson. $16.95, 978-1-63152-049-5. When a life-threatening illness makes it necessary for Virginia Simpson's mother, Ruth, to come live with her, Simpson struggles to heal their relationship before Ruth dies.